Managing Economic Volatility in Latin America

EDITORS
Gaston Gelos and Alejandro Werner

INTERNATIONAL MONETARY FUND

Cataloging-in-Publication Data
Joint Bank-Fund Library

Managing economic volatility in Latin America / edited by
Gaston Gelos and Alejandro Werner. – Washington, D.C. :
International Monetary Fund, c2014.
pages ; cm

Includes bibliographical references and index.

1. Capital movements – Latin America. 2. Foreign exchange reserves – Latin America. 3. Foreign exchange rates – Latin America. 4. Fiscal policy – Latin America. 5. Monetary policy – Latin America. I. Gelos, Gaston. II. Werner, Alejandro M. III. International Monetary Fund.

HG3891.M36 2014

ISBN: 978-1-48436-498-7

Please send orders to:
International Monetary Fund, Publication Services
P.O. Box 92780, Washington, DC 20090, U.S.A.
Tel.: (202) 623-7430 Fax: (202) 623-7201
E-mail: publications@imf.org
Internet: www.elibrary.imf.org
www.imfbookstore.org

Contents

Introduction

Gaston Gelos and Alejandro Werner

After having displayed remarkable resilience during the global financial crisis, many Latin American economies continued to face substantial capital inflows over the last five years, while the commodity exporters among them continued to experience sustained demand for their key products. The recent, more difficult environment for emerging markets, including the capital flow volatility surrounding the uncertainty about the future path of U.S. monetary policy and the economic slowdown in China, however, highlighted the continued challenges related to external factors faced by the region.

This exposure to the external environment poses important policy questions, including how to react to in- and outflows, volatile terms of trade, and related pressures on the exchange rate. This volume presents a collection of novel contributions to this topic, with a special emphasis on Latin America.

Part I deals with some of the fundamental issues related to capital flows and terms-of-trade shocks. Magud and Sosa ask when to worry about real appreciation, taking stock of the vast Dutch disease literature to understand its implications for macroeconomic policy. Interestingly, their comprehensive review reveals that although there is indeed support for the notion that the tradable sector is hurt by a real appreciation, there is much less evidence for a "disease" in the sense of adverse long-term growth effects. This important conclusion provides a cautionary note to policymakers; when thinking about how to react to appreciations owing to positive terms-of-trade shocks or capital inflows, they should beware—as the authors put it—of killing the goose that lays the golden eggs.

Part II covers some key analytical diagnostic questions related to capital inflows issues: assessing reserves adequacy and current account levels. The study by Magnusson Bernard estimates the optimal reserve level for a number of countries in the region using the Jeanne–Rancière (2006) model of optimal reserves and contrasts it with some commonly used benchmarks for reserve adequacy, while also discussing differences in the degree of current account openness and their implications. Another key issue when facing appreciation or depreciation pressures is to be able to assess whether the exchange rate is misaligned, and, more generally, to understand the main drivers of exchange rate movements.

An important element in this context is the estimation of the medium-term or underlying current account balance, for which Perrelli offers an innovative and more robust econometric approach. The author shows that mainstream methods used to estimate the savings-investment norms tend to disregard important features of the data: in these models, the impact of any given policy variable is the same for countries carrying large deficits as for countries enjoying large surpluses. Through the use of the quantile-varying slopes, the econometrician provides a much richer description of the relationships between current account balances and macroeconomic fundamentals in a large panel of heterogeneous countries.

The role of capital flow management policies and exchange-rate regimes in coping with large shocks is explored in Part III. Benelli, Segura-Ubiergo, and Walker focus specifically on one response to capital flows that has received particular attention recently—the introduction of capital restrictions—by examining the impact of the capital inflow tax implemented in Brazil. They find that the measure appears to have shifted the composition of inflows away from portfolio flows and toward derivatives. However, the overall degree of exchange rate pressure remained little changed. Canales-Kriljenko conducts a broad empirical analysis of the role of the exchange rate as a buffer to variations in external conditions, concluding that exchange rate flexibility helps countries dampen the effects of external shocks. This finding underscores the importance of one of Latin America's key macroeconomic achievements over the last 10–15 years, namely a much larger degree of exchange rate flexibility. This has helped the region to weather shocks with much more resilience than in the past.

Part IV explores the effectiveness of fiscal policy in dealing with some of the challenges discussed. Guerson and Melina propose a forward-looking fiscal policy framework that seeks to smooth primary expenditure over the business cycle while remaining consistent with public debt sustainability. Under the policy, a government chooses a budget envelope for the next year such that public debt remains below a preannounced threshold with a specified probability—the authors apply this framework to various Caribbean countries. Empirical simulations for a sample of Caribbean countries show that allowing debt to move within a relatively narrow band achieves significantly smoother primary expenditure paths over the business cycle, in some cases better than those obtained under a structural balance rule. This is a particularly interesting finding for these economies, as they are mostly highly indebted, very open, undiversified, and subject to significant real and financial shocks.

Monetary policy is the focus of Part V. The potential role for monetary policy in the optimal policy response to changes in the external environment depends significantly on country-specific and institutional factors. For example, the financial systems in many economies in Latin America are dollarized to varying degrees, implying limitations for the conduct of monetary policy. However, financial dollarization has declined substantially in some countries in the region in recent years. García-Escribano and Sosa examine the role of different factors—including prudential regulations and the development of the capital market in domestic currency—in driving the process of financial dedollarization for countries that have already fulfilled the main precondition for dedollarization—macroeconomic stability. They find that the exchange rate appreciation, the introduction of prudential measures to create incentives to dedollarize (including an active management of reserve requirement differentials), and the development of a capital market in local currency have contributed to a decline in dollarization. Acosta-Ormaechea and Coble compare the monetary transmission mechanism in four economies that follow inflation targeting (IT)—Chile, New Zealand, Peru, and Uruguay—but differ in their degree of dollarization and financial intermediation, as well as in their history of IT. The evidence suggests that the exchange rate channel is more important in Peru and Uruguay (two highly dollarized economies) than the traditional transmission channels, and that monetary policy has more limited effects on economic activity. Conversely, the traditional interest rate channel is effective in Chile and New Zealand.

Overall, a common thread connects the various chapters in this volume: devising the appropriate response to external shocks in open economies. Although this is not a new challenge for the region, the degree of sophistication of the discussion reflects not only advances in the profession, but also the significant progress in practical policy implementation achieved in many Latin American countries since the crises of the late 1990s and early 2000s.

PART I

Capital Flows and Dutch Disease

CHAPTER 1

Worrying about Currency Appreciation? The Missing Link between Dutch Disease and Growth

NICOLÁS MAGUD AND SEBASTIÁN SOSA

In response to expansionary monetary policy in advanced economies following the 2008–09 global financial crisis, interest rate differentials have triggered a surge in capital inflows to emerging market countries. At the same time, strong growth in emerging market economies, especially in Asia, continues to support commodity prices. While this benign external environment brings opportunities, it also raises some risks and challenges. Capital inflows and higher commodity export prices exert appreciating pressures on domestic currencies (Figure 1.1), which poses policy challenges in many countries out of a concern that a stronger currency would undermine the competitiveness of their tradable sectors and lower growth.

Based on the experience of the Netherlands in the 1960s, a literature on "Dutch disease" was developed in the early 1980s. This literature analyzed the effects of discoveries or price increases of natural resources that result in real exchange rate appreciation, factor reallocation, and de-industrialization. Similar effects may stem from other shocks entailing an increase in foreign exchange inflows, such as capital inflows, aid, and remittances.

Economic growth is usually affected by real exchange rate dynamics, but these effects have been interpreted in different ways. Some views stress that any deviation of the real exchange rate from its fundamental (that is, long-term) value reduces economic growth. Others suggest that, although an overvalued exchange rate hampers growth, an undervalued exchange rate fosters it. In turn, an additional view argues that it is real exchange rate instability that hinders growth. Trying to connect the Dutch disease phenomenon with the relationship between the real exchange rate and growth, a recent view suggests that Dutch disease lowers economic growth. Thus, economic policy should be used to contain any Dutch disease effects.

A previous version of this chapter was published in the *Journal of International Commerce, Economics and Policy*, Vol. 4, No. 2 (April 2013).

Figure 1.1 Commodity Prices, Capital Inflows, Growth, and the Real Effective Exchange Rate in Emerging Markets

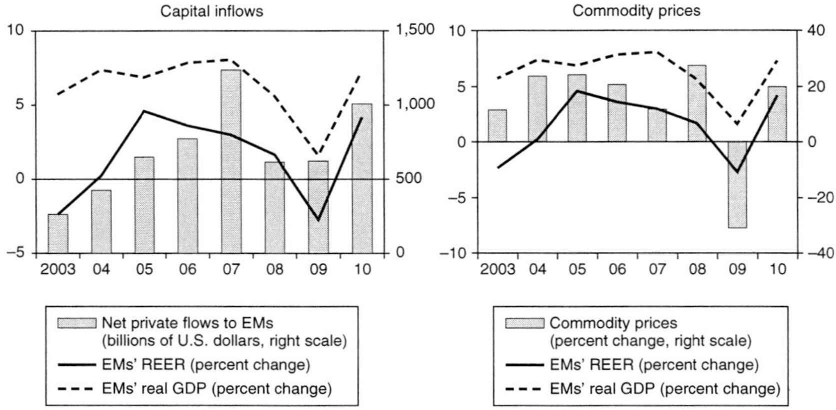

Sources: Institute of International Finance and authors' calculations.
Note: EM = emerging markets; REER = real effective exchange rate.

This chapter examines whether the existing literature provides strong support for the concerns about the potential adverse effects of Dutch disease on long-term growth. To this end, we review the vast literature on Dutch disease and on the relationship between the real exchange rate and growth—two related but distinct concepts. We focus on the theoretical contributions to rationalize the Dutch disease phenomenon and the empirical evidence. We also review the literature on the effects of exchange rate overvaluations and undervaluations on growth. Our survey reviews more than 60 papers (both theoretical and empirical) on these topics. Their main contributions are described below. To make systematic comparisons of the papers' results, we construct simple indices to evaluate their partial and overall implications. In turn, the latter evidence is used to analyze the policy implications of Dutch disease shocks.

We document that Dutch disease does exist in some form. Shocks that trigger foreign exchange inflows (natural resource booms, surges in capital inflows, foreign aid, remittances, etc.) typically appreciate the real exchange rate, generate factor reallocation, and reduce manufacturing output and net exports. However, we do not find evidence that Dutch disease reduces economic growth. We also find that real exchange rate misalignment—in particular when owing to overvaluation—and higher volatility of the real exchange rate lower growth. Regarding the effect of undervaluation of the exchange rate on economic growth, the evidence is mixed and inconclusive.

In principle, Dutch disease is an equilibrium phenomenon reflecting changes in fundamentals, so Dutch disease may not be a disease after all. That said, the policy response to a natural resource boom (or other shocks causing Dutch disease) could play a role in determining the overall impact of the shock. Policy responses should aim at adequately managing the boom and its associated risks. The optimal response would consist of taking advantage of the boom, while dealing with the undesired consequences that it may cause.

DUTCH DISEASE, REAL EXCHANGE RATE APPRECIATION, AND GROWTH: THE MISSING LINK

In the 1960s, the Netherlands discovered natural gas in the North Sea, increasing the country's wealth. As a result, the increase in the price of this commodity acted as a wealth effect, increasing domestic aggregate demand. For a small open economy such as the Netherlands the price of tradable goods was a given. As the price of nontradable goods clears in the domestic market, higher domestic demand increases the relative price of nontradable goods. Thus the Dutch guilder appreciated in real terms, decreasing the country's competitiveness, which, in turn, reduced the other tradable industries' exports. Since then, this type of phenomenon (which could also be triggered by an exogenous increase in the price of a country's existing export, or an increase in capital inflows, foreign aid, or remittances) has been labeled "Dutch disease."[1]

Based on these facts, economic theorists started to develop models to rationalize the effects of these "natural resource shocks." Using conventional models, it was straightforward to show that these shocks (be they in the form of new discoveries or price increases) resulted in an appreciation of the real exchange rate. Assuming a capital-intensive manufacturing tradable sector—as opposed to a labor-intensive nontradable sector—this relative price change triggers factor reallocation—away from manufacturing—and the appreciation of the real exchange rate, decreasing the competitiveness of manufacturing tradable goods. As such, Dutch disease has been also labeled as a resource-based de-industrialization.

Empirical tests of the Dutch disease phenomenon have documented the existence of such a pattern. The evidence shows that natural resource shocks are generally followed by real appreciation and de-industrialization.

While a natural resource boom (or any other shock entailing an increase in foreign exchange inflows) is in principle a positive development owing to wealth effects, there have long been concerns among economists about the potential negative impact of Dutch disease on long-term growth. These concerns are usually based on the idea that the declining (usually manufacturing) tradable sectors may possess some special characteristics that would stimulate growth and welfare in the long term (such as increasing returns to scale, learning by doing (LBD), spillover effects, or other positive externalities).

[1]See *The Economist*, "The Dutch Disease," November 26, 1977, pp. 82–83.

Recently, a new literature focusing on the relationship between the real exchange rate and growth has surged, in some cases proposing new channels. Motivated by the successful experiences of China and other east Asian countries, the view that maintaining an undervalued or "competitive" real exchange rate may foster economic growth has been attracting adherents. This view, linked to the export-led literature as well as to the traditional Dutch disease literature, argues that the operative channel is the size of the (manufacturing) tradable sector. The export-led growth strategy emerged, in part, as a response to the failure of the import substitution growth strategy that started around the 1950s. Given the speed of technological progress, production of manufacturing goods enabled a faster transmission of technology, raising the value-added component of these types of goods—as opposed to basic services that rely on unskilled labor. Banking on the latter, the export-led growth model is based on making an economy grow through exporting manufactures, which will raise a country's wealth much faster than by closing the domestic manufacturing markets and exporting raw materials only, allowing the country to increase its technological degree of sophistication in the process.

Other views link undervalued exchange rates to higher growth through different channels. Dooley; Folkerts-Landau, and Garber (2004), for instance, argue that an overvalued real exchange rate tends to shift demand away from tradable to nontradable goods; thus the real interest rate needs to rise to maintain internal equilibrium, increasing domestic saving rates. Levy-Yeyati and Sturzenegger (2007) point to an alternative channel: an undervalued real exchange rate is associated with lower real wages, leading firms to higher investment, and to higher saving rates to finance them.

The views discussed above suggest that, while real exchange rate overvaluations hurt growth, undervaluations foster it. This contrasts with another position, linked to the Washington Consensus view, which argues that any real exchange rate misalignment implies a sort of disequilibrium that could affect the growth process. According to the latter view, whenever the observed real exchange rate differs from the equilibrium level, welfare is reduced owing to price distortions. Misalignment applies for any deviation of the real exchange rate from its long-term (fundamentals-based) equilibrium. Thus, economic growth would be lower if the real exchange rate is above or below its long-term value, that is, both undervaluation and overvaluation are pernicious to economic growth. For export-led growth, however, only overvaluation decreases growth; undervaluation increases it.

Putting together the concepts elaborated above, it might be tempting to jump to the conclusion that Dutch disease lowers economic growth, and in fact many Dutch disease theorists—as well as some empirical applications—come to this conclusion. However, this needs a strong assumption: that the manufacturing tradable sector is somehow "special." In general, LBD or other types of externalities in this sector have been assumed to obtain theoretical models linking Dutch disease with lower growth. Absent these assumptions, Dutch disease only depicts an equilibrium real exchange rate appreciation reflecting stronger fundamentals and de-industrialization, but would not necessarily be bad for overall growth.

Most of the Dutch disease empirical literature focuses on the impact of foreign exchange inflows on the real exchange rate and the reallocation of resources between the tradable and nontradable sectors, but does not examine the effects on long-term growth, and does not analyze whether the adverse effects associated with Dutch disease offset the beneficial effects of inflows. Research in this area has typically not attempted to directly demonstrate the presence of spillovers or other growth-enhancing qualities in the tradable sector. Hence, the evidence on the negative impact of Dutch disease on growth is still partial, and generally inconclusive. As Sala-i-Martin and Subramanian (2003) argue, the proposition that tradable sectors are "special" or "superior" because of LBD and other positive externalities—a necessary condition for Dutch disease to exert a drag on long-term growth—is "largely unproven."

Concerns about Dutch disease may also derive from the view that real exchange rate overvaluation lowers growth, a result that appears to be supported by the empirical evidence. Evidence on the positive effects that an undervalued real exchange rate may exert growth is mixed, with some studies suggesting that undervaluation actually hurts growth—as argued by the Washington Consensus view. In any case, the real exchange rate appreciation associated with Dutch disease is in principle an equilibrium phenomenon that reflects a change in underlying fundamentals and does not necessarily imply overvaluation, so it is not clear why lower growth should be an unavoidable outcome.

Therefore, even though there is some debate over whether misalignment or overvaluation lowers growth, the channel through which Dutch disease reduces economic growth is not found in the literature (see below). This is quite relevant, as it affects the economic policy discussion.

DUTCH DISEASE AND REAL APPRECIATION: IS THERE ROOM FOR POLICY?

The previous discussion on Dutch disease leads to the following question: is there room for economic policy to avoid real appreciation? But to answer this question, it is necessary first to address an earlier question: is the real exchange rate a policy instrument? In principle, the real exchange rate is a relative price not directly controlled by policymakers. It is rather the outcome of other forces and policies affecting supply and demand. However, as discussed in the next section, it can be somewhat temporarily influenced by certain policies.

While the real exchange rate typically appreciates as a consequence of a natural resource shock, such real appreciation usually represents an equilibrium phenomenon that reflects a change in underlying fundamentals. Therefore, the appreciation should not need to be a cause of concern, and no economic policy response would be required, as there is no misalignment. Following this view, growth will be in line with fundamentals. The export-led growth supporters, however, would claim that there is always a role for economic policy to keep the currency undervalued so as to spur economic growth. Eventually, this is an empirical question—surveyed below—that essentially needs to compare the short-term benefits of an undervalued exchange rate with the long-term costs it might embed.

A real appreciation, however, could result from inconsistent domestic economic policies. For instance, if economic agents take a temporary shock as permanent, the real exchange rate could overshoot and become overvalued, and eventually become unsustainable if not corrected. If economic policy intends to permanently deviate the real exchange rate from its fundamental value, eventually inconsistencies will emerge. The likely effects are that the long-term pain would outweigh the short-term gain.

Therefore, the nature of the shock, or its persistence, is an important factor in determining whether to worry about Dutch disease or not. If the shock is temporary, then there might be a role for economic policy to smooth the impact of the shock and curb the symptoms of Dutch disease. Unfortunately, in some cases it is difficult to determine a priori if the shock is either temporary or permanent.

Therefore, even though Dutch disease could entail an appreciation of the real exchange rate, resource reallocation, and lower productivity in the manufacturing sector, would that imply that undervaluing the exchange rate will prevent Dutch disease and increase economic growth? Not necessarily. As documented below, Dutch disease does exist, but the link between Dutch disease and lower economic growth does not. Therefore, why would there be a role for economic policy to prevent Dutch disease on the basis of sustaining long-term economic growth? Yet the policy response to a natural resource boom (or other shocks causing Dutch disease) will likely affect the final outcome of the shock. The key challenge is how to adequately manage the boom associated with it.

Next, we document what the theoretical and empirical literature has found on these issues. We will then take stock of the literature to derive some policy implications.

THE EXISTING LITERATURE

Dutch Disease: Real Appreciation, Factor Reallocation, and De-Industrialization

Theory

The theoretical literature on Dutch disease is quite extensive. Early contributions include Corden (1981, 1984), Corden and Neary (1982), Van Wijnbergen (1984), Edwards and Aoki (1983), and Haberger (1983). Corden (1981) uses a two-sector economy to illustrate the so-called tradable squeeze, also known as Dutch disease. Using a simple model, he shows how the discovery of natural resources triggers large capital inflows—for example, to finance investments in the natural resource sector—which in turn appreciates the domestic currency. The real appreciation results from two interconnected sources: capital inflows and the increase in demand for nontradable goods (given higher income owing to the discovered resources). Furthermore, expectations of further appreciations increase (speculative) capital inflows, reinforcing the appreciation. The overall effect of the real appreciation is to redirect resources from (traditional) tradable goods to natural resource tradable and nontradable goods. If nominal wages are rigid, this might increase unemployment. To undo these effects, Corden suggests either contracting real domestic expenditures or reducing public debt (in an amount equal to the capital inflows) or, more importantly, spending the proceeds of natural resources to accumulate foreign financial assets.

Corden and Neary (1982) analyze the effects of Dutch disease on income distribution and resource allocation. With a general equilibrium model, they study what they label a "resource movement" and a "spending effect." The former arises as the boom industry affects the marginal productivity of the factors of production—drawing resources out of the non-booming sectors—while the latter increases spending as a result of the wealth effect of the exogenous shock that triggers the boom. Conditional on different factor intensities, the model shows the effects of Dutch disease on income distribution and factor utilization. Corden (1984) extends Corden and Neary (1982) to analyze the effects of immigration, endogenous terms of trade, domestic absorption, and some dynamics.

Van Wijnbergen (1984) includes LBD to study the potential effects of Dutch disease on economic growth. Assuming that economic growth is mainly explained by LBD—mostly through the tradable sector—then Dutch disease will reduce a country's long-term growth. Consequently, there is an argument for responding to Dutch disease shocks by extending a production subsidy to the tradable goods sector. However, the latter results and policy implications depend on having a closed capital account. If the capital account is open, the country can increase its stock of net foreign assets with the Dutch disease revenues, which will counterbalance the real appreciation pressures, thus unwinding the call for production subsidies.

In line with the seminal contributions mentioned above, Edwards and Aoki (1983) discuss whether Dutch disease is a disease in the first place—and show that it is not a disease as long as the real appreciation is permanent and a shift to a new long-term equilibrium. To show this, they model a small open economy subject to an exogenous increase in the price of a commodity export (for example, oil). They show that, in equilibrium, the relative price of (traditional) tradable goods not only decreases with respect to commodity exports, but also with respect to nontradable goods. As a consequence, resources move out of the production of traditional tradable goods into nontradable goods and commodity tradables. The paper then extends Haberger (1983), showing that an overshooting of the exchange rate might arise if an excess supply of money results from the government's monetization of the external shock—which triggers an overshooting of the price of nontradable goods, thus impacting on the real exchange rate. Dutch disease tends to be amplified if the government owns the natural resource, as government expenditures are biased toward nontradable goods and the government spends the revenues. Haberger (1983) also suggests the relevance of not spending the proceeds of the external shock domestically. Hence, he suggests that increasing foreign assets might not only avoid the real appreciation, but also increase the country's long-term growth.

Krugman (1987) introduces dynamic economies of scale into a standard trade model to show conditions under which Dutch disease may appear. However, it is only one of several possibilities in his model—and conditional on the size and duration of the shock. Buiter and Purvis (1983) examine the following as sources of de-industrialization: monetary disinflation, an increase in the price of oil, and a domestic oil discovery. They show that monetary disinflation and an increase in the price of oil will generate real appreciation, thus reducing domestic production of tradable goods. Domestic oil discoveries, however, have more ambiguous effects. They only focus on the demand side part of these shocks, though. They claim that oil shocks are not likely to increase unemployment—as opposed to most of the literature. The latter is based on the assumptions that oil is not an intermediate input—thus not causing long-term impact on the manufacturing sector—and the absence of a nontradable goods sector. An interesting result they obtain is that the increase in the price of oil will also have a negative effect on oil-importing manufacturing output.

Some papers emphasize intertemporal differences of Dutch disease, such as Bruno and Sachs (1982), Chaterji and Price (1988), Arellano and others (2005), and Prati and Tressel (2005). Bruno and Sachs (1982) build a Dutch disease model extended to allow for short-term capital specificity and long-term capital mobility, international capital flows, and intertemporal optimization. By simulating an infinite-horizon economy, the main contribution is to look at the transitional dynamics of Dutch disease shocks. The results confirm the mechanics of Dutch disease and the role for saving the capital inflow generated by Dutch disease: increasing the net foreign assets (NFA) position of the country smoothes the benefits of the Dutch disease shock over time. Chatterji and Price (1988) study the effects of Dutch disease on long-term unemployment. They show that although Dutch disease can increase unemployment in the short term owing to market rigidities, it lowers long-term unemployment. They assume that the quantity of oil production is exogenous, so there is no resource effect but only a spending effect. The labor market rigidity is assumed by a union that sets the wage rate in the tradable goods sector, thus obtaining equilibrium unemployment.

Arellano and others (2005) study the dynamics of foreign-aid-induced Dutch disease in an open economy real business cycle (RBC) model. The usual static effects of Dutch disease are obtained. In the dynamic setting, if foreign aid is a continuous flow, they find that it mainly finances consumption—in line with intertemporal optimization. If financial access is limited, then aid generates fluctuations in investment in order to smooth consumption. Welfare analysis shows that volatility in aid results in a welfare reduction. The paper also presents empirical results on the relationship between foreign aid and the production of goods for export. Results indicate that manufactured good exports, as predicted by the theoretical model, are negatively related to the level of aid, even after controlling for initial endowments, transaction costs, the level of development, and other variables. Prati and Tressel (2005) also focus on Dutch-disease-like effects of international aid. They develop a two-sector open economy model that receives an exogenous flow of foreign aid that can be either consumed or invested in productivity-enhancing public goods. They show a role for macroeconomic policy by adjusting domestic credit—that is, sterilization. The ability of the latter to increase welfare is conditional on the time profile of foreign aid. When foreign aid is mainly front-loaded (back-loaded), a contractionary (expansionary) monetary policy will stimulate savings (consumption), thus smoothing the effects of aid. In the presence of LBD, sterilization might raise productivity and increase future consumption by reducing present consumption—that is, the economy needs tighter monetary policy to increase future growth.

Gylfason, Herbertson, and Zoega (1997) focus on the effects of Dutch disease on the volatility of the real exchange rate, which further lowers productivity and investment in the tradable goods sector. This amplifies the standard Dutch disease effects. They show that abundance of a natural resource tends to inhibit economic growth by reducing investment in human capital. The paper analyzes the case of a flexible exchange rate regime—unlike most of the preceding literature—which can provide insurance to the primary export industry at the expense of increasing exchange rate uncertainty for all other industries. Their findings confirm a statistically significant inverse relationship between the size of the primary sector and economic growth, but not between the volatility of the real exchange rate and growth.

The recent literature has started to dispute the negative implications of Dutch disease. Nkusu (2004) shows that low-income countries that receive foreign aid need not experience Dutch disease. This is the case if countries can draw on their idle capacity to satisfy the demand induced by foreign aid. The author builds a model to specifically analyze the effects of foreign aid in economic growth through the real exchange rate—thus the need to use a Dutch-disease-type model. It shows that if there is factor underutilization—for example, unemployment—the Dutch disease spending effect disappears. Thus, a real appreciation will not affect the tradable sector and it will not reduce growth until the economy returns to full employment—that is, when the spending effect reactivates. Torvik (2001) assumes LBD both in the tradable and nontradable sectors, as well as learning spillovers between sectors. Under these assumptions, the economy depicts a real depreciation in the long term—despite the short-term appreciation—and output and productivity may go either up or down, unlike traditional Dutch disease models. The argument is based on the following: under the LBD and spillover assumptions, in the short term, the higher demand for nontradable goods increases production. This increases the demand for labor in the latter sector. However, LBD and spillovers also increase productivity faster in the nontradable sector. Over time, this implies a reduction in labor demand by the nontradable sector, which in equilibrium requires a real exchange rate depreciation. Furthermore, Matsen and Torvik (2005) show the existence of some level of optimal Dutch disease. This optimal level implies adjusting the national wealth of the Dutch disease that is consumed each period to be lower than current Dutch disease models predict—that is, increase saving—yet positive and increasing over time. As such, if lower growth is observed, it would be part of the optimal growth path. Therefore, the paper shows that the greater the growth generated by the traded sector, the more resources should be spent in the early periods. Making policy endogenous enables the authors to support why some resource-rich countries have been successful while others not: it depends on whether the government generates the intertemporally optimal level of saving.

Focusing on policy reactions to Dutch disease phenomena, Caballero and Lorenzoni (2007) and Lama and Medina (2010) study the impact of exchange rate interventions to contain Dutch disease effects. Caballero and Lorenzoni (2007) analyze the convenience of foreign exchange intervention to prevent real exchange rate appreciation. The key condition is the degree of financial constraint of the export sector. The criterion for intervention, however, is not whether firms go bankrupt but whether these can cause a strong real exchange rate (depreciating) overshooting. If export firms are not financially constrained, only ex post (that is, during the overshooting depreciation) intervention is justified. If these firms are highly financially constrained, on the contrary, ex ante (that is, during the prolonged real appreciation phase) intervention is worthwhile to smooth the overreacting real depreciation. In the model, the overshooting results from the export sector's lack of ability to absorb resources (labor) freed by the nontradable sector—which are channeled by a contraction in real wages that depresses domestic demand. Lama and Medina (2010) analyze the welfare effects of stabilizing the exchange rate—through intervention—to contain the appreciation derived from a Dutch disease shock. Using a stochastic dynamic general equilibrium model with LBD and nominal rigidities, they show that although exchange rate stabilization sustains tradable goods production (that is, it keeps it at an efficient level), it contributes to misallocation of resources and increases the economy's volatility. Thus, welfare decreases in the case of exchange rate intervention. Finally, Bresser-Pereira (2008) claims the government should react to the real appreciation that Dutch disease generates by taxing exports and sales alike to manage the exchange rate, making it clear that the accumulated tax revenues should not be spent domestically. However, he presents no convincing evidence or theoretical model to support his argument.

Applications and Empirical Studies

The empirical literature on Dutch Disease is also extensive. Most of the literature focuses on the impact of higher foreign exchange inflows on the real exchange rate and the reallocation of resources between the tradable and nontradable sectors. Notably, most papers do not examine the effects of the Dutch disease phenomenon on long-term growth—more specifically, they do not analyze whether the adverse effects associated with Dutch disease offset the beneficial effects of inflows.

One strand of the literature focuses on the impact of remittances, generally finding evidence of Dutch disease symptoms. For instance, Lartey, Mandelman, and Acosta (2008) study the existence of Dutch disease effects stemming from remittances, trying to capture both spending and resource movement effects. To this end, they run a set of regressions using the ratio of tradable to nontradable output as the dependent variable, in addition to the standard regressions using the real exchange rate. They use a generalized method of moments estimator to estimate a dynamic panel model, tailored to deal with potential endogeneity in the explanatory variables. Their findings show that an increase in remittances leads to real exchange rate appreciation (spending effect) and a decline in the ratio of tradable to nontradable output (resource movement effect)—two features of the Dutch disease phenomenon. Moreover, they find evidence that these effects are stronger under fixed exchange rate regimes. The authors do not address whether these effects of remittances harm growth and welfare and what policies should be pursued to address them.

Acosta, Lartey, and Mandelman (2009) use Bayesian techniques and data for El Salvador to estimate a dynamic stochastic general equilibrium (DSGE) model of a small open economy to analyze the effects of remittances on resource reallocation and the real exchange rate. The results suggest that a surge in remittances leads to Dutch disease phenomena. This is because higher remittances lead to a decline in labor supply and an increase in consumption demand that is biased toward nontradables. The higher price of nontradables stimulates an expansion of that sector, reallocating labor away from the tradable sector. Using a Bayesian vector autoregression, they find that the empirical results are consistent with the dynamics of the model, in particular regarding the impact of an increase in remittances on nontradable output and the real exchange rate.

Amuedo-Dorantes and Pozo (2004) assess the impact of workers' remittances on the real exchange rate using a panel of 13 Latin American and Caribbean countries. They also find that an increase in remittances leads to a real exchange rate appreciation, with a doubling of remittances appreciating the real exchange rate by 23 percent. In contrast, Rajan and Subramanian (2005) find evidence suggesting that remittances do not create Dutch disease effects.

Another strand of the literature examines the existence of Dutch disease effects stemming from foreign aid. Although there is some evidence of Dutch disease symptoms stemming from aid, that is not an inexorable outcome, and would mainly depend on how aid inflows are actually spent. Moreover, the overall impact on growth would depend on whether spillovers and/or LBD externalities accrue to either tradable or nontradable sectors, and on supply-side effects associated with aid-related investments.

Rajan and Subramanian (2005) analyze why there is no robust association between aid and growth, and suggest that a plausible explanation is that aid may lead to real exchange rate overvaluation, affecting competitiveness in the tradable sector. They find that aid inflows negatively affect a country's competitiveness, as reflected in a decline in the share of labor-intensive and tradable industries in the manufacturing sector. Their results also suggest that the channel is the real exchange rate overvaluation caused by aid inflows. Based on these results, the authors speculate that because the tradable sector is typically the source of productivity improvements, positive spillovers associated with LBD, and scarce foreign exchange earnings that filter through to the rest of the economy, the adverse impact of aid on its competitiveness could retard not just that sector but also the growth of the entire economy. However, they do not show that aid is, on net, harmful to growth. They just provide evidence consistent with a channel that could offset potential beneficial effects of aid.

Rajan and Subramanian (2009) examine the impact of aid on the relative size of and growth in the tradable manufacturing sector, using an approach that exploits the variation within countries and across manufacturing sectors, and corrects for possible reverse causality. They also focus on finding evidence on the channel through which aid might have these effects. They find evidence that aid inflows negatively affect tradable manufacturing sectors, with real exchange rate appreciation being the channel for such effects. Although they do not provide any evidence of causation from manufacturing exports to growth, they speculate that their findings may explain why the evidence about the impact of aid on growth is so ambiguous.

Adenauer and Vagassky (1998) test the existence of Dutch disease symptoms in four CFA zone countries during 1980–92. They find that an increase in aid leads to a real exchange rate appreciation. Then, they examine the channels of aid on a country-by-country basis, focusing on the particular policies followed by each of them. They argue that government policies, consumption levels, and investment are crucial factors in determining the extent of Dutch disease effects in each country. Amuedo-Dorantes and Pozo (2004), in contrast, find no systematic effect of foreign aid on the real exchange rate.

Adam and Bevan (2004) show that the conventional Dutch disease effects of aid may be overturned when productivity spillovers accrue in both the tradable and nontradable sectors. They present a model, calibrated to Ugandan data, where public infrastructure investment generates an intertemporal productivity spillover that may exhibit a sector-specific bias. Their results suggest that, for reasonable values of the parameters regarding the supply-side effects of public expenditure, the traditional Dutch disease effects are not present beyond the short term.

Some studies show that Dutch disease is not an inexorable consequence of aid inflows. For instance, IMF (2005) looks at low-income countries that have experienced a surge in aid inflows and are strong performers in terms of institutions and economic policies (Ethiopia, Ghana, Mozambique, Tanzania, and Uganda), finding that the aid surge was actually accompanied by real exchange rate depreciation, not appreciation. Consistent with real depreciation, export performance was strong in most of the sample, especially Mozambique and Tanzania.

Other studies focus on natural resource booms, associated with either discoveries or price increases. Sachs and Warner (2001) try to explain why countries with large natural resource endowments tend to grow slowly (that is, the natural resource curse). They find evidence that natural-resource-intensive economies tend to have higher price levels (hence higher nontradable prices, assuming roughly similar tradable prices across countries), after controlling for the relationship between price levels and per capita income. They then show that resource-abundant countries tend to have small contributions from export growth in manufactures. They use these results as a potential explanation of the resource curse, by implicitly assuming that a larger manufacturing tradable sector drives long-term growth. However, they do not attempt to show evidence of this relationship. They also discuss other possible explanations for the curse, which relate natural resource abundance with crowding out of entrepreneurial activities or innovation, rent-seeking behavior (voracity effects), and higher corruption. Natural resource countries would thus experience lower innovation, lower entrepreneurial activity, poorer governments, and lower growth.

Sachs and Warner (1999) present a model with natural resources, increasing returns in the spirit of big-push models, and expectations and show that when the increasing-returns-to-scale (IRS) sector is nontradable, a resource boom can indeed pull more goods into that sector, and thereby set off a dynamic growth process. However, when the IRS sector is in tradable manufactures, a resource boom can hurt growth, via the Dutch disease phenomenon. Empirically, they present evidence from seven Latin American countries suggesting that natural resource booms are sometimes accompanied by declining per capita GDP. However, they recognize that they cannot distinguish between several possible channels associated with natural resource booms: Dutch disease, political instability, costs of high variability of export earnings (with imperfect financial and insurance markets), etc.

Gylfason (2001) discusses the concept, existing literature, and case studies of Dutch disease to draw some lessons. In the empirical section, he shows that across countries (1) economic growth varies inversely with natural resource abundance; (2) two different measures of education intended to reflect education inputs and participation are both inversely related to natural resource abundance; and (3) economic growth varies directly with education. Therefore, natural resource abundance seems likely to deter economic growth not only through Dutch disease, rent seeking, and overconfidence that tends to reduce the quality of economic policy and structure, but also by weakening public and private incentives to accumulate human capital. If so, the adverse effects of natural resource abundance on economic growth since the 1960s that have been reported in the literature may in part reflect, and possibly displace, the effect of education on growth.

Larsen (2004) shows that Norway was able to avoid the effects of Dutch disease after the discovery and extraction of oil in the early 1970s, and discusses the policies behind the success. He argues that the factor movement effect was dampened through income coordination: a highly centralized wage formation system made it possible to make the manufacturing sector the wage leader (based on productivity increases). This made it possible to limit wage increases in all sectors from an expanding resource sector. The spending effect, in turn, was curbed because the government shielded the economy by fiscal discipline and investing abroad (through the creation of a petroleum fund). The spillover-loss effect was limited because losses were substituted for by gains in the highly technological off-shore oil extraction sector, which requires more capital than on-land oil extraction. Moreover, social norms, transparent democracy, proper monitoring, an effective judicial system, and the wage negotiation system reduced rent-seeking behavior, limiting the typical negative effects associated with the resource curse.

Ismail (2010) builds a static model. Then he tests it for the existence of Dutch disease using microeconomic data, unlike most of the other studies. Annual data for the period 1977–2004 in 90 countries are used; however, owing to limited availability, this includes only data from the manufacturing sector. With this caveat, he finds that a permanent oil shock results in manufacturing production reductions. Furthermore, these effects seem to be stronger in economies with more open capital accounts. The relative factor price of labor increases with respect to capital. Consequently, capital intensity increases in the oil shock—consistent with his labor-intensive nontradable sector model. Finally, he finds that sectors with higher capital intensity are affected relatively less by these types of shocks.

Spatafora and Warner (1995) look at oil-exporting countries and observe that the real exchange rate tends to appreciate in response to terms-of-trade shocks, but without the existence of Dutch disease. Sala-i-Martin and Subramanian (2003) do not find Dutch disease evidence. Similarly, Gelb (1988), doing a cross-country analysis for oil-exporter countries, finds no evidence of Dutch disease in the manufacturing sector.

Real Exchange Rate and Growth

There is an extensive literature on real exchange rate misalignment and economic growth. Cottani, Cavallo, and Khan (1990), among others, document the existence of a strong negative relationship between per capita GDP growth and two measures of real exchange rate behavior: real exchange instability and real exchange rate misalignment. They find no significant relationship between the purchasing power parity exchange rate and economic growth. Building on Cottani, Cavallo, and Khan, Ghura and Grennes (1993) study the effects of the real exchange rate on growth in sub-Saharan African countries. They confirm the negative relationship between real exchange rate misalignment and instability, and economic growth. For their sample of countries, they also find a negative relationship between the purchasing power parity real exchange rate and growth. In a similar vein, Dollar (1992) finds that existence of a negative relationship between distortions in the real exchange rate and per capita GDP after controlling for the effects of exchange rate variability and the level of investment.

In recent years, a new literature on the level of real exchange rate and growth has emerged, with the view that a depreciated or undervalued exchange rate fosters growth. This view has been motivated by the successful experiences of China and other east Asian countries. Although there is some evidence suggesting that exchange rate overvaluation hinders growth and/or undervaluation stimulates it (Hausmann, Pritchett, and Rodrik, 2004; Prasad, Rajan, and Subramanian, 2007; Levy-Yeyati and Sturzenegger, 2007; Rodrik, 2008; Eichengreen, 2008), the evidence is still limited and far from conclusive. The literature addressing these linkages is still in its infancy, and there is no consensus on the precise channel through which they operate.

A common view—linked to the export-led literature and to the traditional Dutch disease literature—argues that the operative channel is the size of the (manufacturing) tradable sector. In this view, this sector is "special," typically because of externalities associated with export-linked activities (Prasad and others, 2007; Rodrik, 2008). There is, however, little systematic evidence on the specific nature of such externalities, and it is empirically difficult to distinguish between alternative hypotheses. Similarly, although there are a few studies trying to document spillover effects stemming from manufacturing, the evidence is quite inconclusive (Eichengreen, 2008).

Hausmann, Pritchett, and Rodrik (2004) examine episodes of rapid growth accelerations that are sustained for at least eight years, and find that such episodes tend to be associated with increases in investment and trade, and with real exchange rate depreciations.

Prasad, Rajan, and Subramanian (2007) assess the impact of capital inflows on economic growth in nonindustrial economies. Their results show a positive link between current account surpluses and growth, and interpret this as evidence that nonindustrial countries receiving foreign capital inflows have not recorded higher growth rates. They present evidence suggesting that foreign capital inflows can lead to real exchange rate overvaluation, hurting manufacturing exports and thus overall economic growth.

Rodrik (2008) finds that an undervalued real exchange rate has a positive effect on growth, and provides some evidence that the operative channel is the size of the (manufacturing) tradable sector. He then discusses two alternative hypotheses to explain the stylized facts, but is unable to distinguish between them empirically. Finally, he develops a small open economy model where both the tradable and nontradable sectors face an economic distortion. If such distortion is larger in the tradable sector, the size of this sector would be smaller than optimal in equilibrium. Hence, any policy leading to a real exchange rate depreciation would have positive effects on growth.

Berg and Miao (2010) analyze Rodrik (2008) and find an identification problem, as determinants of misalignment are also determinants of growth. In Rodrik's story, undervaluation is good for growth and overvaluation is bad. The so-called Washington Consensus view, on the contrary, considers both types of misalignment to be bad for growth. Berg and Miao show that Rodrik's explanation regarding this symmetry holds. However, Berg and Miao also show that, after controlling for fundamentals, deviations of the real exchange rate from purchasing power parity values, as used in Rodrick (2008), do not explain long-term growth. On the contrary, deviations from fundamental real exchange rates, as in the Washington Consensus view, do explain long-term growth.

Eichengreen (2008) analyzes how the real exchange rate affects economic growth and what the channels are through which this link operates. He states that although there is some evidence suggesting that a competitive real exchange rate may stimulate growth, such evidence is not overwhelming. Moreover, the literature has not yet identified the relevant channels of transmission. In particular, he argues that the evidence on the nature and prevalence of positive externalities associated with export-related activities (or other spillovers stemming from them) is inconclusive and usually indirect. He argues that these results may indicate that a competitive real exchange rate is only a "facilitating condition"—not a sufficient one—that would enable a country to capitalize on certain strong fundamentals (such as a disciplined labor force, a high saving rate, or its attractiveness as a destination for foreign investment). Finally, he notes that while a competitive real exchange rate may play a role in jump-starting growth there are also costs of keeping a weak currency for too long, so it is important to develop an exit strategy.

A second view in the more recent literature links an undervalued exchange rate to growth through an increase in domestic saving. Dooley, Folkerts-Landau, and Garber (2004) argue that a depreciated real exchange rate tends to shift demand away from tradable to nontradable goods, so that the real interest rate needs to rise to maintain internal equilibrium, increasing domestic saving rates. Levy-Yeyati and Sturzenegger (2007) point to an alternative channel: an undervalued real exchange rate is associated with lower real wages, leading firms to higher investment, and to higher saving rates to finance them. They present evidence suggesting that foreign exchange rate intervention has typically been aimed at limiting appreciations rather than depreciations (what they call "fear of appreciation"). After establishing whether such interventions were actually successful in maintaining an undervalued real exchange rate, they examine the effects of "fear of appreciation" on growth in developing economies. They find that fear of appreciation indeed leads to higher long-term growth rates. However, in contrast to the view that points to the relative size and growth of the tradable sector as the relevant channel, they find that higher growth comes from increased domestic saving and investment.

Montiel and Servén (2008), however, argue that the link between the real exchange rate and saving is theoretically and empirically weak. They find no evidence of a positive relationship between a depreciated currency and higher saving rates. Moreover, they claim there is no consensus and no analytical basis in the literature to explain the precise channels through which this link would operate. They also use a standard new open economy model to show that although it is possible to generate a positive impact from a depreciated real exchange rate on saving, the necessary conditions to get this result are quite implausible. Finally, they show that the empirical literature trying to explain international differences in saving rates has not provided evidence on a possible role for the level of the real exchange rate as a potential determinant.

THE LITERATURE REVIEW IN NUMBERS

In this section, we put together the information contained in the papers reviewed in a systematic way, developing some basic indicators. Each of the reviewed papers—either theoretical or empirical—obtains results, for example, on whether Dutch disease exists or not, or if real exchange rate undervaluation increases economic growth, etc. To this end, the papers were divided into two categories: (1) those analyzing Dutch disease; and (2) those studying the effects of the real exchange rate on growth.

Papers focusing on Dutch disease were first separated according the nature of the Dutch disease shock: (1) natural resource/capital inflows; (2) remittances; and (3) foreign aid. Within each category, in turn, each paper was surveyed to find results regarding the following. Do Dutch disease shocks cause:

- a real appreciation?
- lower relative production of tradable goods versus nontradable goods?
- factor reallocation?
- a reduction in the relative productivity of the tradable versus nontradable sectors?
- lower net exports? and
- lower growth?

The papers analyzing the effects of exchange rates on growth were reviewed looking for conclusions regarding the following questions:

- Does misalignment of the real exchange rate lower economic growth?
- Does it make any difference if the misalignment is due to overvaluation?
- Does it make any difference if the misalignment is due to undervaluation?
- Does an appreciation of the real exchange rate (level) decrease economic growth?
- Does a depreciation of the real exchange rate (level) decrease economic growth?
- Does volatility of the real exchange rate misalignment lower economic growth?
- Does volatility of the real exchange rate level lower economic growth?

Figure 1.2 shows the results for the papers analyzing Dutch disease. As mentioned above, the results were separated according to the source of Dutch disease shock. The overall results suggest the following. In more than 80 percent of the cases, Dutch disease shock appreciates the real exchange rate and causes de-industrialization (that is, a decline in the ratio of tradable to nontradable output). In more than 90 percent of the cases, Dutch disease shocks generate factor reallocation and a decrease in the relative productivity of the tradable sector, and in about 75 percent of the cases, exports are reduced. However, and contrary to the common view, no lower growth is observed as a result of Dutch disease in close to 80 percent of the cases. Notably, only a few papers address this question, as most of them focus on real exchange rate appreciation, factor reallocation, and relative output (tradable to nontradable). The results hold regardless of whether the papers are theoretical or empirical, as shown in Figure 1.3.

According to the source of the shock, we observe consistent results (Figure 1.2). For natural resource/capital inflows episodes, the shares are larger in each category. A similar pattern is found for foreign aid shocks. As for remittances, results show a strong indication of real appreciation, but not much net effect on relative tradable/nontradable output or economic growth.

Figure 1.4 presents the results corresponding to the effects of the real exchange rate on growth. There is evidence that real exchange rate misalignment does reduce growth. Of the reviewed observations, 90 percent show that when the misalignment (defined as a deviation from its fundamental value) is due to overvaluation,

Figure 1.2 Literature Review in Numbers: Dutch Disease

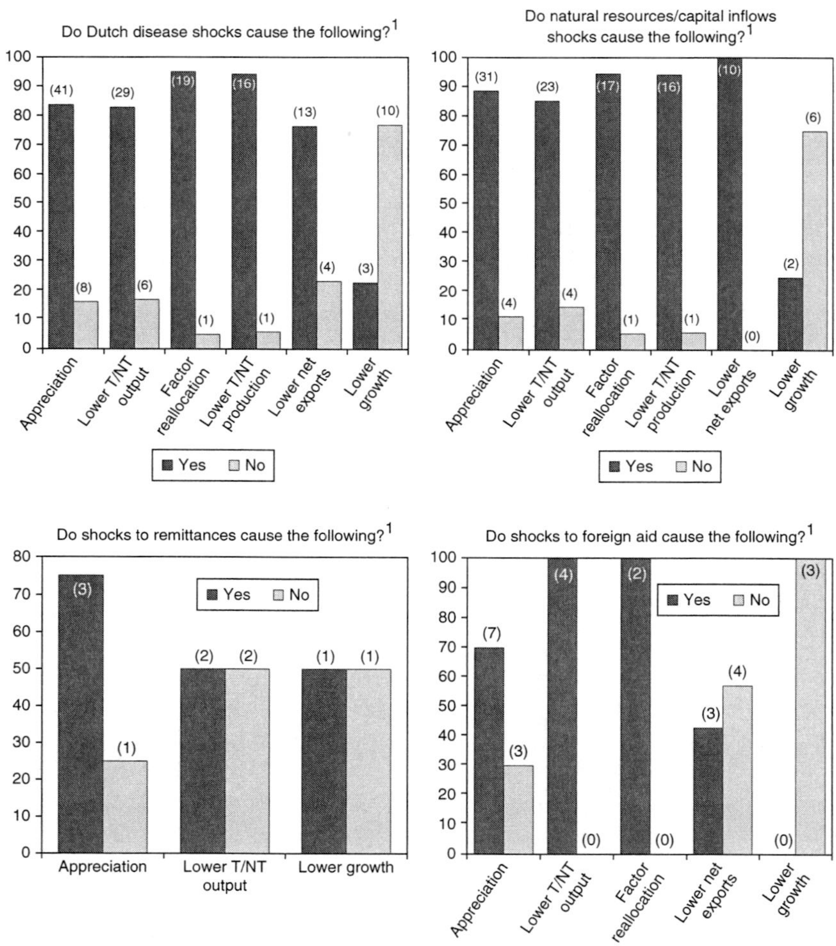

Source: Authors' calculations.

Note: T/NT = tradable/nontradable.

[1]In percent of total observations. Number of observations in parentheses.

Figure 1.3 Literature Review in Numbers: Do Dutch Disease Shocks Cause the Following? Comparing Empirical and Theoretical Papers

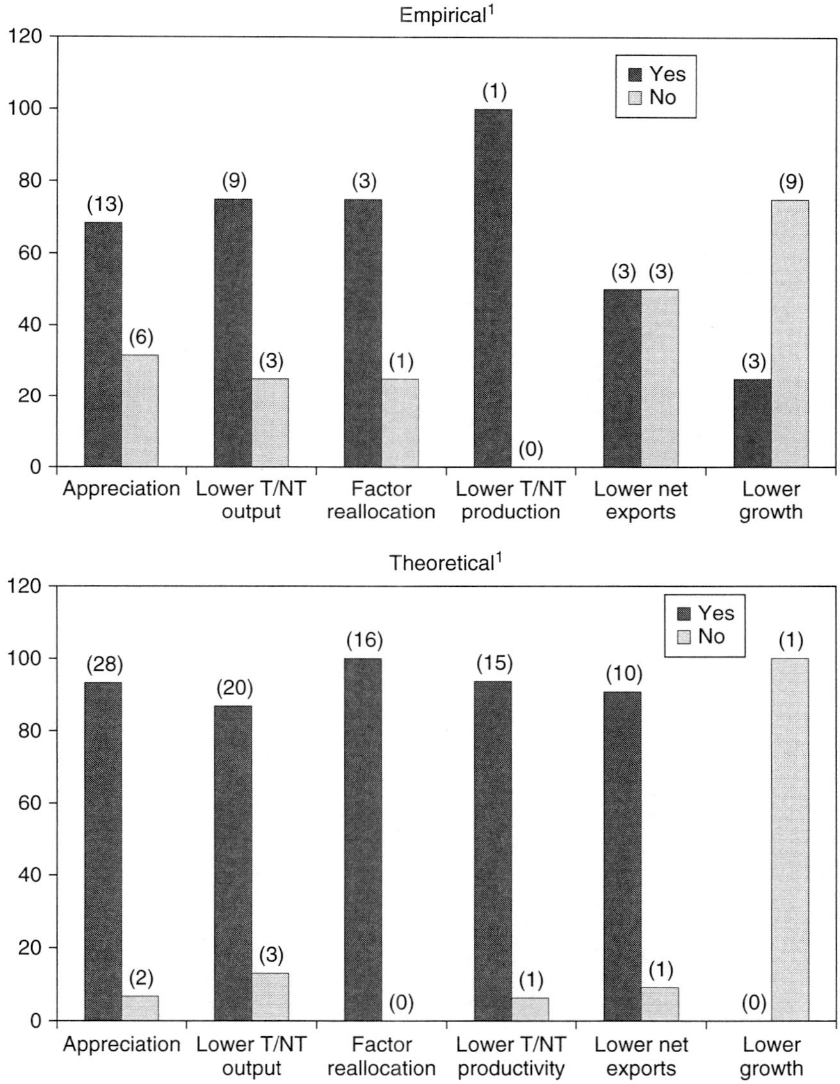

Source: Authors' calculations.
Note: T/NT = tradable/nontradable.
[1]In percent of total observations. Number of observations in parenthesis.

growth is reduced. When the misalignment is due to undervaluation, some results indicate that it lowers growth, but the evidence is broadly inconclusive. If anything, the evidence seems to indicate that misalignment lowers growth. Regarding the exchange rate level, an appreciation appears to reduce growth in 75 percent of the surveyed observations, whereas depreciation seems not to reduce growth in

Figure 1.4 Literature Review in Numbers: Real Exchange Rate and Growth

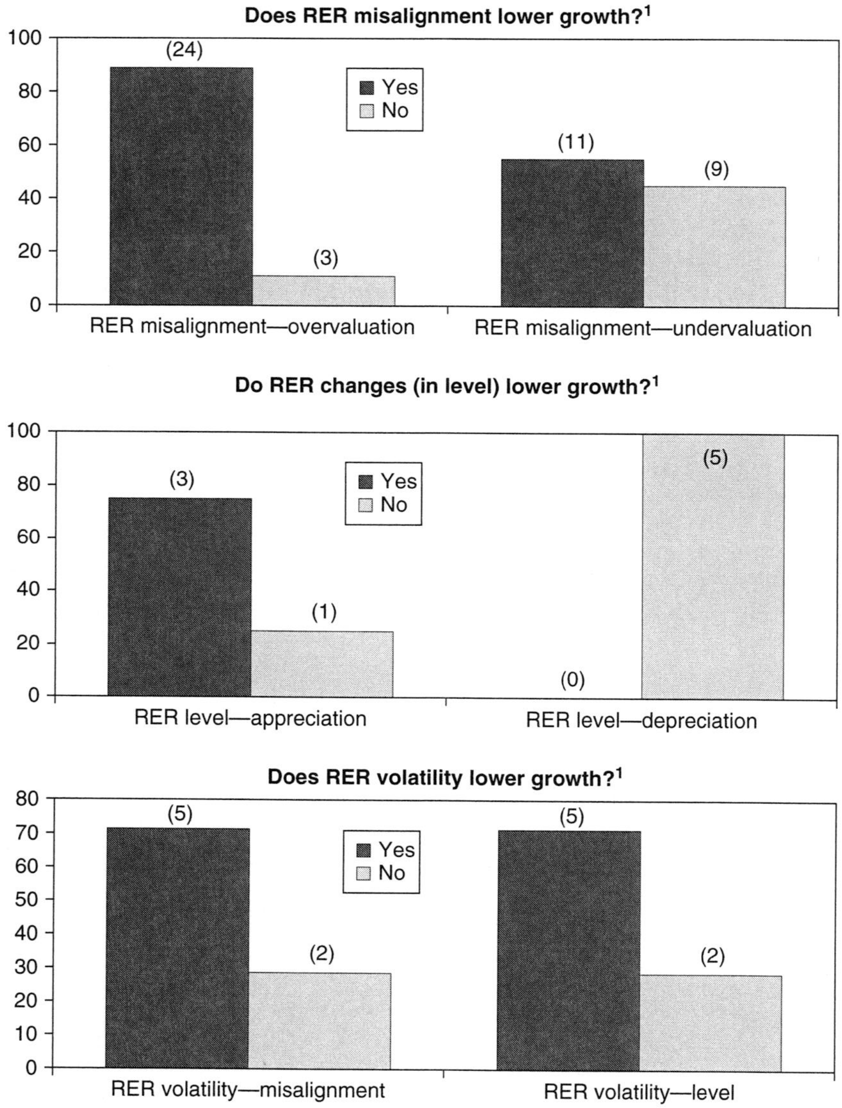

Source: Authors' calculations.
Note: RER = real exchange rate.
[1]In percent of total observations. Number of observations in parentheses.

100 percent of the observations. It should be noted, however, that the majority of the studies addressing the relationship between the real exchange rate and growth focus on misalignment (either overvaluation or undervaluation) and not on the

level of the real exchange rate.[2] Finally, real exchange rate volatility appears to be negative for growth regardless of whether we focus on the volatility of the misalignment or the volatility of the real exchange rate level.

Putting together both pictures, the reviewed literature gives a clear message. On the one hand, Dutch disease does exist—as the real exchange rate appreciates, there is factor reallocation, and production switches away from manufacturing. On the other hand, exchange rate volatility hampers economic growth. Misalignment of the real exchange rate from its fundamental value also lowers growth. Overvaluations (however defined) are always negative for economic growth, but the evidence on undervaluation is inconclusive. Finally, the evidence shows the lack of connection between Dutch disease and economic growth. Dutch disease does exist, but its existence does not imply lower growth. Even though overvaluation may hinder growth, Dutch disease could also be seen as an equilibrium phenomenon in which a country becomes richer.

POLICY DISCUSSION

Should real exchange rate appreciation be a source of concern for policymakers? Should they act to curb Dutch disease effects? If yes, is it owing to concerns about long-term growth? What is policy really capable of doing? In this section, we build on our discussion of the literature to address these questions.

The literature reviewed above reveals that there is little theoretical and empirical basis for the adverse impact of Dutch disease on growth. Although Dutch disease may be accompanied by a contraction of manufacturing tradables, this would not necessarily offset the beneficial effects associated with the positive wealth effect. The policy response should aim at taking advantage of those positive effects, while at the same time mitigating the undesired consequences that it may cause.

A given appreciation of the real exchange rate may have a differential impact on economic growth depending on whether or not it reflects an equilibrium phenomenon. If the appreciation is driven by a permanent change, then it will imply a long-term equilibrium movement, and in principle Dutch disease should not be a concern. However, the real exchange rate could overshoot and become overvalued (for instance, if agents overestimate the persistence of the shock, or in case an excess supply of money results from the government's monetization of the external shock—which triggers an overshooting of the price of nontradable goods). Thus, macroeconomic policy should focus on avoiding overshooting, overheating, and the surge of macroeconomic imbalances that could later become unsustainable.

It is sometimes difficult for policymakers to assess if a certain shock and the corresponding real exchange rate appreciation will be temporary or permanent. If the

---

[2]Although we found 47 studies examining the relationship between real exchange rate misalignment and growth, we found only 9 focusing on the level of the real exchange rate.

authorities treat a permanent shock as temporary and decide, for example, to intervene in the foreign exchange market, they will delay an unavoidable—and desirable—macroeconomic adjustment, resulting also in substantial quasi-fiscal costs owing to sterilization. If, on the contrary, they treat a temporary shock as permanent, they may experience costs in terms of reduced growth. In the particular case of capital inflows shocks, this dilemma has in recent years provided a justification for the use of capital controls in some countries. Use of these controls was based on the belief that they would provide an instrument to limit the cost of accumulating reserves while avoiding a real exchange rate appreciation that may need to be reversed in the future. A discussion on the merits of capital controls is, however, out of the scope of this chapter (see Magud and Reinhart, 2007, for an extensive study on this issue).

Fiscal policy is a natural instrument to help curb Dutch disease effects. In fact, excessive public spending has been a common component of economic mismanagement of booms stemming from positive Dutch disease shocks. Fiscal policy may play a role not only by mitigating the "spending effect" associated with Dutch disease but also by smoothing expenditures to reduce output volatility. A prudent expenditure policy would help by saving part of the increased revenues, which could be used to repay either external debt or to accumulate foreign assets—typically in a sovereign wealth fund to be invested abroad. This would help limit aggregate demand pressures and hence the spending effect, and weaken real appreciation pressures. Directing spending to tradables (imported capital goods, for example) would also help curb the negative impacts of Dutch disease. If there is a presumption that the shock may be temporary, smoothing expenditure over time would help reduce volatility. In this case, a fiscal rule and the use of a stabilization fund could be appropriate.

How the inflow is spent is crucial not only to curb Dutch disease effects, but also to maximize the benefits associated with the positive income shock. It is policymakers' job to ensure that these benefits outweigh any potential adverse effect on long-term growth owing to a contraction of the tradable sector. In this regard, there is a case for improving the quality of expenditures, for example, by promoting investments that would entail positive supply-side effects. Investments that foster productivity and supply of nontradables (such as investments in infrastructure, education, or other activities to improve and expand the availability of skilled labor) would be particularly advantageous.

Norway, after the discovery and extraction of oil in the early 1970s, provides a good example of policies that proved successful in avoiding the effects of Dutch disease. The factor movement effect was dampened through income coordination: a highly centralized wage formation system made it possible to make the manufacturing sector the wage leader (based on productivity increases). This made it possible to constrain wage increases in all sectors from an expanding resource sector. The spending effect, in turn, was curbed because the government shielded the economy by fiscal discipline and invested its savings abroad (through the creation of a petroleum fund). The spillover-loss effect was limited because losses were offset by gains in the highly technological offshore oil extraction sector, which requires more capital than on-land oil extraction. Finally, social norms, transparent democracy, proper monitoring, an effective judicial system, and the wage negotiation system reduced rent-seeking behavior, limiting the typical negative effects associated with the resource curse.

The optimal policy response would depend, to some extent, on the type of shock behind the Dutch disease. For instance, in case of a surge in aid inflows, the creation of a sovereign wealth fund to be held abroad would not make sense. On the contrary, policies would need to focus on ensuring that the increased inflows are spent adequately. Investments with positive supply-side effects, in particular those that would enhance productivity in nontradable sectors, could be helpful to ensure that the increase in aid does not hinder long-term growth.

In case of a positive terms-of-trade or capital inflows shock, policies should focus on mitigating the spending effect and avoiding an excessive increase in aggregate demand, overheating, and inflation pressures—even more so if there is uncertainty about the duration of the shock. Countries that do not want to accept too much real exchange rate appreciation should be ready to tighten fiscal policy. This would be the most reliable way to contain domestic demand, keep inflation in check, and—in the wake of a surge in capital inflows—avoid an excessive deterioration of the current account. Finally, improving financial regulation and supervision could play an important role in helping to contain credit booms or asset bubbles, reducing the likelihood of boom-bust cycles.

CONCLUSION

Concerns about sustained adverse growth effects of real appreciation have been explored for many years, going back at least to the Dutch disease literature of the early 1980s. The debate continues today, including with related recent literature that proposes further links between the real exchange rate and growth—but is still far from resolved. Although the logic of some of the theoretical arguments for this link is clearly established, these arguments lean heavily on special assumptions about the nature of economic growth. And the evidence seems insufficient: to date, with a few exceptions, empirical studies of Dutch disease have focused mainly on how shocks that cause real appreciation may affect the level of traded goods production rather than on whether this sector has a special role in economic growth, or whether it is permanently damaged by temporary episodes of real appreciation. Moreover, although the literature on real exchange rate and growth suggests that an overvalued exchange rate hinders growth, Dutch disease is in principle an equilibrium phenomenon reflecting changes in fundamentals, and not necessarily implying an overvaluation.

Our survey shows that, on the one hand, Dutch disease does exist—as the real exchange rate appreciates, there is factor reallocation, and production switches away from manufacturing. On the other hand, exchange rate volatility hampers economic growth. Misalignment of the real exchange rate from its fundamental value also lowers growth. Overvaluations (however defined) are always negative for economic growth, whereas the evidence on undervaluation is inconclusive.

Should policymakers worry about real exchange rate appreciation? Should they act to prevent appreciation and potential Dutch disease symptoms? As discussed in this chapter, the evidence on the impact of Dutch disease effects on growth is mainly inconclusive. Moreover, it is worth noting that shocks that cause Dutch disease—large capital inflows, export price booms, etc.—are usually associated with periods of economic bonanza. Dutch disease effects are an unintended consequence of foreign exchange abundance, but these negative effects would not necessarily offset the beneficial effects of the inflow. The challenge for policymakers is to adequately manage the boom and its accompanying risks. Therefore, the optimal policy response would consist of taking advantage of the boom, while at the same time dealing with its undesired consequences. When thinking about what to do about Dutch disease, policymakers should beware—in responding to the effects of the disease—of killing the goose that laid the golden egg.

REFERENCES

Acosta, P., E. Lartey, and F. Mandelman, 2009, "Remittances and the Dutch Disease," Federal Reserve Bank of Atlanta Working Paper, 2007–8a (Atlanta: Federal Reserve Bank of Atlanta).

Adam, C., 2005, "Exogenous Inflows and Real Exchange Rates: Theoretical Quirk or Empirical Reality?" paper presented at IMF Seminar on Foreign Aid and Macroeconomic Management, Maputo, Mozambique, March 14–15.

———, and D. Bevan, 2003, "Aid, Public Expenditure and Dutch Disease," CSAE Working Paper 184 (Oxford: Centre for the Study of African Economies, Oxford University).

———, 2004, "Aid and the Supply Side: Public Investment, Export Performance and Dutch Disease in Low Income Countries," Department of Economics Discussion Paper Series 201 (Oxford: Department of Economics, Oxford University).

Adenauer, I., and L. Vagassky, 1998, "Aid and the Real Exchange Rate: Dutch Disease Effects in African Countries," *Intereconomics*, Vol. 33, No. 4, 177–85.

Aguirre, A. and C. Calderon, 2005, "Real Exchange Rate Misalignments and Economic Performance," Central Bank of Chile Working Paper No. 315.

Amuedo-Dorantes, C., and S. Pozo, 2004, "Workers' Remittances and the Real Exchange Rate: a Paradox of Gifts," *World Development 32*, pp. 1407–17.

Arellano, C., A. Bulir, T. Lane, and L. Lipschitz, 2005, "The Dynamic Implications of Foreign Aid and Its Variability," IMF Working Paper 05/119 (Washington: International Monetary Fund).

Barder, O., 2006, "A Policymaker's Guide to Dutch Disease," Center for Global Development Working Paper 91 (Washington).

Berg, A., and Y. Miao, 2010, "The Real Exchange Rate and Growth Revisited: The Washington Consensus Strikes Back?" IMF Working Paper 10/58 (Washington: International Monetary Fund).

Bhalla, S., 2007, "There are no Growth Miracles," paper presented at the 8th Annual NBER-NCAER Neemrana Conference.

Bleaney, M., and D. Greenaway, 2001, "The Impact of Terms of Trade and Real Exchange Rate Volatility on Investment and Growth in Sub-Saharan Africa," *Journal of Development Economics*, Vol. 65 (2), pp. 491–500.

Bosworth, B., S. Collins, and Y. Chen, 1995, "Accounting for Differences in Economic Growth," unpublished manuscript, the Brookings Institution.

Bresser-Pereira, L., 2008, "The Dutch Disease and its Neutralization: a Ricardian Approach," *Brazilian Journal of Political Economy*, Vol. 28, No. 1 (109), pp. 47–71.

Bruno, M., and J. Sachs, 1982, "Energy and Resource Allocation: a Dynamic Model of the 'Dutch Disease,'" NBER Working Paper No. 852 (Cambridge, Massachusetts: National Bureau of Economic Research).

Buiter, W.H., and D.D. Purvis, 1983, "Oil, Disinflation and Export Competitiveness: a Model of the Dutch Disease," in *Economic Interdependence and Flexible Exchange Rates,* ed. by J.S. Bhandari and B.H. Putnam (Cambridge, Massachusetts: MIT Press).

Caballero, R., and G. Lorenzoni, 2007, "Persistent Appreciations and Overshooting: a Normative Analysis," NBER Working Paper No. 13077 (Cambridge, Massachusetts: National Bureau of Economic Research).

Chatterji, M., and S. Price, 1988, "Unions, Dutch Disease and Unemployment," *Oxford Economic Papers,* 40 (2), pp. 302–21.

Corden, W.M., 1981, "The Exchange Rate, Monetary Policy and North Sea Oil," *Oxford Economic Papers,* 33, pp. 23–46.

Corden, W. M., 1984, "Booming Sector and Dutch Disease Economics: Survey and Consolidation," *Oxford Economic Papers,* 36 (3), pp. 359–80.

Corden, W.M., and J.P. Neary, 1982, "Booming Sector and De-industrialization in a Small Open Economy," *Economic Journal,* 92, pp. 825–48.

Cottani, J., D. Cavallo, and S. Khan, 1990, "Real Exchange Rate Behavior and Economic Performance in LDCs," *Economic Development and Cultural Change,* Vol. 39, No. 1 (Oct.), pp. 61–76.

Dollar, D., 1992, "Outward-Oriented Developing Economies Really Do Grow More Rapidly: Evidence from 95 LDCs, 1976-1985," *Economic Development and Cultural Change,* Vol. 40, No. 3 (April), pp. 523–44.

Dooley, M., D. Folkerts-Landau, and P. Garber, 2004, "An Essay on the Revived Bretton Woods System," NBER Working Paper No. 9971 (Cambridge, Massachusetts: National Bureau of Economic Research).

Easterly, William, 2001, "The Middle Class Consensus and Economic Development," *Journal of Economic Growth,* No. 6, pp. 317–35.

Easterly, William, 2005, "National Policies and Economic Growth: A Reappraisal," in *Handbook of Economic Growth,* ed. by Philippe Aghion and Steven Durlauf, Volume 1, Part A., pp. 1015–59.

Edwards, S., and M. Aoki, 1983, "Oil Export Boom and Dutch-Disease: a Dynamic Analysis," *Resources and Energy,* Vol. 5, Issue 3, pp. 219–42.

Eichengreen, B., 2008, "The Real Exchange Rate and Economic Growth," Commission on Growth and Development Working Paper No. 4.

Gelb, A. 1988, "Oil Windfalls: Blessing or Curse?" (Washington: World Bank).

Ghura, D., and T. Grennes, 1993, "The Real Exchange Rate and Macroeconomic Performance in Sub-Saharan Africa," *Journal of Development Economics,* 42, pp. 155–74.

Gylfason, T., 2001, "Lessons from the Dutch Disease: Causes, Treatment, and Cures," Institute of Economic Studies Working Paper 01:06 (Reykjavik).

Gylfason, T., T. T. Herbertson, and G. Zoega, 1997, "A Mixed Blessing: Natural Resources and Economic Growth," *Macroeconomic Dynamics,* Vol. 3, pp. 204–25.

Haberger, A., 1983, "Dutch Disease—How Much Sickness, How Much Boon?" *Resources and Energy 5,* pp. 1–20 (Amsterdam: North-Holland).

Harms, P., and M. Lutz, 2005, "The Macroeconomic Effects of Foreign Aid," in *Development Cooperation—Evaluation and New Approaches,* ed. by H. Ahrens (Berlin: Duncker & Humblot).

Hausmann, R. 1995, "Overcoming Volatility in Latin America," in *Report on Economic and Social Progress in Latin America* (Washington: Inter-American Development Bank).

Hausmann, R., Lant Pritchett, and Dani Rodrik, 2004, "Growth Accelerations," NBER Working Paper No. 10566 (Cambridge, Massachusetts: National Bureau of Economic Research).

Institute of International Finance, 2010, "Capital Flows to Emerging Economies," unpublished (October).

International Monetary Fund, 2005, "The Macroeconomics of Managing Increased Aid Inflows: Experiences of Low-Income Countries and Policy Implications," unpublished (Washington).

Ismail, K., 2010, “The Structural Manifestation of ‘the Dutch Disease’: The Case of Oil Exporting Countries,” IMF Working Paper 10/103 (Washington: International Monetary Fund).
Krugman, P., 1987, “The Narrow Moving Band, the Dutch Disease, and the Competitive Consequences of Mrs. Thatcher,” *Journal of Development Economics*, Vol. 27, pp. 41–55.
Lama, R., and J.P. Medina, 2010, “Is Exchange Rate Stabilization an Appropriate Cure for the Dutch Disease?” IMF Working Paper 10/182 (Washington: International Monetary Fund).
Larsen, E.R., 2004, “Escaping the Resource Curse and the Dutch Disease: When and Why Norway Caught up with and Forged Ahead of Its Neighbors,” Statistics Norway Research Department Discussion Paper 377 (May).
Lartey, E.,F. Mandelman, and P. Acosta, 2008, “Remittances, Exchange Rate Regimes and the Dutch Disease: A Panel Data Analysis,” Federal Reserve Bank of Atlanta Working Paper 2008–12 (Atlanta: Federal Reserve Bank of Atlanta).
Levy-Yeyati, E., and F. Sturzenegger, 2007, “Fear of Appreciation,” World Bank Policy Research Working Paper 4387 (Washington: World Bank).
Loayza, N., P. Fajnzylber, and C. Calderón, 2005, “Economic Growth in Latin America and the Caribbean: Stylized Facts, Explanations, and Forecasts,” World Bank Latin America and the Caribbean Regional Studies Program (Washington: World Bank).
Magud, N. and C. Reinhart, 2007, “Capital Controls: An Evaluation,” in *Capital Controls and Capital Flows in Emerging Economies: Policies, Practices, and Consequences*, edited by Sebastian Edwards (Chicago: University of Chicago Press for the National Bureau of Economic Research).
Magud, N., C. Reinhart, and K. Rogoff, 2007, “Capital Controls: Myth and Reality A Portfolio Balance Approach to Capital Controls,” NBER Working Paper No. 16805 (Cambridge, Massachusetts: National Bureau of Economic Research).
Matsen, E., and R. Torvik, 2005, “Optimal Dutch Disease,” *Journal of Development Economics*, Vol. 78, No. 2, pp. 494–515.
McKinley, T., 2005, “Why Is ‘the Dutch Disease’ Always a Disease? The Macroeconomic Consequences of Scaling up ODA,” International Poverty Centre Working Paper 10, November (New York: United Nations Development Programme).
Montiel, P., and L. Servén, 2008, “Real Exchange Rates, Saving and Growth: Is There a Link?” World Bank Policy Research Working Paper 4636 (Washington: World Bank).
Nkusu, M., 2004, “Aid and the Dutch Disease in Low-Income Countries: Informed Diagnoses for Prudent Prognoses,” IMF Working Paper 04/49 (Washington: International Monetary Fund).
Prasad, E., R. Rajan, and A. Subramanian, 2007, “Foreign Capital and Economic Growth,” NBER Working Paper No. 13619 (Cambridge, Massachusetts: National Bureau of Economic Research).
Prati, A., and T. Tressel, 2005, “Aid Volatility and Dutch Disease: Is There a Role for Macroeconomic Policies?” IMF Working Paper 06/145 (Washington: International Monetary Fund).
Rajan, R., and A. Subramanian, 2005, “What Undermines Aid’s Impact on Growth?” IMF Working Paper 05/126 (Washington: International Monetary Fund).
Rajan, R., and A. Subramanian, 2009, “Aid, Dutch Disease, and Manufacturing Growth,” Center for Global Development Working Paper 196 (Washington: Center for Global Development).
Razin, O., and S.M. Collins, 1997, “Real Exchange Rate Misalignment and Growth,” NBER Working Paper No. 6174 (Cambridge, Massachusetts: National Bureau of Economic Research).
Rodrik, D., 2008, “The Real Exchange Rate and Economic Growth,” *Brookings Papers on Economic Activity: Fall 2008* (Washington: Brookings Institution).
Sachs, J.D., and A.M. Warner, 1999, “The Big Push, Natural Resource Booms and Growth,” *Journal of Development Economics*, 59, pp. 43–76.
———, 2001, “The Curse of Natural Resources,” *European Economic Review*, Vol. 45, pp. 827–38.
Sackey, H.A., 2002, “External Aid Flows and the Real Exchange Rate in Ghana,” AERC Research Paper 110 (Nairobi: African Economic Research Consortium).

Sala-i-Martin, X., and A. Subramanian, 2003, "Addressing the Natural Resource Curse: An illustration from Nigeria," NBER Working Paper No. 9804 (Cambridge, Massachusetts: National Bureau of Economic Research).

Spatafora, N., and A. Warner, 1995, "Macroeconomic Effects of Terms of Trade Shocks," IMF Policy Research Working Paper 1410 (Washington: International Monetary Fund).

Stijns, J.P., 2003, "An Empirical Test of the Dutch Disease Hypothesis Using a Gravity Model of Trade," unpublished (Berkeley: University of California).

Torvik, R., 2001, "Learning by Doing and the Dutch Disease," *European Economic Review*, Vol. 45, No. 2, pp. 285–306.

Usui, N., 1998, "Dutch Disease and Policy Adjustments to the Oil Boom: A Comparative Study of Indonesia and Mexico," *Resources Policy*, 23 (4), pp. 151–62.

Van Wijnbergen, S., 1984, "The 'Dutch Disease': A Disease After All?" *Economic Journal*, Vol. 94, No. 373, pp. 41–55.

Vos, R., 1998, "Aid Flows and Dutch Disease in a General Equilibrium Framework for Pakistan," *Journal of Policy Modelling*, Vol. 20, No. 1, pp. 77–109.

Younger, S., 1992, "Aid and Dutch Disease: Macroeconomic Management When Everybody Loves You," *World Development*, Vol. 20, No. 11, pp. 1587–97.

Williamson, J., 2008, "Exchange Rate Economics," Peterson Institute for International Studies Working Paper 08–3 (Washington: Peterson Institute for International Studies).

PART II

Assessing Reserve Adequacy and Current Account Levels

CHAPTER 2

International Reserve Adequacy in Central America

KRISTIN MAGNUSSON BERNARD

International reserve accumulation has recently grown rapidly, reaching 17 percent of global GDP in 2011, which represents a fourfold increase over 10 years. During this time, emerging market holdings rose to 32 percent of GDP.[1] This extensive accumulation of foreign reserves has naturally prompted questions regarding what benefits countries have from international reserve holdings, and whether current levels can be justified on economic grounds.

One long-standing view of the rationale for holding international reserves is to insure against balance of payments shocks. Commonly used rules of thumb for reserve adequacy investigate whether international reserves cover some external commitments, for example, three months of imports for countries with limited access to capital markets, or measures of potential capital flight, such as short-term external debt at residual maturity and current account deficits. Alternatively, the actual demand for international reserves has been studied using variants of the "buffer stock model," treating reserves as a resource for smoothing consumption in the face of sudden stops of external credit and the output falls that often accompany it (Frenkel and Jovanovic, 1981). This strand of literature typically finds that the size of reserve holdings is positively related to income volatility, openness, and financial depth (Edwards, 1983; Flood and Marion, 2002; Obstfeld, Shambaugh, and Taylor, 2008). Previous literature has also tried to find an "optimal" level of international reserves by weighing the aforementioned benefits of international reserves for mitigating falls in domestic consumption during balance of payments crises against the cost of holding reserves—for example, the interest rate differential between long-term debt issued to finance reserves and the return on reserves (Jeanne and Rancière, 2006; Gonçalves, 2007; Valencia, 2010).

Using the above-mentioned frameworks, several authors have concluded that the recent reserve holdings of most emerging markets are hard to justify on economic grounds, and that other factors, such as export-oriented growth strategies, might be at play (Dooley, Folkerts-Landau, and Garber, 2003). Recent evidence from Asia and Latin America suggests that the overaccumulation of international reserves in one country might then have prompted others to follow suit through an attempt to "keep up with the Joneses" (Cheung and Qian, 2009; Cheung and Sengupta, 2011).

[1]The figure is 26 percent of GDP if China is excluded.

Most research on the international reserve coverage has so far concentrated on large emerging markets and advanced economies. This chapter will instead focus on small non-dollarized economies in Central America, that is, Costa Rica, the Dominican Republic, Guatemala, Honduras, and Nicaragua.[2] Our motivation is twofold. First, to provide evidence on reserve coverage for the region—which is lacking—and smaller emerging markets in general.[3] Second, to shed light on the appropriateness of the different commonly used methods for assessing reserve adequacy for smaller and less financially integrated emerging markets than those previously studied, including the possible presence of "keeping up with the Joneses" effects.

Our focus region also displays other features that make it an interesting testing ground for assessing reserve adequacy. Compared with some of their larger and more advanced emerging market peers, the Central American economies have, on the one hand, relatively little short-term external debt, suggesting a smaller vulnerability along that dimension. On the other hand, the share of dollar-denominated deposits to total deposits is about 45 percent on average in the region—well above the levels of dollarization in the five largest economies in Latin America and other emerging markets. This gives rise to risks of large deposit withdrawals during crises, which needs to be taken into account when assessing reserve adequacy and has received little attention in the literature.[4]

RULES OF THUMB FOR RESERVE COVER

Central America has increased its reserve cover in recent years, though the extensions of coverage were much smaller than those of other emerging markets.[5] Although gross international reserves increased by more than 50 percent during 2000–08 in Central America, they jumped threefold in the five largest Latin American economies and sixfold in a larger global sample of emerging markets, as seen from Figure 2.1. In fact, the rules of thumb that follow suggest that Central America's reserve cover could be strengthened further.

Maybe the most traditional rule of thumb—generally used for countries with limited access to capital markets—is that international reserves should equal three months of imports. As seen from Figure 2.2, this level is barely reached by Central American economies, but exceeded by a wide margin both by the larger economies in Latin America and the full sample of emerging markets.

---

[2]El Salvador and Panama were fully dollarized for the period studied, and the notion of international reserves is hence not readily applicable to them. Belize belongs to Central America, but was excluded owing to its smaller size compared with the other economies in the sample.

[3]An exception is Canales-Kriljenko (2008), who uses a version of the Jeanne and Rancière (2006) model to assess optimal reserve adequacy for the Dominican Republic.

[4]Gonçalves (2007) is a notable exception.

[5]International reserve holdings are defined in the standard way, that is, as the sum of gold, SDR holdings, and foreign exchange. Because our analysis does not cover 2009, the exceptional SDR allocation in that year does not affect this measure.

Figure 2.1 Evolution of International Reserves

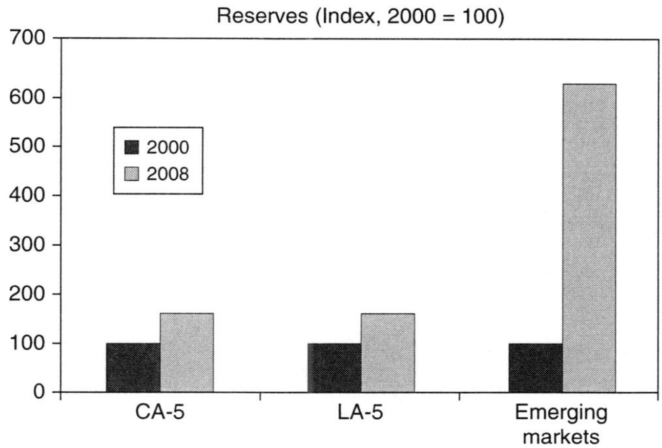

Source: IMF, International Financial Statistics database.
Note: CA-5 = the five largest economies in Central America; LA-5 = the five largest economies in Latin America.

Figure 2.2 Reserve-to-Import Ratios

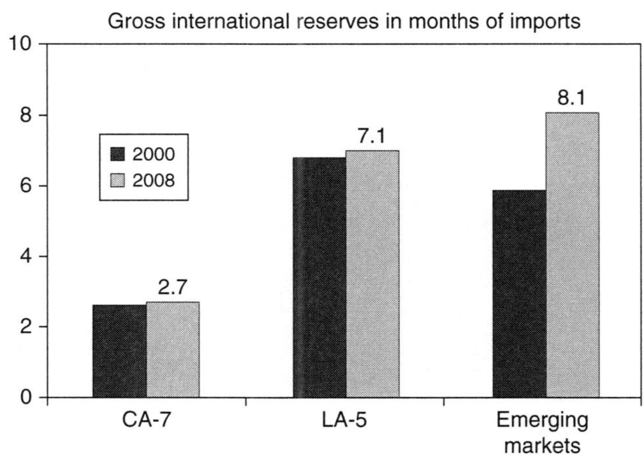

Source: IMF, International Financial Statistics database.
Note: CA-7 = Central American economies; LA-5 = the five largest economies in Latin America.

Alternatively, the so-called Greenspan-Guidotti rule states that gross international reserves should cover short-term external debt measured on a residual maturity basis, that is, public and private external debt maturing over the next 12 months (Greenspan, 1999). This rule is often extended to also take into account current account deficits to proxy for total external financing needs and give a more extensive picture of possible capital flight. As seen from Figure 2.3,

Figure 2.3 Ratio of Reserves to Short-Term Debt and the Current Account Deficit

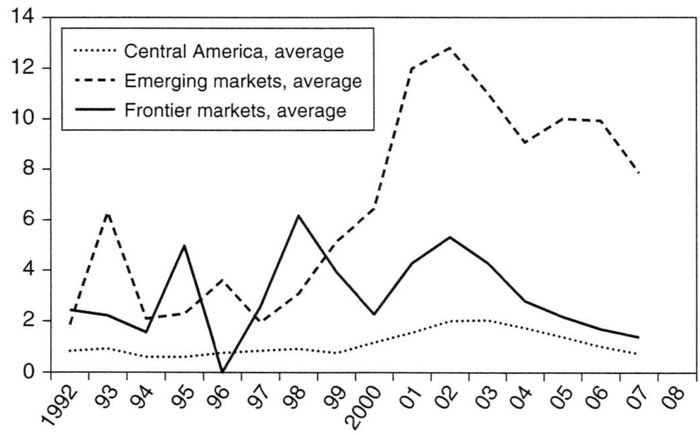

Source: IMF, International Financial Statistics database; and World Economic Outlook database.
Note: Emerging markets refer to countries covered by the JP Morgan EMBI index, except Algeria and Brazil; Frontier markets are countries included in the MSCI Barra Frontier Market Index.

Central America falls short of the benchmark, despite its relatively modest external debt levels, and in contrast to other emerging markets.

Another often-used rule of thumb is to compare international reserves with the stock of broad money, usually M2. Traditionally, a cover of 5–20 percent of broad money has been considered adequate, but more recently, for example, Obstfeld, Shambaugh, and Taylor (2008) have argued that a sufficient "war chest" should cover up to 50 percent. Regardless of the precise level deemed appropriate, Figure 2.4 shows that Central America again is below comparators in this dimension. Moreover, one needs to take into account the relatively low level of financial intermediation in the region; in Central America, the ratio of broad money to GDP stands at roughly 40 percent, compared with an average of 70 percent for the larger sample of emerging market economies.

Taken together, the above benchmarks suggest that Central America's reserve cover is on the low side both in an absolute sense and when compared with emerging market peers on the Latin American continent and elsewhere.

Reserve Demand Regressions

The rules of thumb presented in the previous section were provided to offer a benchmark regarding the adequacy of international reserves; but another angle for analyzing international reserves would be to try to explain what has motivated a country to accumulate a certain stock. Indirectly, this approach can also shed light on whether the time variation in international reserve coverage can be justified because of changes in, for example, macroeconomic fundamentals, or whether there is excessive accumulation or rundown of reserves during certain

Figure 2.4 Gross Reserves to Broad Money

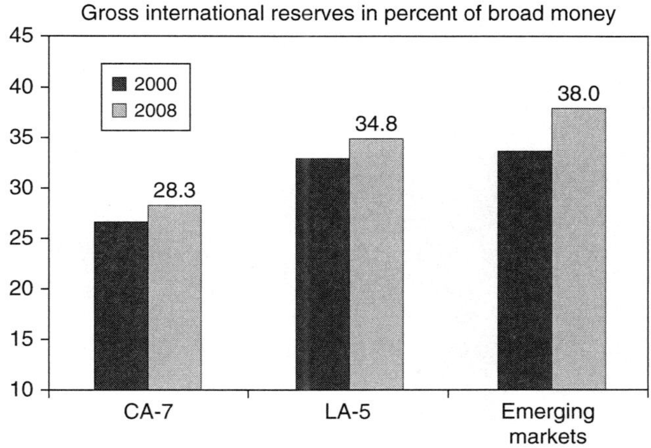

Source: IMF, International Financial Statistics database.
Note: CA-7 = Central American economies; LA-5 = the five largest economies in Latin America.

time periods. This strand of literature has often used variants of the "buffer-stock model" (Frenkel and Jovanovic, 1981), which considers international reserves a resource for smoothing consumption in the face of sudden stops.

The amount of reserves a country needs naturally varies with its characteristics. Countries experiencing relatively higher income volatility over extended periods may opt for higher reserve holdings owing to their larger utility from income insurance. As pointed out by Edwards (1983) and Flood and Marion (2002), countries with fixed exchange rate regimes also need larger reserve holdings to defend the parity of their domestic currency vis-a-vis the currency they have pegged to. The secular move toward more exchange rate flexibility during past decades should then, all else being equal, have resulted in lower international reserve holdings around the world, whereas in fact the opposite happened. One reason for reserve holdings to remain high is that de facto exchange rate flexibility could be lower than de jure measures, or that some countries classified as floaters hold international reserves to occasionally intervene in the foreign exchange market and influence their floating exchange rates.

Other factors argued that matter for reserve demand correspond more directly to balance of payments needs. Closely linked to the Greenspan-Guidotti rule, Radelet and Sachs (1998) argued that short-term foreign currency debt is an important source of vulnerabilities, and hence a potentially important determinant of reserve demand. Calvo (1996) first suggested that a country's vulnerability to crisis should be measured by the size of its money supply, as it is a natural upper limit on the extent of possible asset withdrawal. Obstfeld, Shambaugh, and Taylor (2008) further investigated the need to protect the domestic banking system and credit markets through international reserves. They argue that the rationale for holding reserves increases in more financially open economies, as risks multiply with the possible combination of currency mismatches and deposit withdrawals, both of those currently held in foreign currencies and through an increased demand for exchanging domestic deposits into hard currency. Given that domestic bond markets are often thin in emerging markets, international reserves are then argued to be one of the few means of financing available to a government in times of crisis. Key variables for reserve demand would then be measures of financial depth and openness of the economy, which the authors investigate both in a theoretical model and an econometric analysis.

Reserve demand might also stem from motives other than economic fundamentals. Peer or "Joneses" effects are meant to capture precautionary or mercantilist hoarding by one economy that may induce competitive hoarding by other economies in the same region, as found by Cheung and Qian (2009). If a market is viewed as having inadequate reserve coverage compared with its peers, it might be more vulnerable to capital outflows by market participants in times of economic crisis.

We follow the methodology of Obstfeld, Shambaugh, and Taylor (2008) and investigate reserve demand in a panel of 52 emerging market economies for the period 1993–2008.[6] More specifically, we estimate the following models:

$$Y_{it} = X_{it}'\alpha + \delta D1_i + \gamma D1_i * J_{it-1} + \theta D2_{it} + \varepsilon_{it}, \quad i = 1 \ldots N; t = 1 \ldots. T$$

where i denotes economies (N = 52) and t denotes time (T = 16). Y_{it} is the reserves-to-GDP ratio of economy i at time t. X_{it}' is the vector of economic variables used to explain reserve demand. $D1_i$ is a dummy taking on the value 1 for Central American countries. $D2_{it}$ takes on the value 1 in years when country i experienced a crisis, defined as a reversal of the current-account-to-GDP ratio by more than 5 percentage points. The presence of peer effects is investigated by defining "Joneses" variables for economy i as follows:

$$J_{it} = \sum_{i \neq k} Y_{kt}$$

where Y_{kt} is the reserves-to-GDP ratio of economy k at time t. For smaller countries, it is however not clear whether size matters, and the relevant comparators are other smaller emerging markets or the largest countries in the region. To allow for both possibilities, we sum respectively over the other small emerging markets in the region, and only the five largest economies.[7] Following Cheung and Qian (2009), we lag the "Joneses" variable to take into account lack of contemporaneous data on other countries' reserve levels.

Table 2.1 shows that our findings are in line with previous studies: reserve demand is positively related to openness and GDP volatility, and negatively

[6]All data sources can be found in Appendix 2.1.

[7]Brazil, Chile, Colombia, Mexico, and Peru.

TABLE 2.1

Reserve Demand Regressions. Dependent Variable: GIR/GDP

Variable	Coefficient	T-stat.
Log (population)	–0.008*	–1.97
Openness[1]	0.117***	9.82
Exchange rate flexibility[2]	–0.241*	–1.87
GDP volatility[3]	0.101*	1.37
Central America dummy	–0.024*	–1.40
FDI/GDP	0.191***	2.90
Short-term debt/GDP	0.031*	1.71
Jones2*CA dummy	0.004***	3.55

Source: Author's calculations.
[1]Defined as (exports + imports)/GDP.
[2]Defined as the period standard deviation of the NCU/dollar exchange rate, over the period average.
[3]Defined as the period standard deviation of real GDP over the period average.
***, **, * denote results significant at the 1, 5, and 10 percent significance levels (one-sided t-tests).
Note: FDI = foreign direct investment; GIR = gross international reserves.

related to exchange rate flexibility. The largest effect on reserve demand comes from exchange rate flexibility; raising the period standard deviation of the nominal national currency/U.S. dollar exchange rate by one unit is associated with a decreased reserve/GDP ratio of about 25 percentage points. The effects of a 1 percentage point increase in the openness of the economy, defined as the ratio of exports and imports to GDP, or the FDI/GDP ratio, have effects on the reserve-to-GDP ratio close to that size. Contrary to previous studies, we find no significant effect of financial depth on reserve demand.

The level of total external debt as well as crisis dummies have the expected positive sign but are not found to significantly affect reserve demand in a consistent manner, which is also in line with existing work (Obstfeld, 2008). Raising the short-term debt-to-GDP ratio is, however, found to increase the reserve-to-GDP ratio by about 3 percentage points, suggesting that the maturity structure of debt matters. The "Joneses" variables have the expected positive sign, suggesting that increased reserve accumulation by peers affects country *i*'s reserve demand upward. However, only the reserve levels in the large emerging markets seem to matter, in that an increase in the reserve-to-GDP ratio of the five largest economies in Latin America on average increases the reserve-to-GDP ratio of a Central American economy by 0.5 percentage point the following year, but there is no significant effect of reserve accumulation in other Central American economies.

Taken together, Central America stands out as having lower reserve ratios after controlling for the standard demand drivers in the literature, as indicated by a significant, negative coefficient of a dummy for the region that can be interpreted as the reserve-to-GDP ratio on average being about 2 percentage points lower in Central America, after controlling for other relevant factors.

All estimated coefficients, as well as different specifications and robustness checks, can be found in Appendix 2.2.

MODELS OF OPTIMAL RESERVES

The econometric analysis in the previous section can be criticized for lacking microfoundations, that is, for not discussing whether actual reserve holdings are optimal from the perspective of rational utility-maximizing agents. This section hence focuses on reserve optimality from a consumption insurance perspective, balancing the benefits of holding reserves when sudden stops in external credit occur with the quasi-fiscal costs of doing so. However, the focus on external debt links this framework to the Greenspan-Guidotti rule and the reserve demand models in the previous section.

Although the early literature discussing reserve optimality emphasized vulnerabilities stemming from external short-term debt, recent work has expanded the definition. As mentioned earlier, bank dollar deposits are an important source of fragility in Central America, and thus we use the Gonçalves (2007) dollar deposit extension of the Jeanne and Rancière (2006) framework for assessing the role of reserves for consumption insurance. As pointed out by Valencia (2010), another reason for accumulating precautionary reserves is to insure against volatile terms-of-trade developments. This option is, however, mainly relevant as a tool for revenue management for commodity exporters—which the Central American economies we focus on are not.[8]

The model features an intertemporal optimization problem of a small open economy hit by sudden stops in capital flows. Notice that this model neither studies the role of reserves for actually reducing the likelihood or cost of a crisis nor the effects on borrowing costs. These benefits are, however, typically found to be insignificant or only present at low reserve-to-GDP ratios, and hence the costs and benefits of holding reserves are thought to be well approximated by the model (Blanchard, Faruqee, and Das, 2010; Llaudes, Salman, and Chivakul, 2010).

In the model, reserves are held to smooth consumption over time. This role of international reserves can be inferred from a few accounting relationships. First, note that real domestic absorption in an open economy can be written as the difference between real domestic output and the trade balance:

$$A_t = Y_t - TB_t \tag{2.1}$$

where the trade balance, in turn, can be written as:

$$TB_t = -KA_t - IT_t + \Delta R_t \tag{2.2}$$

where KA_t is the financial account, IT_t is income and transfers from abroad, and $\Delta R_t = R_t - R_{t-1}$ is the change in reserves. Equations (2.1) and (2.2) can be combined to obtain an expression for decomposing domestic absorption into domestic output, the financial account, income from abroad, and accumulation or decumulation of reserves:

$$A_t = Y_t + KA_t + IT_t - \Delta R_t \tag{2.3}$$

[8]In theory, commodity importers could naturally also use reserves to insure against terms-of-trade shocks; in practice, they have less frequently been used against volatile commodity prices.

A sudden stop is characterized by a cut in external credit, resulting in a sharp fall of the capital account KA_t, all else being equal, inducing a fall in domestic absorption. If the sudden stop is accompanied by a fall in output, Y_t, the effects on domestic absorption will be amplified. Reserves can, however, be used for example to repay external debt that is not rolled over, alleviating the need to cut domestic absorption, and thus provide consumption insurance.

Based on a partial equilibrium framework, a main advantage of the model is that it has a closed form solution.[9] For simplicity, all variables in the model are scaled by GDP. The government welfare maximization problem results in first-order conditions that can be manipulated to obtain the optimal level of reserves as a fixed fraction of the level of output, ρ:

$$\rho = \lambda + \gamma - \frac{p^{1/\sigma} - 1}{1 + (p^{1/\sigma} - 1)(1 - \delta - \pi)} \left(1 - \frac{r - g}{1 + g} \lambda - (\delta + \pi)(\lambda + \gamma) \right) \quad (2.4)$$

where:

ρ = optimal reserves-to-output ratio

$\lambda = (\alpha(1 - \varphi)\,\lambda_{DEP} + \lambda_{DEBT})$ sum of external debt λ_{DEBT}, defined as external debt coming due on a residual maturity basis over the next 12 months, and possible deposit withdrawals $\alpha(1 - \varphi)\,\lambda_{DEP}$, that is, deposit obligations not covered by banks' liquid foreign assets

φ = share of dollar deposits covered by banks' liquid foreign assets

α = share of dollar deposits backed by the government

γ = output cost of a crisis

σ = coefficient of relative risk aversion

δ = term premium

π = probability of crisis

r = risk-free interest rate

g = real growth rate of (potential) output

$p = 1 + \delta/[\pi\,(1 - \delta - \pi)]$ is the liquidity premium generated by a crisis (if $\delta = 0$, $p = 1$, that is, domestic consumption is perfectly insured against the risk of a crisis).

To get the intuition behind this formula for the optimal reserve-to-GDP ratio, it is useful to examine an approximation, which can be obtained by setting $\delta + \pi = r - g = 0$ in Equation (2.4), implying:

$$\rho = \lambda + \gamma - \left(1 - \left(1 + \frac{\delta}{\pi} \right)^{1/\sigma} \right) \quad (2.5)$$

This approximation illustrates that the optimal level of reserves increases one-for-one with the amount of short-term external debt λ and the output cost of a crisis γ, and declines with the opportunity cost of holding reserves $(1+ \delta/\pi)$.

[9]The full model can be found in Appendix 2.3.

If the term premium δ is equal to zero, then reserves should be optimally set to the level that perfectly smoothes the impact of a crisis on domestic consumption, that is, $\lambda + \gamma$, the "full insurance" optimum. If the output cost of a crisis is zero ($\gamma = 0$), then $\rho = \lambda$, or optimal reserves should equal short-term external debt. Otherwise, the optimal level of reserves also increases with the probability of a sudden stop, π, and the risk aversion parameter σ, and declines with the term premium δ.

To take into account the importance of dollar deposits, we follow Gonçalves in assuming that the optimal level of foreign reserves should also cover a significant fraction of foreign currency deposits' withdrawal from the banking sector. Lacking country-specific information for government backing of foreign currency deposits, we use the Gonçalves value of 30 percent, referring to the 2001 Uruguay crisis. But unlike Gonçalves, we do not distinguish between the government's coverage of resident and nonresident deposits, owing to lack of data regarding this split for the countries we study. To give an upper bound on the interval in which reserve coverage can be considered optimal according to the model, we also present results for the case when the government fully insures all U.S. dollar deposits.

We also stick with the original Jeanne and Rancière model, and do not take into account valuation effects on international reserves through possible depreciation of the real exchange rate. Although Gonçalves argues that by increasing foreign currency liabilities, such a depreciation likely leads to further drops in consumption and thus a higher marginal benefit of holding reserves, Jeanne and Rancière have shown that the optimal level of foreign reserves is not significantly affected by the real exchange rate. In a model with depreciation, the same amount of foreign reserves provides more insurance in terms of a domestic consumption buffer when the economy faces a sudden stop—that is, the marginal benefit of foreign reserves goes down, and these two effects offset each other.

Parameters

To compare the results for Central America with relevant peers, that is, small- to middle-sized emerging markets for which data are available, we perform the exercises in this section for Armenia, Bolivia, Bulgaria, Costa Rica, the Dominican Republic, Guatemala, Honduras, Nicaragua, Paraguay, Romania, and Uruguay.

The non-country-specific model parameters are common to the Jeanne and Rancière (2006) and Gonçalves (2007) papers and are relatively standard (Table 2.2). The risk aversion parameter is set at 2, a standard estimate in the business cycle literature. The risk-free short-term dollar interest rate is set at 5 percent, roughly corresponding to the average U.S. three-month Treasury bill rate over the past decades. The term premium is assumed to be 1.5 percent, close to the average difference between the yield on 10-year U.S. Treasury bills and the federal funds rate over the same period. (Country-specific debt levels λ, potential output growth rates g, and estimated output losses γ are available from the author on request.) Regarding the calculated probabilities of crisis π, Jeanne and Rancière use a cross-country probit model to arrive at an estimate of 10.2 percent, that

TABLE 2.2

Non-Country-Specific Model Parameters

Term premium, δ	1.5 percent
Risk-free rate, *r*	5 percent
Coefficient of relative risk aversion, σ	2
Deposit coverage, α	30–100 percent

Sources: Jeanne and Rancière (2006); and Gonçalves (2007).

is, that the average emerging market experiences a crisis every 10 years. For countries experiencing a crisis during the two decades for which we have data, we used the implied probability (for example, one crisis during this period would result in a probability of 5 percent), while the Jeanne and Rancière estimate was used for the remaining countries. We discuss the importance of this and other parameters for the results later in the sensitivity analysis section.

Results

This section discusses actual reserve-to-GDP ratios versus the optimal levels spelled out by the Jeanne and Rancière model, as well as the Gonçalves model, with 30 percent and full government backing of U.S. dollar deposits, respectively. For the Jeanne and Rancière model, data were available to calculate the optimal level of reserves for the period 1993–2008. Results for the Gonçalves model could only be obtained for 2003–08, the longest time period for which we could get data on dollar deposits and private banks' liquid foreign assets. Because of lags in data publication for short-term external debt, we were not able to cover the 2009 crisis—when several of the countries in our sample used considerable amounts of their foreign reserves to meet balance of payments needs; thus, numbers on actual reserves should be considered as upper bounds.

Optimal reserve levels according to the Jeanne and Rancière model vary widely across time and countries, as seen from the time series plots in Appendix 4. Although some countries—such as Armenia—show little time series variation in their optimal reserves over the time period under study, others—such as Bulgaria—display dramatic variation. Moreover, while the optimal levels of reserves are steadily declining for some countries, for example, Bolivia, Honduras, and Nicaragua, the model predicts increasing need for reserves in other countries such as Armenia, Bulgaria, Costa Rica, and Romania.[10]

The figures in Table 2.3 below refer to time averages for 2003–08 to avoid results being contaminated by outliers. As seen from the table, actual reserve levels are in many cases close to, but typically exceeding, those spelled out by the Jeanne and Rancière model, and especially so for the more financially integrated emerging markets in the sample, for example, Bulgaria, Costa Rica, the Dominican Republic, Romania, and Uruguay.

[10]Romania has had a currency board for much of the period under study, which has implications for optimal reserve coverage: it is mainly included for its similarity in terms of macroeconomic characteristics to the Central American sample.

TABLE 2.3
Actual versus Optimal Reserves (percent of GDP); Time Averages, 2003–08

			Gonçalves (no depreciation effects)	
	Actual	Jeanne and Rancière	30 percent Guarantee	Full Guarantee
Costa Rica	10.2	8.2	14.8	21.6
Dominican Republic	3.4	4.9	5.8	9.6
Guatemala	11.0	6.4	8.7	15.8
Honduras	19.1	7.3	7.9	12.7
Nicaragua	13.2	17.7	21.7	44.4
Armenia	6.0	13.8	14.4	15.6
Bolivia	16	2.5	2.7	4.3
Bulgaria	28.9	24.9	. . .	. . .
Paraguay	14.4	11.3	11.7	12.3
Romania	15.2	16.7	19.0	24.4
Uruguay	13.6	11.3	12.8	17.7

Source: Author's calculations.
Note: . . . = no data available.

As discussed earlier, the assumptions of the model will lead to always prescribing low reserve levels for countries with short-term low external debt levels, such as Bolivia, Guatemala, and Honduras.[11] The discrepancy between actual and optimal reserves is especially striking for Bolivia. As mentioned earlier, Bolivia's current high level of international reserves is usually considered the result of the recent natural resource boom and associated motivation to insure against terms-of-trade shocks, together with few alternatives for investing export revenues other than accumulating international reserves (Valencia, 2010).

If both dollar deposits and short-term external debt are taken into account, actual reserves are lower than optimal reserves for the majority of the countries in Central America, even if the government only backs one-third of deposits not covered by banks' liquid foreign assets. In the extreme case of full dollar deposit insurance, Honduras is the only country in the Central America region whose reserves are still higher than the optimal levels, as further shown by Figure 2.5.

Sensitivity Analysis

This section shows how the level of optimal reserves depends on the calibrated parameters. The graphs in this section refer to results from the Jeanne and Rancière model for Costa Rica and the year 2008. Another country, or including dollar deposits, would have given a similar picture but of course different levels.

[11]Notice, however, that while all of Guatemala's public external debt is long term, shortterm external debt in 2009 constituted 90 percent of banks' external debt (in the form of credit lines with foreign banks) and 40 percent of nonfinancial private sector external debt.

Risk Aversion Parameter, σ

As seen from Figure 2.6, more elevated risk aversion increases the value of consumption insurance and hence the level of optimal reserves. Increasing σ from 2 to 5, for example, on average increases the average optimal reserve-to-GDP ratio by about 4 percent for our sample. For the Central American economies, the increase is somewhat larger, about 5 percent on average.

Term Premium, δ, and Lower Risk-Free Rate, r

Figure 2.6 also shows that a lower term premium decreases the opportunity cost of holding reserves, and thus pushes up the optimal reserve-to-GDP ratio. If the

Figure 2.5 Optimal versus Actual Reserve Levels

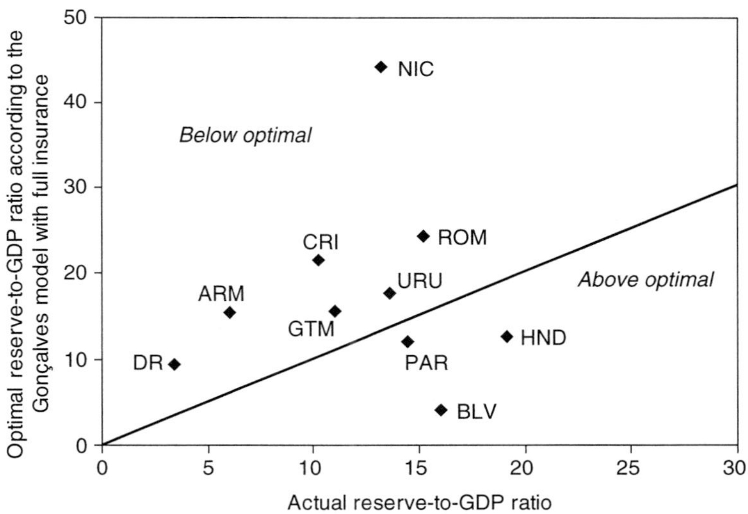

Source: Author's calculations.
Note: Refers to time averages for the years 2003–08. ARM = Armenia; BLV = Bolivia; CRI = Costa Rica; DR = Dominican Republic; GTM = Guatemala; HND = Honduras; NIC = Nicaragua; PAR = Paraguay; ROM = Romania; URU = Uruguay.

Figure 2.6 Risk Aversion Parameter and Term Premium

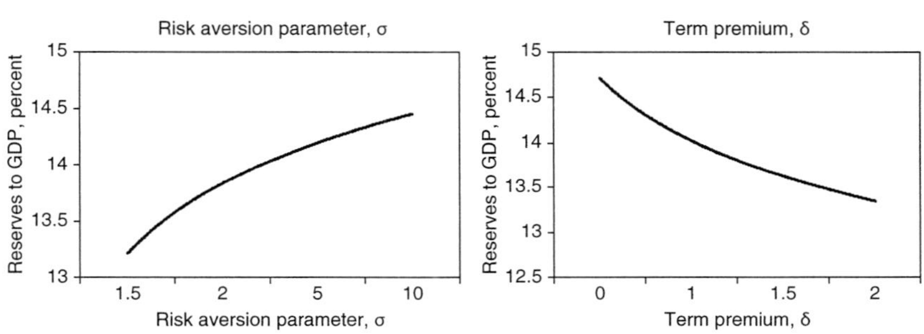

Source: Author's calculations.

term premium were to fall 150 basis points from 1.5 to 0, the average optimal reserve-to-GDP ratio would increase by almost 7 percent. Again, the increase is larger for the Central American economies—more than 8 percent. Varying the risk-free rate has similar effects.

Probability of a Crisis, π

A higher probability of a crisis increases the marginal benefit of reserves in the case of a sudden stop, as seen from Figure 2.7. If the crisis probability estimated by Jeanne and Rancière—10.2 percent—were to fall by half to 5 percent, this would lower the average reserves-to-GDP ratio by close to 11 percent. Given that the Central American economies have relatively low crisis probabilities compared with other economies in the sample in the benchmark parameterization, lowering the crisis probability to 5 percent would decrease their optimal reserve-to-GDP ratio by less—to about 8 percent.

Size of Output Loss, γ

With a greater output loss, the need for consumption insurance naturally increases, and with it the optimal reserve-to-GDP ratio. Figure 2.7 shows that if the countries studied were to experience an output drop the size of Mexico's in 1994, –6.5 percent, the average increase in the optimal reserve-to-GDP ratio would be almost 70 percent for the Central American economies versus 40 percent for the full sample. If the same group of countries had a similar output loss to Uruguay in 2001, −14 percent, the optimal reserve-to-GDP ratio would in fact double, that is, increase by 104 percent for the Central American economies and by 68 percent for the full sample. This striking result, which is in contrast to the findings in, for example, Gonçalves (2007), is because the Central American economies did not experience such dramatic output losses during the period we studied, and the effects of increases in the output loss parameter are quite dramatic.

Figure 2.7 Probability of a Crisis and Size of Output Loss

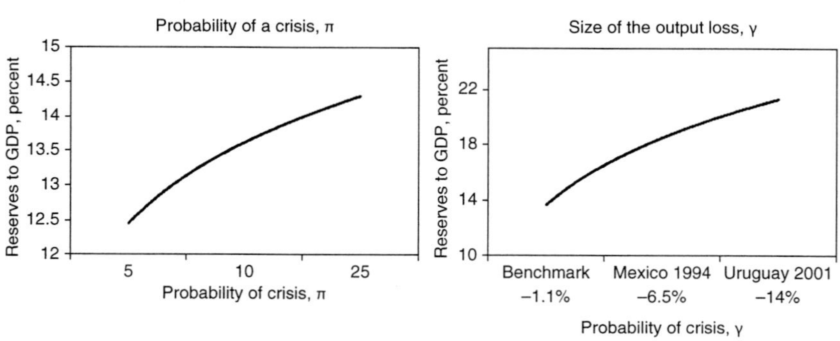

Source: Author's calculations.

CONCLUSION

This chapter has applied a host of methods to discuss adequacy and demand drivers for international reserves in Central America and a comparator group of emerging markets. Our results show that the region scores relatively low on traditional reserve benchmarks such as reserves to months of imports or short-term external debt and current account positions. We also find that after controlling for determinants of reserve demand commonly found in the literature, such as openness of the economy, exchange rate flexibility, financial depth, and external debt stocks, in a panel data framework with a large sample of emerging markets, Central America stands out as having significantly lower reserve-to-GDP ratios. We, however, find evidence of a "keeping up with the Joneses" effect, that is, that the Central American countries in our sample take into account the reserve accumulation of the large emerging markets in Latin America when making policy decisions.

We also investigate optimal reserve-to-GDP ratios using the framework developed by Jeanne and Rancière (2006) and Gonçalves (2007), and again find that the actual reserve levels in Central America in many cases are lower than those prescribed by the model as optimal insurance against a sudden stop of credit and withdrawal in part of dollar deposits.

The costs of reserve accumulation, such as the relatively low return on international reserves, quasi-fiscal costs stemming from sterilization operations, and the potential valuation losses associated with exchange rate movements, are non-negligible. Taken together, the results in this chapter, however, suggest that further reserve accumulation is an important policy option for the economies in Central America. But it is neither an uncomplicated option nor the only alternative. First, it is important that further reserve accumulation not be seen as compromising the inflation-targeting credibility of the countries that have committed to such regimes. The results from the reserve demand regressions also suggest that the need to accumulate foreign reserves could be mitigated by, for example, allowing for higher exchange rate flexibility and by bringing down short-term external debt. Moreover, several of the Central American countries studied swiftly accessed liquidity support from the IMF during the crisis. Given the increasing flexibility of IMF lending facilities and the usually temporary need for increased reserve coverage in times of heightened uncertainty, multilateral reserve pools remain not only the cheapest but also in other respects an attractive means to obtain international reserves.

APPENDIX 2.1. DATA SOURCES

TABLE A2.1

Variable	Source
Stylized facts	
International reserves	IMF, International Financial Statistics Database
Broad money (M2)	IMF, International Financial Statistics Database
GDP, real and nominal	World Economic Outlook Database
Current account deficit	World Economic Outlook Database
Private short-term foreign currency debt	Global Development Finance Database
Public short-term foreign currency debt	Global Development Finance Database
Foreign currency deposits	Global Development Finance Database
Total deposits	IMF, International Financial Statistics Database
Imports	World Economic Outlook Database
Exports	World Economic Outlook Database
CPIS portfolio investment	IMF, International Financial Statistics Database
Regression analysis	
Population	World Economic Outlook Database
Nominal effective exchange rate	IMF, International Financial Statistics Database
Foreign direct investment	World Economic Outlook Database
Exports	World Economic Outlook Database
External debt	Global Development Finance Database
Optimal reserves models	
Banks' liquid foreign assets	National authorities
Reserve requirements on foreign exchange deposits	National authorities
SDR holdings	IMF, International Financial Statistics Database

Note: CPIS = Coordinated Portfolio Investment Survey.

APPENDIX 2.2. RESULTS FROM RESERVE DEMAND REGRESSIONS

TABLE A2.2

Reserve Demand Regressions. Dependent Variable: GIR/GDP						
Variable	**Coefficient/T-statistic**					
Population (log)	−0.009**	−0.013***	−0.008*	−0.010**	−0.005***	−0.008*
	(−1.96)	(−2.73)	(−1.86)	(−2.29)	(−2.36)	(−1.97)
Openness[1]	0.043***	0.0.031***	0.108***	0.103	0.127***	0.117***
	(6.15)	(4.60)	(9.62)	(8.79)	(12.35)	(9.82)
Exchange rate volatility[2]	−.235**	−0.449***	−0.401*	0.206*	−0.181*	−0.241*
	(−3.24)	(−3.74)	(−4.60)	(−1.70)	(−1.75)	(−1.87)
GDP volatility[3]	0.073**	0.591*	0.0391	0.1 31	0.090	0.101*
	(2.36)	(1.81)	(1.21)	(1.46)	(1.20)	(1.37)
Financial depth[4]	−0.0003	−0.0001*	−0.0001*	−0.000*	−0.000*	−0.000*
	−(0.93)	(−0.90)	(−0.29)	(−1.20)	(−1.24)	(−.1.87)
Central America dummy	−0.0122*	−0.134***	−0.028*	−0.029	−0.045*	−0.024
	(−1.74)	(−3.29)	(−1.54)	(−1.51)	(−1.74)	(−1.40)
Jones1*CA dummy[5]	0.004	0.003	0.001	0.005	0.002	0.001
	(1.08)	(0.93)	(0.39)	(1.03)	(0.60)	(0.28)
Jones2*CA dummy[6]	0.008***	0.006***	0.004***	0.004***	0.006***	0.004***
	(5.15)	(3.68)	(2.74)	(3.17)	(4.29)	(3.55)
FDI/GDP		0.36***	0.165***	0.190***	0.332***	0.191***
		(4.65)	(2.57)	(2.95)	(3.17)	(2.90)
Total debt/GDP			0.009*	0.006		
			(1.76)	(1.12)		
Short-term debt/GDP					0.039**	0.031*
					(2.26)	(1.71)
Crisis dummy					0.004	0.94
					(1.08)	(0.69)

[1]Defined as (exports + imports)/GDP.
[2]Defined as the period standard deviation of the NCU/dollar exchange rate, over the period average.
[3]Defined as the period standard deviation of real GDP over the period average.
[4]Defined as M2/GDP. Refers to the time period 1993–2008 and a panel of 52 emerging markets.
[5]Average of other Central American economies in sample.
[6]Average of LA-5 economies.
Note: FDI = foreign direct investment; GIR = gross international reserves. ***, **, and * denote results significant at the 1, 5, and 10 percent significance levels (one-sided t-tests). Robust standard errors appear in parentheses.

APPENDIX 2.3. THE JEANNE AND RANCIÈRE (2006) MODEL

Consider a small open economy in discrete time, $t = 0, 1, 2 \ldots$. There is one single good, consumed both domestically and abroad. The only source of uncertainty in the model is the risk of a sudden stop, that is, an exogeneous loss of access to credit.

The domestic economy consists of a private sector and a government, where the former is modeled as a representative consumer subject to the budget constraint

$$C_t = Y_t + L_t - (1 + r_t)\, L_{t-1} + Z_t \qquad \text{(A1)}$$

where Y_t is domestic output, L_t is the foreign debt of the representative consumer, and Z_t is a transfer from the government. The interest rate r_t is constant, and the representative consumer does not default on his/her external debt.

Output and private external debt both grow at the same constant rate g, until the sudden stop occurs. In a sudden stop, debt cannot be rolled over and output falls by a fraction γ below its long-term growth path or potential growth rate. The consumer is assumed only to hold short-term external debt, and L_t hence falls to zero in a sudden stop. After the sudden stop, L_t stays at zero, and output resumes its long-term growth rate.

The probability of a sudden stop occurs with probability π in each period. After the sudden stop, all uncertainty is resolved, and the economy resumes growing at $g < r$. For simplicity, only one sudden stop is assumed, although the results can be extended to multiple occurrences.

We denote with the superscripts b, d, and a the periods *before*, *during*, and *after* the sudden stop. By denoting λ as the level of private external debt as a share of ouput in the pre-sudden-stop period, the following set of equations sums up the assumptions so far:

$$Y_t^b = Y_t^a = (1+g)^t Y_0, Y_t^d = (1-\gamma)(1+g)^t Y_0 \qquad \text{(A2)}$$

$$L_t^b = \lambda(1+g)^t Y_0, L_t^d = L_t^a = 0, \qquad \text{(A3)}$$

where, as mentioned earlier, λ is the level of private external debt as a share of output in the pre-sudden-stop period.

Unlike the private sector, the government can issue a long-term security that does not have to be repaid in a sudden stop. This security is in the form of a bond that yields one unit of the single good for every period leading up to the sudden stop, and zero thereafter. The life expectancy of the bond is $1/\pi$ and falls accordingly with the probability of a sudden stop.

Before a sudden stop, the price of the security is equal to the sum of the present discounted value of the unit of good it pays in the next period (with certainty) and the expected market value of the security,

$$P = \frac{1}{1+r+\delta}[1+(1-\pi)P] \qquad \text{(A4)}$$

which, after solving for P and assuming the price of the security is constant before the sudden stop and zero thereafter, and that there is a positive term premium δ,[12] becomes

$$P = \frac{1}{1+r+\delta} \quad \text{(A5)}$$

The long-term sercurity is used to finance a stock of international reserves

$$R_t = PN_t \quad \text{(A6)}$$

where N_t is the number of securities issued by the government in period t. Given that the government is assumed unable to issue any long-term security during the sudden stop, all reserves must be accumulated prior to that time.

When we substitute N_t and N_{t-1} from the government's budget constraint using Equation (A6)

$$Z_t + R_t + N_{t-1} = P(N_t - N_{t-1}) + (1 + r)R_{t-1} \quad \text{(A7)}$$

we get an expression for the transfer before the sudden stop

$$Z_t^b = -\left(\frac{1}{P} - r\right)R_{t-1} = -(\delta + \pi)R_{t-1}. \quad \text{(A8)}$$

The transfer is negative; that is, the government taxes the representative consumer to pay for reserve holdings, and this cost is proportional to the sum of the term premium and the probability of a sudden stop.

In the event of a sudden stop, the government transfers the remaining reserves (net of the last payment on the long-term bond) to help the consumer pay the external debt that cannot be rolled over,

$$Z_t^d = (1 - \delta - \pi)R_{t-1} \quad \text{(A9)}$$

The assumption $\delta + \pi < 1$ ensures that this transfer is positive. After the sudden stop, the government becomes inactive: R_t, N_t, and Z_t equal zero.

Using Equations (A8) and (A9) to substitute Z_t from Equation (A4), we obtain expressions for the level of domestic consumption before, during, and after the sudden stop,

$$C_t^b = Y_t^b + L_t^b - (1+r)L_{t-1}^b - (\delta + \pi)R_{t-1} \quad \text{(A10)}$$

$$C_t^d = (1-\gamma)Y_t^b - (1+r)L_{t-1}^b + (1 - \delta - \pi)R_{t-1} \quad \text{(A11)}$$

$$C_t^a = Y_t^a \quad \text{(A12)}$$

[12]The term premium does not include the default premium; it is instead included in the sudden stop probability π.

From Equations (A11) and (A12), the trade-off involved in choosing the optimal level of reserves is clear, as well as the consumption insurance role played by reserves. By increasing R_{t-1}, consumption can be increased during the sudden stop, but it is lowered if no sudden stop occurs.

The model is closed by assuming that the government maximizes the welfare of the representative consumer:

$$U_t = \Sigma_{S=0,...,+\infty}(1 + r)^{-s}\, u(C_{t+s}) \tag{A14}$$

where the utility function is characterized by constant relative risk aversion:

$$u(C) = \frac{C^{1-\sigma} - 1}{1-\sigma} \tag{A15}$$

The government chooses the level of reserves R_t so as to maximize U_t in each period t before the sudden stop. The optimal level of reserves in period t maximizes the expected utility of period $t + 1$ consumption:

$$R_t = \arg\max\,(1-\pi)u(C^b_{t+1}) + \pi u(C^d_{t+1}) \tag{A16}$$

and C^b_{t+1} and C^d_{t+1} given by Equations (A10) and (A11).

The first-order condition is given by the following:

$$\pi(1-\delta-\pi) = (1-\pi)(\delta+\pi)u'(C^b_{t+1}) \tag{A17}$$

The left-hand side of Equation (A17) is given by the product of the probability of the occurrence of a sudden stop and the marginal benefit of reserves in the event of a sudden stop, which is equal to the probability of no sudden stop times the marginal cost of holding reserves.

The above first-order condition can be manipulated to obtain a closed-form expression for the optimal level of reserves. Denoted by p_t, the marginal rate of substitution between consumption in the respective states of sudden stop and no sudden stop, or the liquidity premium of reserves in the event of a sudden stop, is as follows:

$$p_t \equiv \frac{u'(C^d_t)}{u'(C^b_t)} \tag{A18}$$

According to the first-order condition (17), when reserves are set at optimal, this marginal rate of substitution should be constant and equal to:

$$p_t \equiv \frac{1-\pi}{\pi}\frac{\delta+\pi}{1-\delta-\pi} = 1 + \frac{\delta}{\pi(1-\delta-\pi)} \tag{A19}$$

If the term premium δ is equal to zero, then p is equal to 1, implying that domestic consumption is perfectly insured against the risk of a sudden stop, $C^d_t = C^a_t$.

If the term premium is strictly positive, then $p > 1$, and domestic consumption is lower in a sudden stop.

We use the first-order condition $(C_t^d) - \sigma = p(C_t^b)^{-\sigma}$ and the expressions for C_t^d and C_t^b to show that the optimal level of reserves during normal times is a fixed level of output:

$$R_t = \rho Y_{t+1}^b \tag{A20}$$

By using Equation (A20) with Equations (A2) and (A3), together with the first-order condition and the expressions for C_t^d and C_t^b, one can solve for the optimal-reserve-to-GDP ratio ρ:

$$\rho = \lambda + \gamma - \frac{p^{1/\sigma} - 1}{1 + (p^{1/\sigma} - 1)}\left(1 - \frac{r - g}{1 + g}\right)\lambda - (\delta + \pi)(\lambda + \gamma) \tag{A21}$$

A good approximation to the exact formula, in the range of parameter values considered in the calibration, can be obtained by setting $\delta + \pi = r - g = 0$ in the last term of Equation (A21):

$$\rho = \lambda + \gamma - (1 - p^{1/\sigma}) \tag{A22}$$

This approximate formula shows that the optimal level of reserves is increasing one for one with the amount of short-term debt and the output cost of a sudden stop. As noted earlier, if the term premium is equal to zero, then p is equal to 1, and reserves should be set to the level that perfectly smoothes the impact of the sudden stop on domestic consumption, $\rho = \lambda + \gamma$. The optimal level of reserves falls with an increase in ρ, which in turn could be caused by a decrease in the probability of a sudden stop, π, or an increase in the term premium δ. An increase in the risk aversion parameter σ decreases $p^{1/\sigma}$ and raises the optimal level of reserves.

Note that in this model, the optimal level of reserves could be lower and higher than the Greenspan-Guidotti rule, which states that the ratio of reserves to short-term debt should be equal to 1, that is:

$$\rho = \lambda$$

which means that consumption is perfectly smoothed in a sudden stop if there is no output cost. As shown by Equation (A22), the optimal level of reserves spelled out by the model could be higher or lower than this rule. As captured by γ, on the one hand, the optimal level could be higher because reserves smooth the impact of the output loss. On the other hand, the optimal level could be lower, owing to the cost of reserves captured by $(1 - p^{1/\sigma})$.

APPENDIX 2.4. OPTIMAL RESERVES ACCORDING TO THE JEANNE AND RANCIÈRE (2006) MODEL (PERCENT OF GDP)

Figure A2.1

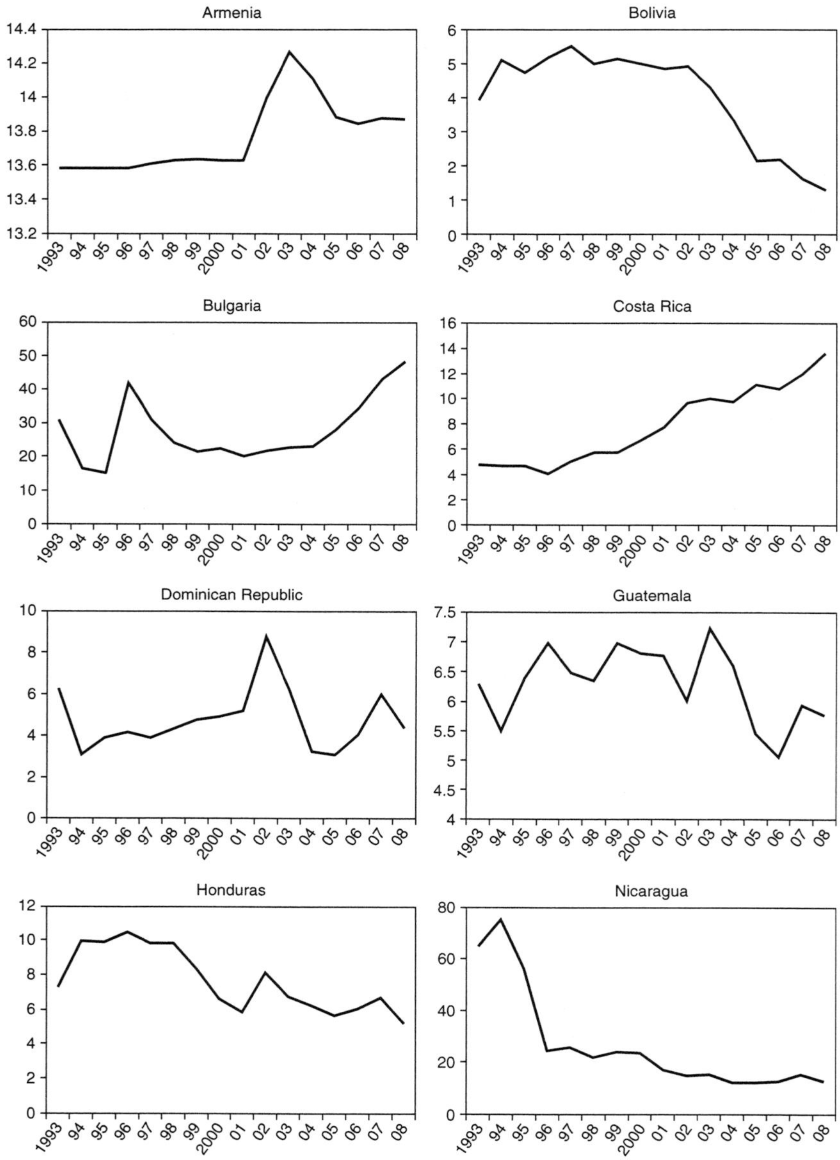

Figure A2.1 (Concluded)

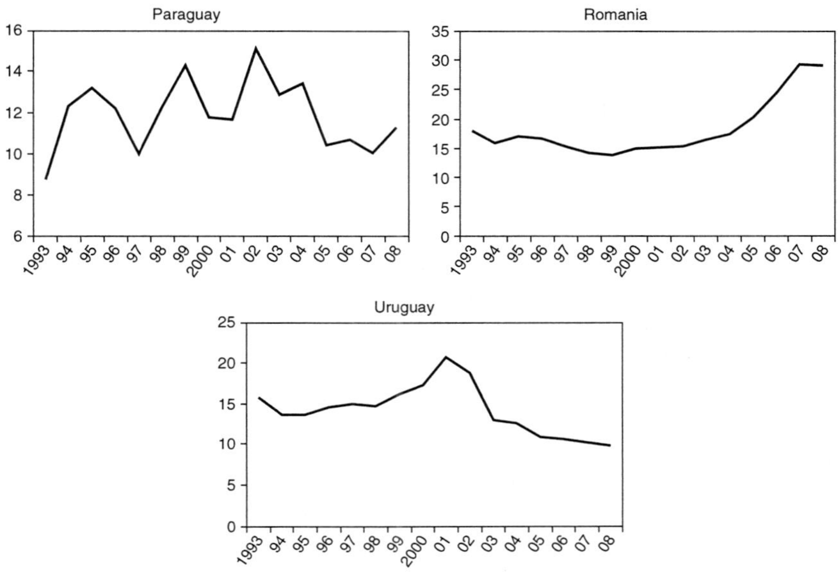

Source: Author's calculations.

REFERENCES

Blanchard, Olivier, Hamid Faruqee, and Mitali Das, 2010, "The Initial Impact of the Crisis on Emerging Market Countries," *Brookings Papers on Economic Activity* (Washington: Brookings Institution).

Calvo, Guillermo, 1996, "Capital Flows and Macroeconomic Management," *International Journal of Finance and Economics*, Issue 3 (July), pp. 207–23.

Canales-Kriljenko, Jorge Ivan, 2008, *Estimating Optimal Reserves in the Dominican Republic*, Selected Issues Paper (Washington: International Monetary Fund).

Cheung, Yin-Wong, and Xingwang Qian, 2009, "Hoarding of International Reserves: Mrs. Machlup's Wardrobe and the Joneses," *Review of International Economics*, 17(4), pp. 777–801.

Cheung, Yin-Wong, and Rajerswari Sengupta, 2011, "Accumulation of Reserves and Keeping Up with the Joneses: The case of LATAM Economies," *International Review of Economics and Finance*, 20, pp. 19–31.

Dooley, M., D. Folkerts-Landau, and P. Garber, 2003, An essay on the revived Bretton Woods system, NBER Working Paper No. 9971 (Cambridge, Massachusetts: National Bureau of Economic Research).

Edwards, Sebastian, 1983, "The Demand for International Reserves and Exchange Rate Adjustments: The Case of LDCs, 1964–1972," *Economica*, No. 50 (August), pp. 269–80.

Flood, Robert, and Nancy Marion, 2002, "Holding Reserves in an Era of High Capital Mobility," IMF Working Paper 02/62 (Washington: International Monetary Fund).

Frenkel, Jacob, and Boyan Jovanovic, 1981, "Optimal International Reserves: A Stochastic Framework," *Economic Journal No. 91* (June), pp. 507–14.

Gonçalves, Fernando M., 2007, "The Optimal Level of Foreign Reserves in Financially Dollarized Economies: The Case of Uruguay," IMF Working Paper 07/265 (Washington: International Monetary Fund).

Greenspan, Alan, 1999, "Currency Reserves and Debt," remarks before the World Bank Conference on Recent Trends in Reserves Management, Washington, D.C. http://www.federalreserve.gov/boarddocs/speeches/1999/19990429.htm.

Jeanne, Olivier, 2007, "Benefits and Costs of International Reserves: The Balance Sheet Approach," IMF Research Department manuscript (Washington: International Monetary Fund).

———, 2007, "International Reserves in Emerging Market Countries: Too Much of a Good Thing?" Manuscript prepared for the March 2007 panel of the Brookings Papers on Economic Activity (Washington: Brookings Institution).

Jeanne, Olivier, and Romain Rancière, 2006, "The Optimal Level of International Reserves for Emerging Market Economies: Formulas and Applications," IMF Working Paper 06/299 (Washington: International Monetary Fund).

Llaudes, Ricardo, Ferhan Salman, and Mali Chivakul, 2010, "The Impact of the Great Recession on Emerging Markets," unpublished (Washington, International Monetary Fund).

Obstfeld, Maurice, Jay C. Shambaugh, and Alan M. Taylor, 2008, "Financial Stability, the Trilemma, and International Reserves," NBER Working Paper No. 14217 (Cambridge, Massachusetts: National Bureau of Economic Research).

Radelet, Steven, and Jeffrey Sachs, 1998, "The Onset of the East Asian Financial Crisis," *Asian Crisis and International Solutions*, Chapter 20 (Cambridge, Massachusetts: National Bureau of Economic Research).

Valencia, Fabian, 2010, "Precautionary Reserves: An Application to Bolivia," IMF Working Paper 10/54 (Washington: International Monetary Fund).

CHAPTER 3

Estimating Current Account Norms in Latin American Emerging Markets: A Quantile Regression Approach

ROBERTO PERRELLI

A key tool to assess the equilibrium exchange rate is based on the estimation of the savings-investment balance (current account norms). These norms are projected on a set of macroeconomic fundamentals and demographic characteristics for a panel of heterogeneous countries. In the traditional estimation methods, the contribution of each fundamental for the savings-investment balance is constant across countries. In this chapter, we propose an alternative approach—the quantile regression (QR)—that captures the unobserved heterogeneity over time and across countries, delivering coefficients that vary throughout the sample. The QR results suggest that the responses of the current account norms to changes in the fiscal and oil balances are much higher at the tail end of the conditional distribution than at the average.

A central issue in the analysis of international trade imbalances and external competitiveness is the assessment of the equilibrium exchange rate of trade partners. One of the main methodologies used to assess exchange rate misalignments is the macroeconomic balance framework developed by researchers at the International Monetary Fund.[1] The macroeconomic balance approach evaluates whether prevailing exchange rates and policies are consistent with medium-term internal and external equilibrium.

The theoretical foundations of the macroeconomic balance approach to exchange rate assessment were developed in the initial years of the IMF,[2] and the methodology has been at the core of IMF economists' work ever since. For instance, one of its most prominent applications in the early years was the assessment of the degree of overvaluation of the pound sterling in 1967. Over the last six decades, the

[1]For a broader discussion, see Polak (1995), Isard and Faruqee (1998), and Lee and others (2008).

[2]As developed by Nurkse (1945), Meade (1951), and Metzler (1951).

methodology has been continuously refined by IMF researchers; the set of policy variables has been expanded; and the sample of countries now covers 54, including advanced, newly industrialized, and emerging market economies. Extensions of the method to oil-exporting countries and to tourism-dependent economies have also emerged in recent years.

The macroeconomic balance approach assesses the degree of exchange rate misalignment by comparing the savings-investment norm (that is, the savings-investment balance that would prevail under equilibrium) with the projected current account balance over the medium term and under existing policies. The distance between the two is known as the current account gap, and provides a good sense of the direction of misalignment (for example, overvaluation or undervaluation) as well as the degree of exchange rate adjustment that would be necessary to bring the underlying current account balance closer to the savings-investment norm.

The precise magnitude of the exchange rate misalignment, usually taken with a grain of salt by IMF economists, is computed by dividing the current account gap by the elasticities of exports and imports to marginal changes in the real effective exchange rate. Higher ratios imply that larger exchange rate adjustments would be necessary to shift the underlying current account toward the savings-investment norm.

In this chapter, we focus on the estimation of the savings-investment norms in the macroeconomic balance approach, leaving the discussion on trade elasticities for a separate work (Perrelli, 2011). In the estimation of the savings-investment norms, researchers have been considering that each policy variable included in the model has a constant impact on the current account balance of all economies in the sample. As the macroeconomic balance approach has extended its sample to a large set of heterogeneous economies, these methods tend to neglect a great deal of heterogeneity not captured by the explanatory variables (henceforth simply called unobserved heterogeneity). In addition, these methods rely on stringent distributional assumptions (normality) of the residuals.

This chapter aims to supplement the existing methods of estimation of the savings-investment norms with the quantile regression approach. Quantile regressions offer an alternative view of the impact of policy variables on exchange rate assessments of heterogeneous countries. The quantile regression approach provides a flexible framework where normality and identically independently distributed errors are not required. In the quantile regression approach, the model coefficients (slopes) can vary according to the quantiles (for example, percentiles) of the conditional distribution of the dependent variable, capturing the unobserved heterogeneity neglected by traditional models, and providing a more complete assessment of the role of the policy variables in the determination of the savings-investment norms. The approach may be quite useful for countries at the tail end of the conditional distribution of current account balances—for example, those with larger deficits or larger surpluses—where the unobserved heterogeneity is expected to be more accentuated than around the mean.

THE MACROECONOMIC BALANCE APPROACH TO ASSESSING THE EQUILIBRIUM EXCHANGE RATE

The macroeconomic balance approach to assessing the equilibrium exchange rate aims to evaluate whether prevailing exchange rates and policies are consistent with medium-term internal and external equilibrium. The approach is based on seminal work of Nurkse (1945), Meade (1951), and Metzler (1951). In early applications of the method, the exchange rate was assessed by comparing the underlying current account with the net capital flows (Isard and Mussa, 1998). By the mid-1990s, when the IMF established the Consultative Group on Exchange Rate Issues (CGER) to coordinate analytical work on the topic, the macroeconomic balance framework involved a sample of 22 advanced economies.[3] Owing to limited access to capital markets, emerging market economies were not included in that sample. In the last decade, the approach was adapted to include countries with extended access to international capital markets and enhanced data standards, enlarging the sample from 22 countries to 54 countries. Recent advances to the methodology include adaptation of the model to oil-exporting countries (Bems and de Carvalho Filho, 2009) and to tourism-dependent small open economies (Piñeda, Cashin, and Sun, 2009).

The approach is based on the well-known national accounts identity that the savings-investment (S-I) balance equals net exports (that is, the external current account balance, CAB). It relies on an adjustment process function where movements in the real effective exchange rate (REER) of a given country would be gradually reflected in its CAB. All else being equal, an upward change in the country's REER would be associated with a loss of international competitiveness and therefore with a deterioration of its external current account position. The opposite is also true (see Figure 3.1).

A lynchpin of the methodology is the accurate assessment of the savings-investment norm, that is, the savings-investment balance that would prevail if the REER were at its equilibrium level (solid vertical line in Figure 3.1). Once that is obtained, one is able to identify the distance between the underlying CAB and the S-I norm. This distance, often called the current account gap, determines the direction of the exchange rate misalignment and helps to quantify the amount of exchange rate adjustment necessary to bring the underlying current account balance closer to the savings-investment norm.

The size of the exchange rate adjustment is assessed in three steps: (1) estimation of the S-I norm and the current account gap; (2) estimation of the elasticities of exports and imports to marginal changes in the REER; and (3) calculation of the ratio of the current account gap and the elasticities. The estimated results are used as an

---

[3]Namely Australia, Austria, Belgium, Canada, Denmark, Finland, France, Germany, Greece, Ireland, Italy, Japan, Luxembourg, Netherlands, New Zealand, Norway, Portugal, Spain, Sweden, Switzerland, the United Kingdom, and the United States.

Figure 3.1 REER, Savings-Investment Norm, and the Adjustment Process Function

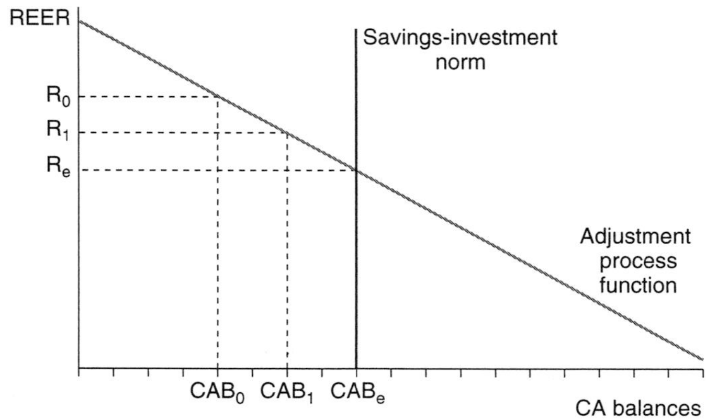

Source: Author's calculations.

indicator of the degree of exchange rate misalignment. In this chapter, we concentrate on the first step of the macroeconomic balance approach, leaving the study of import and export elasticities for future work.

Note that the speed and path of the exchange rate adjustment toward a level consistent with its equilibrium are not yielded by the macroeconomic balance approach; neither do these aspects have a prominent role in the exercise. Instead, the approach provides a measurement of how distant the underlying current account balance is from the savings-investment norm (that is, the savings-investment balance at the equilibrium exchange rate), and by how much the real effective exchange rate would have to adjust to bring them together.

Determinants of the Savings-Investment Norm

The savings-investment norm is determined empirically by a set of macroeconomic fundamentals, demographic aspects, and country individual characteristics that are viewed as having a substantial impact on the long-term patterns of internal and external savings across countries. Although the REER is clearly associated with movements in the underlying current account, by design the S-I norm is orthogonal to changes in the REER (thus the vertical line in Figure 3.1 above), and serves as a benchmark to gauge signals of exchange rate misalignments.

The econometric estimation of the S-I norm involves the following set of variables (as described in Lee and others, 2008):

- *Fiscal balance:* the ratio of the general government balance to GDP.
- *Real growth of purchasing power parity-GDP per capita:* included only for emerging market economies.
- *Old-age dependency ratio:* the ratio of the population above 65 years to the population between 30 and 64 years.

- *Population growth:* the annual population growth rate of each economy.
- *PPP-GDP per capita:* a proxy for relative income, measured as the ratio of per capita purchasing power parity (PPP) income to the U.S. level, both in constant 2000 international U.S. dollars.
- *Oil balance:* the ratio of oil balance to GDP.
- *Asian crisis:* dummy variable for Asian emerging markets for the 1997–2004 period, namely China, Hong Kong SAR, India, Indonesia, Korea, Malaysia, the Philippines, Singapore, Taiwan Province of China, and Thailand.
- *Banking crisis:* dummy variable for banking crisis episodes. Obtained from Demirgüç-Kunt and Detragiache (2005) and Gruber and Kamin (2005).
- *Financial center:* dummy variable indicating if the country is a financial center.
- *Initial NFA:* the ratio of net foreign assets (NFA) to GDP prevailing at the beginning of each four-year period. It uses the NFA data from Lane and Milesi-Ferretti (2007).

We note that four of these variables enter the econometric model as deviations from the averages for trading partners: (1) fiscal balance; (2) old-age dependency ratio; (3) population growth; and (4) real growth of PPP-GDP per capita. The justification is that the S-I norm of a given country would only be affected by these variables if they changed relative to its trading partners. The remaining variables enter the model as described above.

Also, the inclusion of the fiscal balance as a determinant of the savings-investment norm relies on the assumption that the hypothesis of Ricardian equivalence does not hold in the sample (Isard and Mussa, 1998). Simply put, if a country promoted a policy adjustment that reduced its fiscal deficit, the private savings in that country could decline but not enough to fully offset the improvement in public savings. Therefore, the fiscal adjustment would have a positive impact on the savings profile of the country, which would be reflected in a movement to the right of the S-I norm curve (Figure 3.2).

The intuition behind the other variables is more straightforward. Higher growth rates of real PPP-GDP per capita (relative to trading partners), on the one hand, are associated with faster economic growth and elevated investment needs, which contribute to a deterioration of the S-I norm. On the other hand, a higher level of PPP-GDP per capita (relative to the U.S. standards) suggests a more advanced stage of economic development, normally characterized by slower economic growth and lower investment needs, thus positively associated with higher S-I norms.

A higher old-age dependency ratio and population growth (relative to trading partners) are expected to decrease national savings and thus to have a negative impact on the S-I norm. Higher oil balances, as displayed by oil-exporting countries, are positively associated with higher S-I norms. Currency and banking crises are positively associated with S-I norms owing to the forced external adjustment, sudden stop, and lack of external financing faced by the crisis

Figure 3.2 Non-Ricardian Effect of Fiscal Adjustment on Savings-Investment Norm

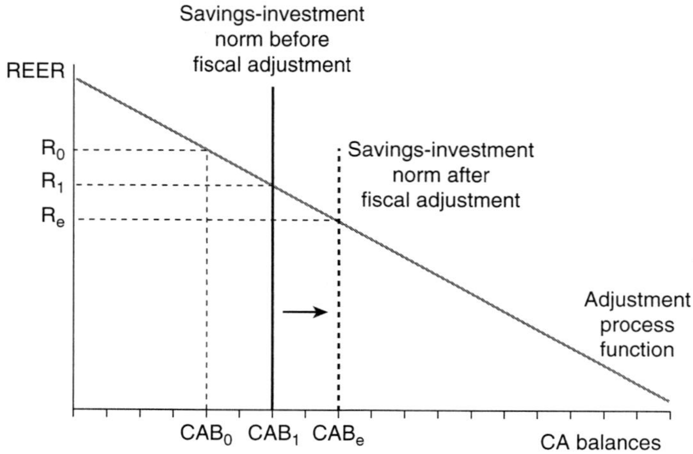

Source: Author's calculations.

countries. Being a financial center is a proxy for net creditor positions and is thus related to higher S-I norms.[4] And countries with a higher initial NFA position have lower external indebtedness and tend to present higher current account balances.

One of the models also includes the lagged dependent variable (that is, the lagged current account balance in percent of GDP) as an explanatory variable in the regression. This variable is expected to have a positive sign due to the persistence of the current account balances in the sample.

Data and Econometric Models

The latest edition of the macroeconomic balance approach, as described in Lee and others (2008), uses a sample of the following 54 countries, including advanced, newly industrialized, and emerging market economies: Algeria, Argentina, Australia, Austria, Belgium, Brazil, Canada, Chile, China, Colombia, Croatia, the Czech Republic, Denmark, Egypt, Finland, France, Germany, Greece, Hong Kong SAR, Hungary, India, Indonesia, Ireland, Israel, Italy, Korea, Japan, Luxembourg, Malaysia, Mexico, Morocco, the Netherlands, New Zealand, Norway, Pakistan, Peru, the Philippines, Poland, Portugal, Russia, Singapore, the Slovak Republic, Slovenia, South Africa, Spain, Sweden, Switzerland, Taiwan Province of China, Thailand, Tunisia, Turkey, the United Kingdom, the United States, and Venezuela.

[4]In the sample, six economies are considered financial centers: Belgium, Hong Kong SAR, Luxembourg, the Netherlands, Singapore, and Switzerland.

The data cover the period from 1973 to 2004, and are structured in eight blocks of four-year averages: 1973–76; 1977–80; 1981–84; 1985–88; 1989–92; 1993–96; 1997–2000; and 2001–04. The estimation methods used in the macroeconomic balance approach are the pooled ordinary least squares (OLS—where the sample is treated as a cross section of 432 observations), and the fixed-effects regression (where the sample is treated as a panel with 54 cross sections and eight time series).[5]

The savings-investment norms are obtained according to three econometric models:

- *Pooled OLS with lagged current account balance:* in this model, besides the variables listed above, Lee and others (2008) mention the inclusion of country-specific dummy variables for six mid-sized economies and four Asian crisis countries, with their need justified by statistical tests.[6]
- *Pooled OLS with initial net foreign assets:* the same variables as above are applied, except that the lagged current account balance is replaced by the initial net foreign assets position.
- *Fixed effects:* owing to the standard cross-section dummies, other time-fixed indicators (for example, being a financial center) are naturally dropped. The model also excludes variables that present a high correlation with the cross-section dummies, such as banking crisis and PPP-GDP per capita (relative to the U.S. standards). Finally, the model excludes the initial NFA and the lagged current account balance from the list of explanatory variables.

Results of these models are discussed in detail below (see the section on Results), along with the estimates provided by the quantile regression models.

THE QUANTILE REGRESSION FRAMEWORK

Mainstream methods used to assess the equilibrium exchange rate estimate the impact of macroeconomic fundamentals on the savings-investment balance (current account norm) of a representative country (for example, the "average" country), without appropriately assessing the role of fundamentals at the tail end of the conditional distribution of the dependent variable. By delivering coefficients that are constant throughout the sample, these models restrict the role of explanatory variables to a mere "location-shift" of the conditional distribution of the dependent variable, neglecting important features of the data. In other words, these methods assume that the explanatory variables would change the mean but not other aspects of the conditional distribution of the dependent variable. Given the diversity of countries we deal with in international economics, it is important to evaluate the effects of the covariates not only on the average response but also on the outstanding ones. The quantile regression approach was

[5]The data are available on request.

[6]The dummies for mid-sized economies are for Australia, Chile, Israel, New Zealand, Sweden, and Thailand. The dummies for the Asian crisis economies are for Korea, Malaysia, Singapore, and Thailand.

introduced by Koenker and Bassett (1978a) as a supplement to traditional econometric techniques. Rather than focusing on the conditional mean, the QR approach offers a characterization of the entire conditional distribution of the dependent variable. It is based on the principle of ranking optimization, where the dependent variable (response), given a set of explanatory variables (covariates), is ranked according to the quantile where it is located in the conditional distribution. Given its rank nature, the QR estimates of the regression coefficients are robust to outliers in the dependent variable.

The QR regression does not require that the error term follow a normal distribution (or any parametric profile) because it is more efficient than traditional least squares estimators in the presence of non-normal residuals.

Econometric Setup

Let Y be a random variable with distribution function $F(y) = \Pr(Y \leq y)$. For $\tau \in (0,1)$, the τ-*th* quantile is defined as $Q(\tau) = \inf\{y: F(y) \geq \tau\}$. Simply put, an observation situated in the τ-*th* sample quantile is greater than τ percent of the observations. Well-known unconditional quantiles include the median ($\tau = 0.5$) and the first and third quartiles (respectively, $\tau = 0.25$ and $\tau = 0.75$).

Next, consider a basic linear (in parameters) regression model:

$$y_i = X_i' \beta + u_i$$

for $i = 1, \ldots, n$, where β is a $K \times 1$ vector of coefficients, X is a $n \times K$ matrix of explanatory variables, y is the response variable, and u is the $n \times 1$ vector of residuals. In the present application, y would represent the current account norm, and X would be the matrix of macroeconomic fundamentals, demographic factors, and country-specific dummies. In traditional estimation methods, such as the OLS, the vector of coefficient $\hat{\beta}$ is found through the minimization of the sum of the squared residuals. In contrast, the vector of coefficients in the QR setup is obtained by the solution of the following asymmetric penalty function:

$$\min_{\beta \in \Re^K} \left[\sum_{i \in \{ i: y_i \geq X_i' \beta \}} \tau \left| y_i - X_i' \beta \right| + \sum_{i \in \{ i: y_i < X_i' \beta \}} (1-\tau) \left| y_i - X_i' \beta \right| \right]. \tag{3.1}$$

The asymmetric penalty function above is equivalent to the weighted sum of the absolute values of the residuals, where the weights vary according to each quantile (τ). The QR coefficients $\hat{\beta}(\tau)$ are the solution to Equation (3.1) and naturally depend on each τ of the conditional distribution of the dependent variable $F(y|X) = \Pr(Y \leq y|X)$.

A special case of Equation (3.1) is the least absolute deviation (LAD) estimator, where $\tau = .5$ and the penalty function becomes symmetric, collapsing simply to:

$$\min_{\beta \in \Re^K} \sum_{i=1}^{n} \left| y_i - X_i' \beta \right|. \tag{3.2}$$

In this special case, the QR model fits the median response on a set of covariates (the asymmetric distribution of the LAD estimator is discussed in Koenker and Bassett, 1978b).

Interpretation of the Quantile Regression Slopes

The following empirical application is used in this chapter: we estimate regression coefficients for a grid of quantiles spanning from the 10th to the 90th percentile (by increments of 1 percent) of the conditional distribution of the explanatory variable (the current account norms). Although the OLS regression yields a $K \times 1$ vector of estimated coefficients (slopes) $\hat{\beta}$, the QR provides a matrix of coefficients $\hat{\beta}(\tau)$ with dimension $K \times \ell(\tau)$, where $\ell(\tau)$ is the length of the grid of quantiles selected to be estimated by the model (in the present application, the length of this grid is $\ell(\tau) = 90 - 10 + 1 = 81$).

Just as the OLS coefficient $\hat{\beta}_k$ measures the impact of marginal changes in x_k on the mean of the conditional distribution of y, the QR coefficient $\hat{\beta}_k(\tau)$ captures the impact of marginal changes in x_k on the τ-*th* quantile of the conditional distribution of y. As τ spans the entire sample, $\hat{\beta}_k(\tau)$ captures the impact of x_k at each sample quantile, providing a much richer description of the relationship between x_k and y. Conversely, the OLS coefficient is constant throughout the sample.

In the empirical application below, we display the estimates of the QR coefficients, and the respective confidence intervals, for a long range of quantiles of the conditional distribution of y. To compare, we plot the OLS coefficients as horizontal lines (fixed values) for all quantiles in the sample.

Unobserved Heterogeneity and Interquartile Differences in Slopes

The unobserved heterogeneity neglected by the traditional regression models can be captured by the QR coefficients at each quantile of the conditional distribution. Latent factors are embedded in the quantile regression coefficients, in the sense that a given explanatory variable is allowed to interact with the unobserved heterogeneity and present different effects throughout the sample.

Some researchers find it useful to assess the statistical significance of the changes in the slopes $\hat{\beta}_k(\tau)$ over the grid of quantiles. In this regard, a common test in the QR framework is the estimation of the degree of variability of $\hat{\beta}_k(\tau)$ between the first and the third quartiles. Rejecting the null hypothesis—that $\hat{\beta}_k(\tau = .75) - \hat{\beta}_k(\tau = .25) = 0$—is a good indicator that the variability of the slopes is significant. The test can be extended to other quantiles.

RESULTS

In this section, we supplement the econometric results obtained from the mainstream methods currently used in the macroeconomic balance approach (see Lee and others, 2008) with the quantile regression estimates.

The exchange rate assessment conducted by the macroeconomic balance approach is based on three models of the savings-investment norm: (1) a pooled OLS with a lagged current account balance among the explanatory variables; (2) a pooled OLS with the initial net foreign assets replacing the lagged current account balance as an explanatory variable; and (3) a fixed-effects panel regression, which includes cross-section-specific dummies but drops the lagged current account balance, the initial NFA, and time-fixed dummies such as the financial center indicator.

Overall, the three models have high goodness of fit (R-squares up to 64 percent). In addition, in the three models, the most prominent policy variables have the expected sign and are statistically significant. Nevertheless, compared with the actual data (that is, current account balances), the models deliver fitted values that have density distributions more concentrated around the sample mean. As seen in Figure 3.3, almost 20 percent of the fitted results lie around the sample mean (a deficit close to 1 percent for all models), but the actual data have half of that mass around that region.

The compression of the conditional distributions of the fitted values toward the mean is also reflected in the standard deviations and in other relevant rank measures, as can be observed in Table 3.1. For instance, the standard deviation of the actual current account balances is 30 percent higher than those of the current account balances fitted by mainstream methods. The interquartile range, measured as the difference between the lower and upper quartiles—a robust metric for the spread in the central region of the distribution—is also about 30 percent higher in the actual data. To better understand the reasons for this compression, we take a closer look at the coefficients estimated by each model, and compare them with quantile regression estimates.

In Table 3.2, we display the results for the pooled OLS model with the lagged dependent variable (Model 1). In addition, we provide quantile regression estimates of that specification at five selected percentiles of the conditional distribution of the

Figure 3.3 Conditional Distribution of Current Account Norms for CGER Countries

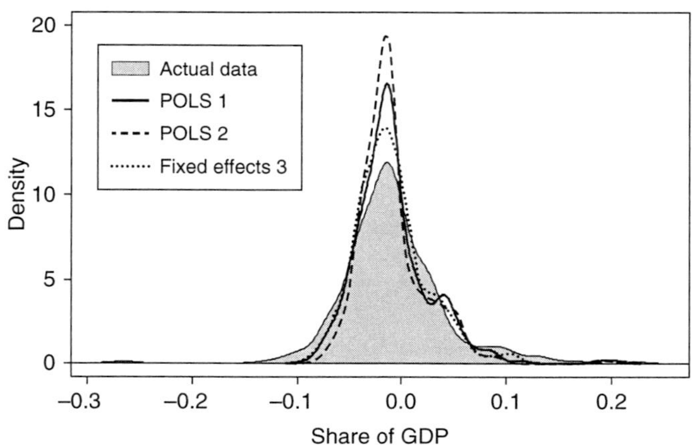

Source: Author's calculations.
Note: CGER = Consultative Group on Exchange Rate Issues; POLS = pooled ordinary least squares. See text for discussion of models.

TABLE 3.1

Summary Statistics of the Fitted Values of the Savings-Investment Norms[1]

	Actual Data	Model 1	Model 2	Model 3
		(Percent of GDP)		
Mean	–0.9	–0.9	–0.9	–0.9
Standard deviation	4.7	3.6	3.3	3.6
Minimum	–26.5	–8.8	–7.7	–8.5
Lower quartile	–3.5	–3.1	–2.9	–3.3
Median	–1.3	–1.3	–1.5	–1.5
Upper quartile	1.2	0.7	0.3	0.6
Maximum	22.5	20.4	20.8	20.6

Source: Author's calculations.
[1]Model 1 is the pooled ordinary least squares (OLS) with lagged current account balance; Model 2 is the pooled OLS with the initial net foreign assets; and Model 3 is the fixed effects panel regression.

TABLE 3.2

Current Account Norm—Estimates Including Lagged Current Account Balance

Dependent Variable: **Current Account Balance**

		Quantile Regression				
Explanatory Variables:	**POLS**	**tau = 0.1**	**tau = 0.25**	**tau = 0.5**	**tau = 0.75**	**tau = 0.9**
Fiscal balance	0.189	0.219	0.160	0.068	0.144	0.217
	0.043***	0.084***	0.078**	0.072	0.061**	0.084***
Real growth of PPP-GDP per capita	–0.157	–0.027	–0.166	–0.156	–0.180	–0.177
	0.079**	0.164**	0.110	0.098	0.149	0.210
Old-age dependency ratio	–0.125	–0.113	–0.175	–0.075	–0.020	–0.181
	0.048***	0.117	0.062***	0.053	0.063	0.107*
Population growth	–1.034	–1.093	–1.159	–0.600	–0.468	–1.100
	0.405***	0.616**	0.559**	0.447	0.510	0.672
PPP-GDP per capita	0.020	0.038	0.026	0.017	0.002	0.007
	0.011*	0.018**	0.012**	0.012	0.012	0.024
Oil balance	0.169	0.088	0.134	0.200	0.235	0.208
	0.030***	0.082	0.081*	0.058***	0.054***	0.067***
Asian crisis	0.034	0.044	0.035	0.033	0.042	0.013
	0.006***	0.011***	0.011***	0.012***	0.016**	0.017
Banking crisis	0.010	0.014	0.008	0.006	0.014	0.028
	0.007	0.013	0.010	0.008	0.012	0.016*
Lagged current account balance	0.366	0.355	0.455	0.437	0.399	0.376
	0.089**	0.070***	0.078***	0.073***	0.085***	0.110***
Financial center	0.031	0.010	0.024	0.032	0.038	0.055
	0.004***	0.009	0.009**	0.008***	0.011***	0.016***
Constant	–0.003	–0.027	–0.016	–0.002	0.007	0.021
	0.004	0.006***	0.005***	0.005	0.005	0.011*
R-squared	0.643	n.a.	n.a.	n.a.	n.a.	n.a.

Source: Author's calculations.
Note: POLS = pooled ordinary least squares; PPP = purchasing power parity. (***) significant at 1 percent; (**) significant at 5 percent; and (*) significant at 10 percent.

current account balances: the 10th (lowest decile), the 25th (lower quartile), the 50th (median), the 75th (upper quartile), and the 90th (highest decile).

Countries with current account balances situated below the lower quartile correspond to cases with larger current account deficits. Conversely, countries with current account balances above the upper quartile correspond to cases with the highest current account surpluses. More interestingly, countries may switch their rank over time—for example, a fast-growing economy with current account deficits below the lower quartile in the 1980s could be enjoying surpluses and be placed at the top quartile in the 2000s. Nevertheless, in light of the gradual adjustment (high persistence) of current account balances, deficit-prone countries are expected to remain associated with lower quantiles (whereas surplus economies are expected to remain at the upper quantiles) of the conditional distribution of the response.

The results indicate that, although in most cases, the coefficients present the expected sign at these quantiles, their magnitude and statistical significance change substantially throughout the quantiles. For instance, the coefficient for the fiscal balance has a higher magnitude for the countries located at the tail end of the conditional distribution rather than at the center.

A more insightful view is provided in Figure 3.4, where we plot the quantile regression coefficients for each of the policy variables on a grid of quantiles that

Figure 3.4 Quantile Regression Estimates for Pooled Ordinary Least Squares Model with Lagged Current Account Balance

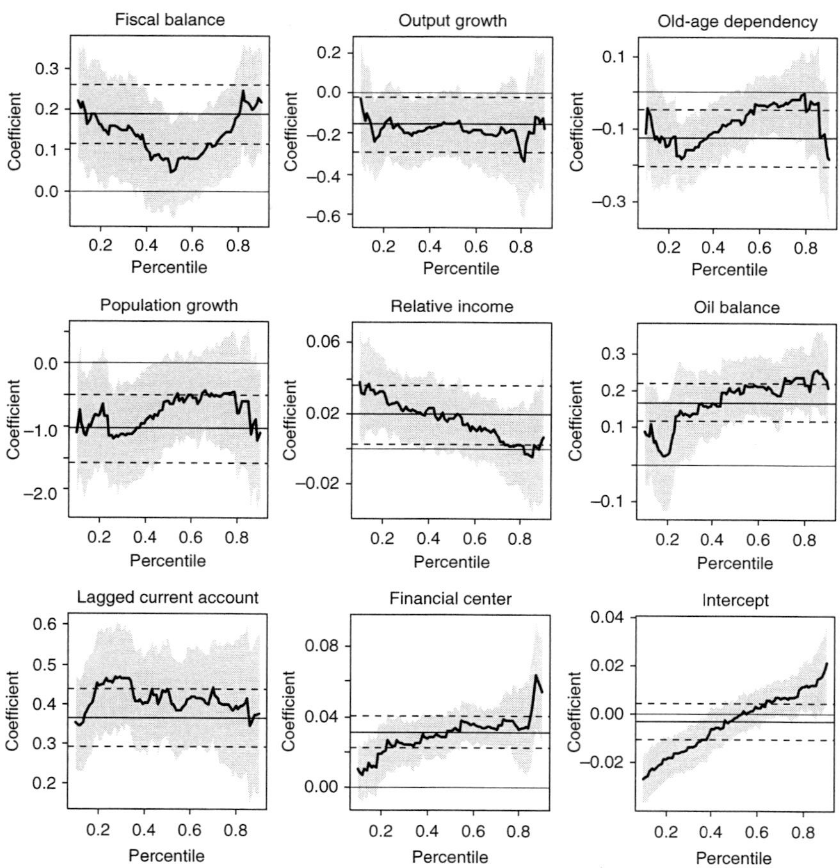

Source: Author's calculations.
Note: For simplicity, the coefficients for country and time dummies are not plotted above.

spans from the 10th to the 90th percentile, in increments of 1 percent. The point estimates of $\hat{\beta}(\tau)$ are represented by the solid black line in each panel chart. Their respective confidence intervals, based on bootstrapped standard errors, are represented by the shaded gray area. For comparison, the estimated coefficients from the pooled OLS model are plotted as solid red lines (and the boundaries of their respective confidence intervals are plotted as dashed red lines). As the pooled OLS coefficients are constant for the entire conditional distribution of the dependent variable, these lines are horizontal.

The results suggest that coefficients of the fiscal balance are almost three times higher at the tail end of the distribution (where the external imbalances reside) than in the center, with the $\hat{\beta}(\tau)$ function U-shaped. The lagged current account balance has a somewhat stable contribution to the dependent variable, explaining between 35 percent and 45 percent of its variation—an elevated degree of persistence for all quantiles.

In Table 3.3 and Figure 3.5, we present the quantile regression coefficients for the econometric specification of the pooled OLS model with the initial net foreign assets (Model 2).

The convex shape of the fiscal balance impact is observed again. Also, the contribution of the oil balances to the current account—which in Model 1 was

TABLE 3.3

Current Account Norm—Estimates Including Initial Net Foreign Assets Position

Dependent Variable: **Current Account Balance**

		Quantile Regression				
Explanatory Variables:	**POLS**	**tau = 0.1**	**tau = 0.25**	**tau = 0.5**	**tau = 0.75**	**tau = 0.9**
Fiscal balance	0.198	0.230	0.159	0.082	0.145	0.226
	0.056***	0.083***	0.090*	0.074	0.073**	0.080***
Real growth of PPP-GDP per capita	−0.208	−0.343	−0.326	−0.236	−0.228	−0.168
	0.095**	0.174**	0.118***	0.116**	0.117**	0.209
Old-age dependency ratio	−0.142	−0.094	−0.169	−0.178	−0.087	−0.073
	0.062**	0.099	0.065**	0.059***	0.051*	0.086
Population growth	−1.213	−1.230	−1.454	−1.329	−0.577	−0.831
	0.472***	0.529**	0.634**	0.504***	0.504	0.552
PPP-GDP per capita	0.024	0.033	0.023	0.017	0.011	0.009
	0.015	0.019*	0.012*	0.014	0.013	0.024
Oil balance	0.231	0.190	0.210	0.187	0.296	0.310
	0.035***	0.073***	0.064***	0.053***	0.060***	0.060***
Asian crisis	0.061	0.099	0.067	0.044	0.047	0.038
	0.007**	0.041**	0.031**	0.026*	0.023**	0.023*
Banking crisis	0.008	0.003	0.008	0.006	0.019	0.013
	0.007	0.017	0.011	0.009	0.010*	0.010
Net foreign assets	0.025	0.018	0.030	0.036	0.034	0.014
	0.010**	0.014	0.011***	0.008***	0.010***	0.016
Financial center	0.026	−0.005	0.022	0.032	0.031	0.066
	0.008***	0.023	0.015	0.009***	0.009***	0.019***
Constant	−0.001	−0.032	−0.020	−0.003	0.013	0.023
	0.006	0.008***	0.006***	0.005	0.006**	0.010**
R-squared	0.553	n.a.	n.a.	n.a.	n.a.	n.a.

Source: Author's calculations.

Note: POLS = pooled ordinary least squares; PPP = purchasing power parity. (***) significant at 1 percent; (**) significant at 5 percent; and (*) significant at 10 percent.

an upward sloped curve with the quantiles—is now quite flat for most of the sample, with a peak in the upper quartile. This suggests that there is a degree of interaction between oil balance and initial net foreign balance that was not captured in Model 1.

The contribution of the initial net foreign assets position tends to be smaller at the tail end of the conditional distribution, implying that for high deficit and high surplus countries, the initial NFA position is less important for determination of external balances than for the rest of the sample. In fact, the coefficients for the initial NFA position are only statistically different from zero along the interquartile range.

Figure 3.5 Quantile Regression Estimates for Pooled Ordinary Least Squares Model with Initial Net Foreign Assets (NFA) Position

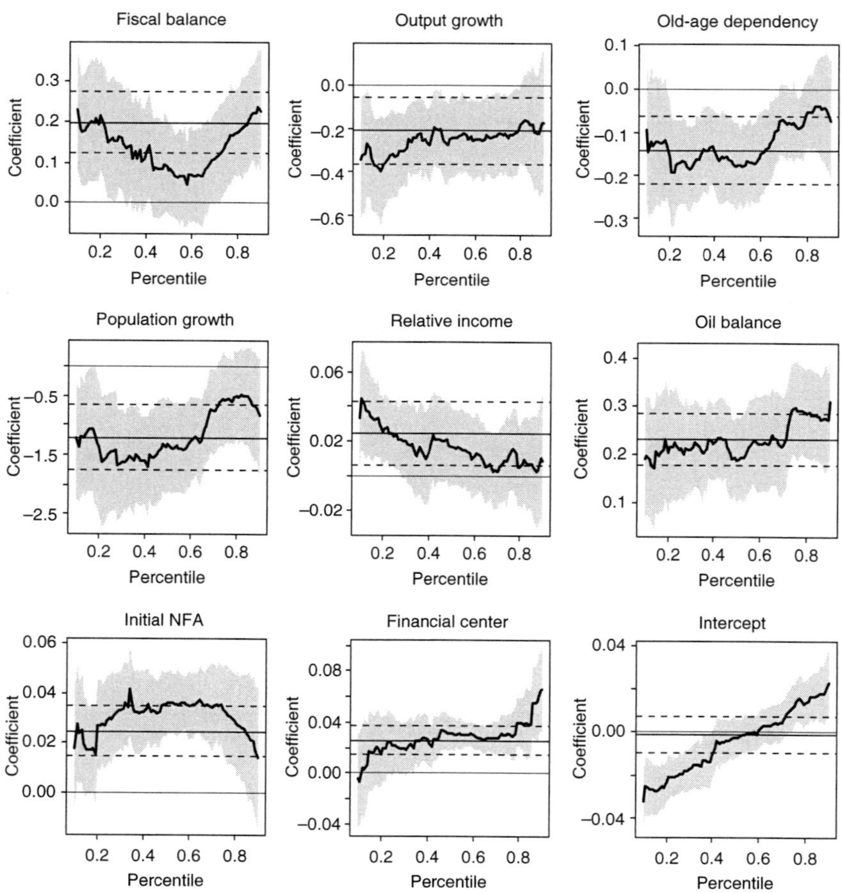

Source: Author's calculations.
Note: For simplicity, the coefficients for country and time dummies are not plotted above.

Also, the contribution of the output growth (real growth of PPP-GDP per capita) is close to the pooled OLS estimates for most percentiles. However, the contribution of the relative income (PPP-GDP per capita relative to the U.S. standard) declines substantially with the quantiles in both models, even crossing the zero boundary (that is, changing sign) at the upper quantiles of the first model.

With regard to the behavior of countries' demographic factors, both the old-age dependency ratio and the population growth tend to oscillate within the boundaries of the confidence interval delimited by the pooled OLS method. However, in Model 2, they tend to have a smaller impact on the surplus countries than on the rest of the sample.

Finally, the financial center dummy presents a higher impact in the upper quantiles, supporting the theoretical view that financial centers tend to run current account surpluses (albeit in 17 percent of the cases, a financial center presented a current account deficit).

In Table 3.4 and Figure 3.6, we present the coefficients for the econometric specification of the fixed-effects panel regression (Model 3). Coefficients are identical to those obtained from a pooled OLS regression with a dummy variable for each cross section. Hence, the quantile regression framework is applied in a similar way as in Models 1 and 2.

The results of the fixed-effects model are more streamlined, as the model forcefully drops time-fixed dummy variables (such as the financial center indicator) owing

TABLE 3.4

Current Account Norm—Estimates Based on Fixed-Effects Panel Regression

***Dependent Variable:* Current Account Balance**

		Quantile Regression				
Explanatory Variables:	**POLS**	**tau = 0.1**	**tau = 0.25**	**tau = 0.5**	**tau = 0.75**	**tau = 0.9**
Fiscal balance	0.314	0.294	0.257	0.235	0.188	0.285
	0.087***	0.097***	0.093***	0.090***	0.086**	0.094***
Real growth of PPP-GDP per capita	−0.268	−0.199	−0.183	−0.183	−0.112	−0.139
	0.198	0.143	0.129	0.134	0.138	0.171
Old-age dependency ratio	−0.234	−0.308	−0.231	−0.168	−0.259	−0.209
	0.128*	0.143**	0.125*	0.111	0.152*	0.181
Population growth	−0.470	−1.568	−1.941	−1.457	−0.931	−1.283
	1.153	0.849*	0.946**	0.702**	0.738	0.965
Oil balance	0.306	−0.001	0.234	0.250	0.354	0.341
	0.096***	0.134	0.123**	0.110**	0.101***	0.123***
Asian crisis	0.067	0.094	0.077	0.061	0.052	0.043
	0.007***	0.043**	0.040*	0.035*	0.031*	0.029
Constant	−0.002	−0.040	−0.019	−0.004	0.010	0.013
	0.009	0.013***	0.013	0.011	0.011	0.013
R-squared	0.633	n.a.	n.a.	n.a.	n.a.	n.a.

Source: Author's calculations.

Note: POLS = pooled ordinary least squares; PPP = purchasing power parity. (***) significant at 1 percent; (**) significant at 5 percent; and (*) significant at 10 percent.

Figure 3.6 Quantile Regression Coefficients for Fixed-Effects Panel Regression

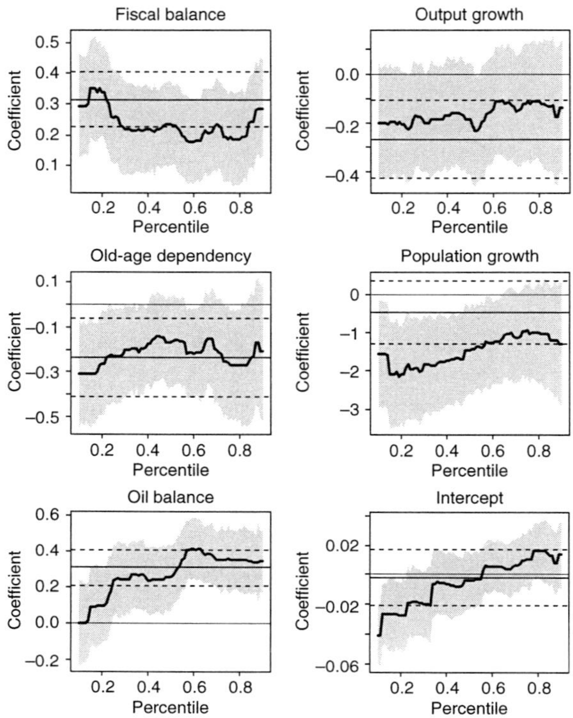

Source: Author's calculations.
Note: For simplicity, the coefficients for country and time dummies are not plotted above.

to perfect correlation with the cross-section dummies. In addition, explanatory variables that present high (but not perfect) correlation with the cross-section dummies, are not part of the original macroeconomic balance approach (fixed-effects panel regression).

The quantile regression estimates for the fixed-effects model confirm the convex shape of the fiscal balance contribution to the current account, as well as the higher impact of the oil balances on the current accounts of countries that present larger surpluses.

Interestingly, the quantile regression estimates of the impact of output growth on the current account balances are systematically lower (in absolute values) than as estimated by the fixed-effects model. The opposite happens to the contribution of population growth.

Finally, the role of the old-age dependency ratio is quantitatively similar in both approaches.

AN APPLICATION TO LATIN AMERICAN EMERGING MARKETS

A useful application of the quantile regression framework regards the estimation of current account norms for Latin American emerging markets. To illustrate the heterogeneity among these countries, as well as in comparison with non–Latin American economies included in the CGER analysis, in Figure 3.7, we plot the percentiles of each country's current account balance at each point in time. Large current account deficits are associated with lower percentiles; the opposite is true for sizable surpluses. These percentiles also vary over time, such that current account reversals are well captured by these statistics.

In Figure 3.7, panel A, we see that the current account balances of Brazil, Chile, Colombia, and Mexico very often lie between the 25th and the 75th percentiles, known as the interquartile range (shaded area). In contrast, the current account balances of Argentina, Peru, and Venezuela are usually located far away from the center of the distribution, as illustrated in Figure 3.7, panel B. This phenomenon is related to both cyclical and structural features of these countries during each sub-period of the sample. Such degree of differentiation sometimes is not fully captured by the CGER panel data regressions.

Econometric models that neglect heterogeneity over time and across countries may yield estimates of current account norms that tend to be much closer to the sample average than warranted by a country-year's specific characteristics. In these cases, supplementing the CGER models with the quantile regression approach helps to uncover the neglected heterogeneity. To illustrate this point, in Table 3.5, we list five Latin American episodes of current account balances outside the interquartile range. In all of them, the current account norm based on the quantile regression model fitted for the specific percentile of each observation ("quantile norm") was associated with narrower current account gaps (that is, smaller

Figure 3.7 Latin America: Percentiles of Current Account Balances, 1985–2004

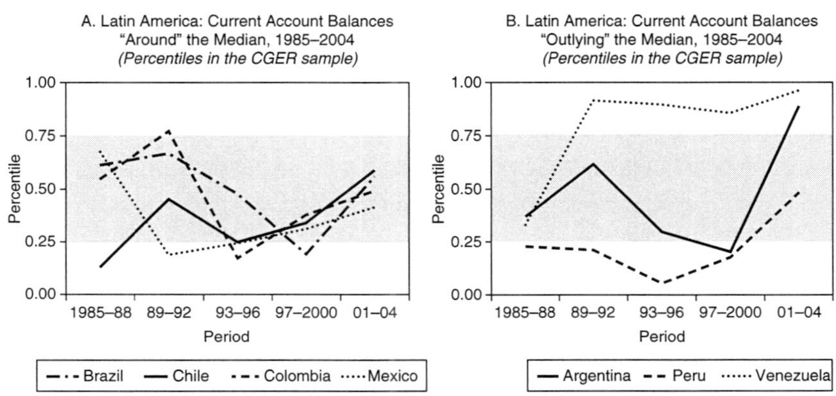

Source: IMF staff calculations.
Note: CGER = Consultative Group on Exchange Rate Issues.

TABLE 3.5

Latin America: Selected Episodes of Current Account Balances "Outlying" the Median, 1985–2004

	Period	Episode Percentile	Current Account Balance	CGER Norm	Quantile Norm	CGER Gap	Quantile Gap
			(Percent of GDP)				
Brazil	1997–2000	0.19	–4.2	–1.5	–3.7	–2.8	–0.5
Colombia	1993–96	0.17	–4.4	–0.3	–3.1	–4.2	–1.4
Mexico	1993–96	0.24	–3.5	–0.4	–2.4	–3.1	–1.2
Peru	1989–92	0.21	–4.0	–1.6	–4.0	–2.4	0.0
Venezuela	1989–92	0.91	4.8	1.9	7.0	2.9	–2.2

Source: Author's calculations.

Note: CGER = Consultative Group on Exchange Rate Issues. The CGER norm corresponds to the fitted value according to the pooled ordinary least squares model described in Table 3.2, whereas the quantile norm refers to the fitted value for the respective percentile of the episode, based on the quantile regression specification of Table 3.2. The gap refers to the difference between the actual current account balance and the fitted current account norm acording to each method.

differences between the actual current account balance and the estimated norm) than the respective estimates of the CGER norm. All else being equal, the quantile regression gaps suggest a lower degree of exchange rate misalignment in Latin American economies than what would be expected from the examination of the CGER gaps during these episodes.

CONCLUSION

In this chapter, we provided an alternative framework to estimate the savings-investment norms used in the macroeconomic balance approach to assess exchange rate misalignments. The quantile regression approach provides a flexible framework to evaluate the contribution of policy variables and demographic characteristics on the determination of current account balances.

Mainstream methods used to estimate the savings-investment norms tend to disregard important features of the data, yielding fitted values that are compressed toward the mean. In these models, the contribution of each explanatory variable is fixed for all quantiles of the conditional distribution of the current account balances. These models show that the impact of any given policy variable is the same for countries carrying large deficits (that is, countries in the lower quantiles) as for countries enjoying large surpluses (those in the higher quantiles of the conditional distribution of current account balances).

The quantile regression estimates provided in this chapter supplement those from traditional models by providing slopes that vary according to the quantile of the conditional distribution of the current account balances. Through the use of the quantile-varying slopes, the econometrician provides a much richer description of the relationships between current account balances and macroeconomic fundamentals in a large panel of heterogeneous countries.

Our results indicate that the contribution of fiscal balances to the current account tends to be higher at the tail end of the conditional distribution of current account balances (that is, where countries with the largest external imbalances are located). In addition, we found that the contribution of oil balances tends to be more accentuated in the upper quantiles. Important nonlinearities in the role of output growth and demographic characteristics were also discussed.

In an empirical application to Latin American emerging markets, we find that during periods of sizable deficits or surpluses, the current account norms based on the quantile regression approach are broadly associated with narrower current account gaps (less exchange rate misalignment) than suggested by the CGER macroeconomic balance approach. This finding may reflect the ability of the quantile regression framework to capture unobserved heterogeneity over time and across countries.

REFERENCES

Bems, Rudolfs, and Irineu de Carvalho Filho, 2009, "Exchange Rate Assessments: Methodologies for Oil Exporting Countries," IMF Working Paper 09/281 (Washington: International Monetary Fund).

Chinn, Menzie, and Eswar Prasad, 2003, "Medium-Term Determinants of Current Accounts in Industrial and Developing Countries: An Empirical Exploration," *Journal of International Economics*, Vol. 59, No. 1, pp. 47–76.

Demirgüç-Kunt, Asli, and Enrica Detragiache, 2005, "Cross-Country Empirical Studies of Systemic Bank Distress: A Survey," IMF Working Paper 05/96 (Washington: International Monetary Fund).

Gruber, Joseph, and Steve Kamin, 2005, "Explaining the Global Pattern of Current Account Imbalances," International Finance Discussion Paper No. 846 (Washington: Board of Governors of the Federal Reserve System).

Isard, Peter, and Hamid Faruqee, eds., 1998, *Exchange Rate Assessment: Extensions of the Macroeconomic Balance Approach*, Occasional Paper 167 (Washington: International Monetary Fund).

Isard, Peter, and Michael Mussa, 1998, "A Methodology for Exchange Rate Assessment," in *Exchange Rate Assessment: Extensions of the Macroeconomic Balance Approach*, edited by Peter Isard and Hamid Faruqee, Occasional Paper 167 (Washington: International Monetary Fund), chapter 2.

Koenker, Roger, 2005, *Quantile Regression (Econometric Society Monographs)* (Cambridge, Massachusetts: Cambridge University Press).

———, and Gilbert Bassett, 1978a, "Regression Quantiles," *Econometrica*, Vol. 46, pp. 33–50.

———, 1978b, "The Asymptotic Distribution of the Least Absolute Error Estimator," *Journal of the American Statistical Association*, Vol. 73, pp. 618–22.

Koenker, Roger, and Kevin Hallock, 2001, "Quantile Regression," *Journal of Economic Perspectives*, Vol. 15, pp. 143–56.

Lane, Philip, and Gian Maria Milesi-Ferretti, 2007, "The External Wealth of Nations Mark II: Revised and Extended Estimates of Foreign Assets and Liabilities, 1970–2004," *Journal of International Economics*, Vol. 73, No. 2, pp. 223–50.

Lee, Jaewoo, Gian Maria Milesi-Ferretti, Jonathan Ostry, Alessandro Prati, and Luca Antonio Ricci, 2008, *Exchange Rate Assessments: CGER Methodologies*, Occasional Paper 261 (Washington: International Monetary Fund).

Meade, James E., 1951, *The Theory of International Economic Policy Volume One: The Balance of Payments* (London: Oxford University Press).

Metzler, Loyd A., 1951, "Wealth, Saving, and the Rate of Interest," *Journal of Political Economy*, Vol. 59, pp. 93–116.

Nurkse, Ragnar, 1945, "Conditions of International Monetary Equilibrium," *Princeton Essays in International Finance*, No. 4 (Princeton, New Jersey: Princeton University).

Perrelli, Roberto A., 2011, "Extending the Macroeconomic Balance Assessment of the Equilibrium Exchange Rate—A Quantile Regression Approach," unpublished (Washington: International Monetary Fund).

Piñeda, Emilio, Paul Cashin, and Yan Sun, 2009, "Assessing Exchange Rate Competitiveness in the Eastern Caribbean Currency Union," IMF Working Paper 09/78 (Washington: International Monetary Fund).

Polak, Jacques, 1995, "Fifty Years of Exchange Rate Research and Policy at the International Monetary Fund," *IMF Staff Papers*, Vol. 42, pp. 734–61.

Taylor, Alan, 2001, "A Century of Current Account Dynamics," *Journal of International Money and Finance*, Vol. 21, pp. 725–48.

PART III

The Role of Macroprudential Policies and Exchange Rate Regimes

CHAPTER 4

Brazil's Experience in Managing Capital Inflows: The Role of Capital Controls

ROBERTO BENELLI, ALEX SEGURA-UBIERGO, AND W. CHRISTOPHER WALKER

This chapter presents Brazil's experience in managing capital flows. It discusses the Brazilian authorities' use of a broad range of instruments to deal with capital inflows, including foreign exchange (FX) intervention, macroprudential tools, fiscal adjustment, and capital controls. Although it is difficult to separate the individual effects of each policy measure, they seem to have collectively reduced the speed of exchange rate appreciation. Capital controls have affected mostly the composition of flows (higher foreign direct investment [FDI] and less fixed-income portfolio investment), rather than the overall quantity of flows. The IOF (Imposto sobre Operações Financeiras) also appears to have curtailed incentives for carry trades.

Brazil's recent experience managing capital inflows has generated a substantial amount of interest, reflecting both the nation's prominence as a major emerging market and the fact that it has been one of the front-runners in adopting capital flow management measures (CFMs). This chapter provides a comprehensive account of Brazil's recent experience by reviewing the authorities' policy response to the surge in capital inflows in the recovery from the global financial crisis. Given the difficulty in identifying empirically the effect of CFMs—and hence a proper counterfactual of what might have happened to capital inflows under different policy responses—this chapter refrains from strong causal inferences, but rather relies on a variety of empirical facts to disentangle the possible impact of CFMs.[1] The chapter is organized in three sections, beginning with some stylized facts about capital inflows into Brazil in the period 2009–11, followed by a description of authorities' policy response, and concluding with an assessment of the role and effectiveness of capital controls.

[1]This is particularly the case in assessing the impact of capital control measures such as the IOF, which is highly endogenous. In addition, the absence of a sufficiently long time series precludes obtaining robust results with the use of econometric techniques.

STYLIZED FACTS ON CAPITAL INFLOWS

Strong economic growth prospects for Brazil in the aftermath of the global crisis reinforced structural factors (including high nominal interest rates), resulting in large capital inflows and strong appreciation pressures (Figures 4.1 and 4.2). In 2010, gross capital inflows[2] exceeded US$150 billion (6.8 percent of 2010 GDP), compared with US$92 billion in 2009. Gross capital inflows remained strong in 2011, exceeding US$15 billion per month.

Deep capital markets and high interest rates make Brazil one of the preferred destinations for capital flows to emerging market economies. Brazil's equity market is one of the world's ten largest by market capitalization, containing several globally known firms, such as Petrobras, Vale, Embraer, and Odebrecht. The sovereign bond market is also deep, featuring a variety of maturities and types of bonds, including fixed-rate, floating-rate, inflation-linked, and foreign-currency-linked bonds. The total stock of domestic bonds outstanding exceeds US$900 billion. As a result, Brazil is a bellwether, attracting a large share of total inflows to emerging and developing economies and reflecting global views toward such economies as an asset class (Figure 4.3).

Foreign investors' interest in Brazil is also influenced by the large derivatives market. Volume trading in the market for derivatives tripled from 2003 to 2011, transforming the domestic BM&F futures market into one the largest clearinghouses for derivatives in the world. The market for most classes of derivatives is liquid out to maturities of more than two years, with most of the trading concentrated in

Figure 4.1 Gross Capital Inflows (Billions of U.S. dollars; 3-month moving average)

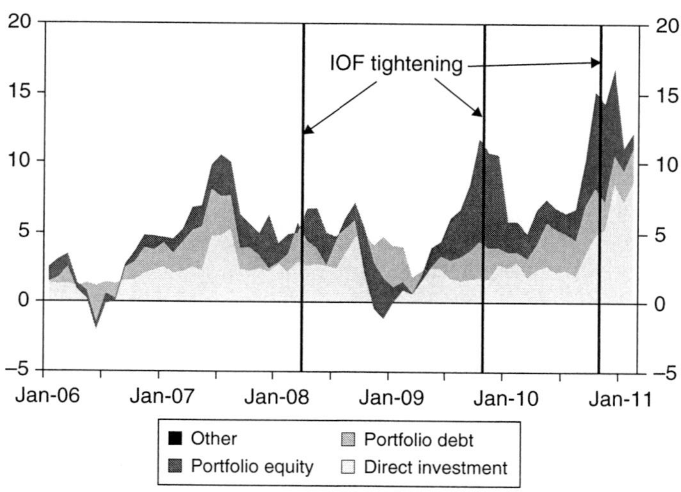

Source: IMF staff calculations.
Note: IOF = Imposto sobre Operações Financeiras.

[2]Gross capital inflows are defined as foreigners' net direct investment plus portfolio investment and other flows.

Figure 4.2 Foreign Investment (Billions of U.S. dollars; monthly average)[1]

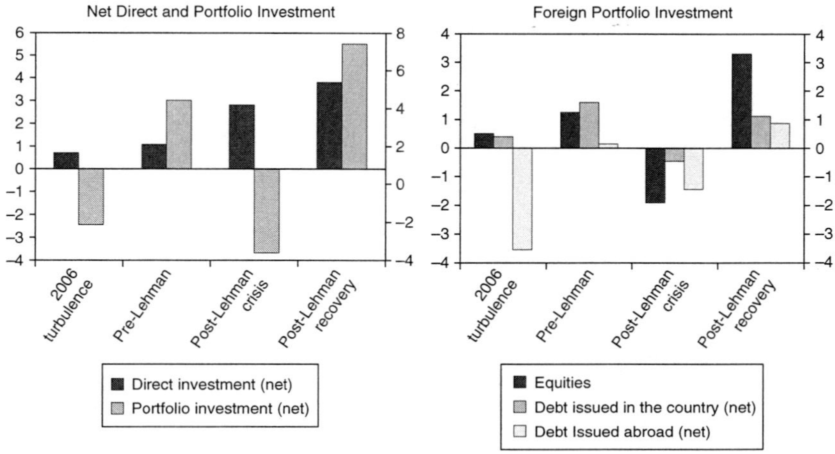

Source: IMF staff calculations.

[1]"2006 turbulence" indicates the period from April 2006 through June 2006; "Pre-Lehman" indicates the period from July 2006 through August 2008; "Post-Lehman crisis" indicates the period from September 2008 through March 2009; "Post-Lehamn recovery" indicates the period from April 2009 to date.

Figure 4.3 Flows to Brazil: Share to and Correlation with Emerging Markets

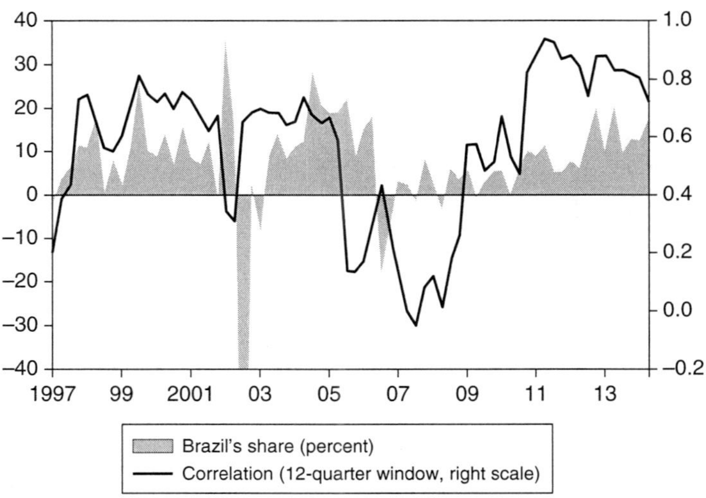

Source: IMF staff calculations.

interest-rate and currency-based derivatives. There is also an active offshore market in nondeliverable currency forwards (NDFs) in the Brazilian *real*, centered on banks located in New York. There are offshore markets as well for several other "access" products that allow foreign investors to trade as if they were in Brazil. These include credit-linked notes and derivatives based on Brazilian interest rates, all settled in U.S. dollars.

As a result, Brazil has dominated capital inflows to Latin America, and accounted for a large share of global equity issuance in 2010. This was due in part to the record Petrobras issuance in the third quarter that year.[3] In addition to FDI and equity flows, fixed-income inflows were steady during most of 2010, reflecting both "real money" flows as well as retail flows (especially from Japan), while external corporate bond issuance rose to near-record highs.

POLICY RESPONSE

The Brazilian authorities used a broad range of measures to manage the surge in capital inflows, including exchange rate appreciation, reserve accumulation, and fiscal adjustment, as well as macroprudential and CFM measures.

Rationale for Managing Capital Flows

Large inflows in the context of a flexible exchange rate system and open capital account can lead to strong swings in the exchange rate. The Brazilian *real* appreciated by more than 40 percent against the U.S. dollar between December 2008 and July 2011, while the real effective exchange rate reached a level stronger than before the financial crisis (when it had already reached its highest level in 30 years). As a result of this rapid appreciation, exchange rate valuation assessments showed that the Brazilian *real* was substantially overvalued (Figure 4.4).

Large capital inflows also raise the risk of disruptive sudden stops (Ostry and others, 2011). Such stops tend to be highly synchronized across countries, particularly among countries with open capital accounts. Brazil, in particular, has in the past experienced firsthand the consequence of volatile capital flows. This "excessive" volatility is well captured by an exercise that compares actual capital flows to Brazil with their predicted value based on a panel regression of capital flows to a range of pull and push factors (Figure 4.5).[4]

Reserve Accumulation

The Brazilian *real* would likely have appreciated even further without strong FX intervention (Figure 4.6). In this regard, the central bank (Banco Central do Brasil, or BCB) stepped up its intervention in both the spot and forward markets during the period of heavy inflows, often holding daily (or even twice-daily) auctions. From December 2008 to July 2011, Brazil's stock of foreign reserves rose by more than $139 billion, to $346 billion. The BCB also intervened in the onshore forward market, buying U.S. dollars forward against the *real*.

Fiscal Adjustment

Although fiscal adjustments are generally understood to be aimed at maintaining debt sustainability and containing inflation, their positive effect as a tool to deal with large capital inflows should not be underestimated. In 2011, the combination of budgetary adjustment and reductions in quasi-fiscal activities (including transfers

[3]Foreigners' subscribed participation in the recapitalization of Petrobras amounted to US$14 billion.
[4]The details underpinning this panel regression analysis are provided in IMF (2011).

Figure 4.4 Gross and Net Capital Inflows

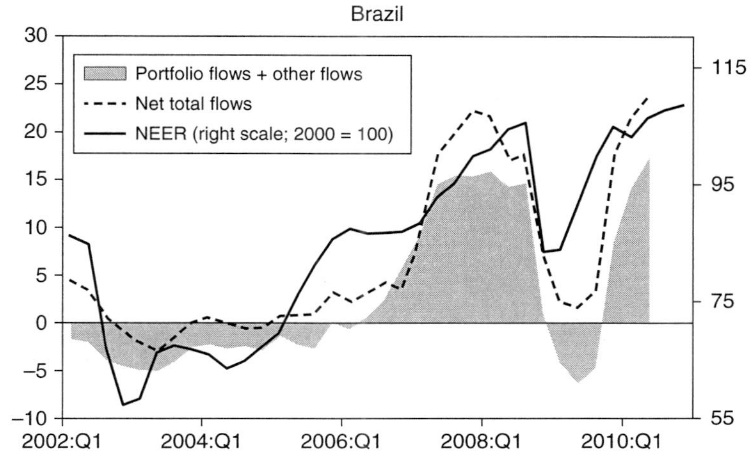

Source: IMF staff calculations.
Note: NEER = nominal effective exchange rate.

Figure 4.5 Predicted and Actual Capital Inflows

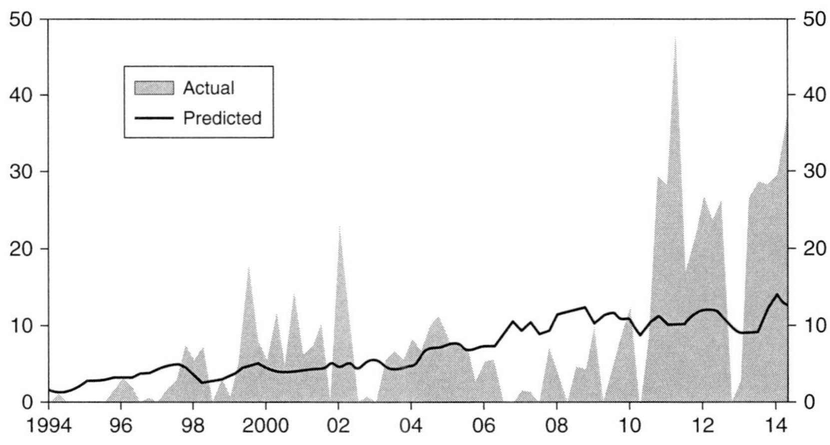

Source: IMF staff calculations.

from the Treasury to the national development bank) was equivalent to a structural fiscal adjustment of about 2 percent of GDP. As in many other emerging markets, the difficulty of estimating fiscal multipliers and the interest rate channel of monetary policy makes it difficult to assess trade-offs between monetary and fiscal policy. This uncertainty is reflected in the broad range of responses in a poll of domestic analysts conducted by the BCB (Figure 4.7). However, this survey also suggested that, according to the mode of the response distribution, a 1.2 percent of GDP fiscal adjustment announced would be equivalent to about 120 basis points of otherwise necessary monetary tightening that would have attracted even more inflows.

Figure 4.6 Nominal Exchange Rate, Central Bank Interventions, and IOF Imposition

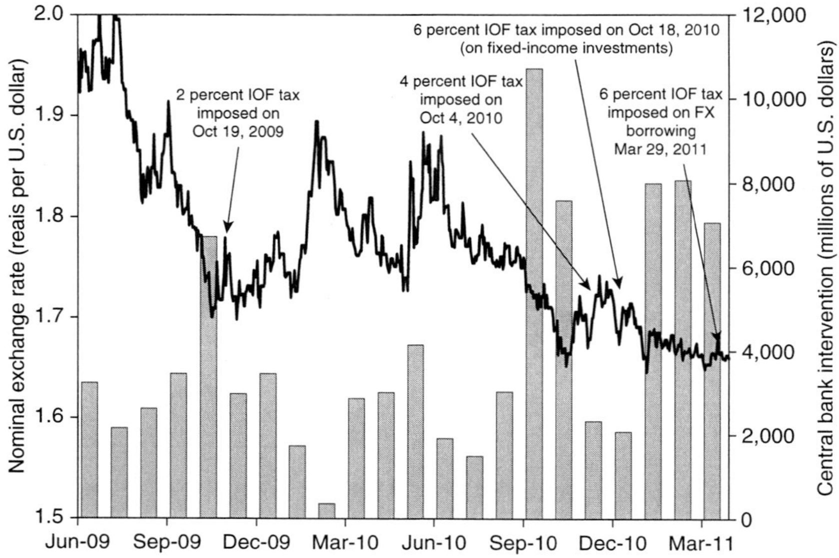

Source: IMF staff calculations.
Note: FX = foreign exchange; IOF = Imposto sobre Aperaçóes Financeiras.

Figure 4.7 Change in Policy Rate Equivalent to Fiscal Measures

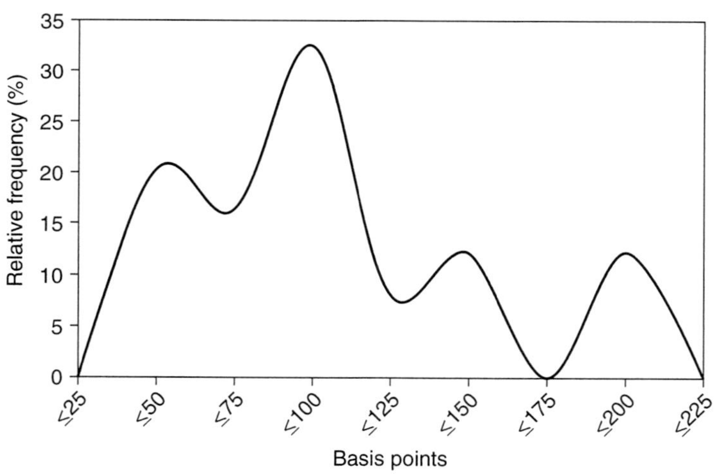

Source: Central Bank of Brazil, based on a survey of market participants.

Macroprudential Instruments

In January 2011, the BCB introduced reserve requirements that sought to limit the short U.S. dollar positions of banks. The BCB noted that this measure was designed to reduce leverage in the system, particularly for banks with restricted

Figure 4.8 Change in Policy Rate Equivalent to Macroprudential Measures[1]

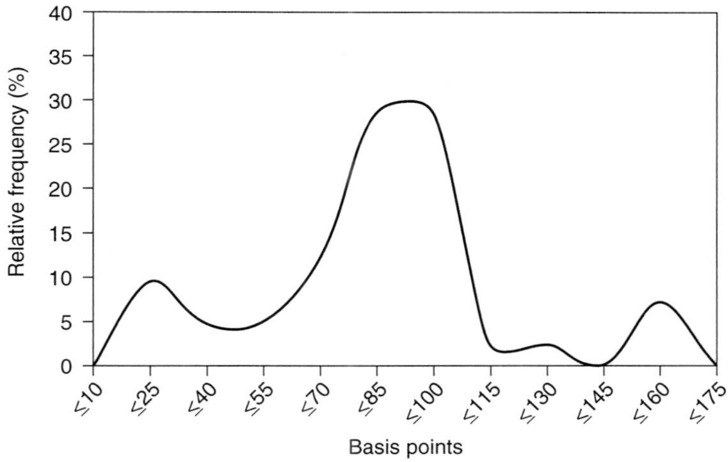

Source: Central Bank of Brazil, based on a survey of market participants.
[1]Refers to a single change in policy rate (effective for four quarters).

Tier I capital but easy access to international liquidity. The measure required banks to deposit the equivalent of 60 percent of their short U.S. dollar positions—a form of short-term U.S. dollar borrowing—in cash at the central bank, at no interest. By accessing offshore U.S. dollar liquidity, domestic banks could facilitate the carry trade via the domestic currency futures market[5] (see Appendix 4.1 for a description of the mechanisms of this trade). Besides reducing foreign currency leverage, the measure increased the cost to banks of becoming counterparties to other investors in the derivatives market, thus affecting carry trade liquidity. Banks' short dollar positions decreased in the wake of this action.

The authorities also introduced other macroprudential measures aimed at restraining credit growth and further reducing incentives for external borrowing by banks. In December 2010, the BCB raised bank capital requirements for most consumer credit operations with maturities over 204 months, which apply primarily to car loans. The BCB also raised unremunerated reserve requirements on time deposits from 15 percent to 20 percent. The additional (unremunerated) reserve requirements for banks' sight deposits were increased from 8 percent to 12 percent.

Although these measures were not designed specifically to deal with capital inflows, to the extent that they reined in credit growth and aggregate demand, they could help manage flows. This was of particular importance in light of the fact that, given Brazil's already high interest rates by international standards,

[5]Because the IOF applied only to actual payments made in derivatives transactions, rather than to the notional amount of the transactions, carry trading via futures became more attractive vis-à-vis outright purchase of domestic fixed-income securities.

further increases in the policy rate would have attracted more capital inflows. Thus, while prudential measures are directed at maintaining stability, they also complement monetary policy by having a moderating influence on demand. In a survey, the BCB found that market participants believed, on average, these macroprudential measures were equivalent to an increase of about 90 basis points in the policy rate.

Capital Flow Management Measures

In response to heavy postcrisis inflows in 2009, Brazil imposed an entry tax on foreign purchases of domestic bonds and equities. The tax, known as the IOF (*Imposto sobre Operações Financeiras*), was imposed on October 19, 2009, at a rate of 2 percent on purchases by foreigners of domestic bonds and equities. Other types of capital inflows, including direct investment and foreign currency borrowing abroad by Brazilian banks and firms, were not initially affected. The finance ministry announced that the measure was intended to combat speculation in capital markets and to counteract the appreciation of the *real*, which it viewed as damaging export industries and employment. Rapid credit growth or monetary policy considerations were not cited as issues at the time of the introduction of the IOF.

Strong capital inflows and appreciation pressures prompted the authorities to adopt a battery of new measures, tightening potential loopholes in the IOF, over the course of 18 months (Table 4.1).

TABLE 4.1

Regulatory Changes Affecting the IOF

October–November 2010	The initial IOF was raised twice in October 2010, but only for flows into debt securities. It was first raised to 4 percent on October 5 and increased further to 6 percent on October 19. The authorities subsequently announced its extension to margin calls on derivative positions. New regulations were shortly introduced to register as new operations flows that initially came into equities (taxed at 2 percent) and subsequently migrated to debt securities (thereby avoiding the higher 6 percent tax), as well as the conversion of IOF-exempt purchases of American Depository Receipts traded at the New York Stock Exchange into stocks traded at the Sâo Paulo Bovespa stock market.
March 2011	On March 28, the IOF was extended to foreign borrowing by corporations and banks for loans with a maturity of less than 360 days. One week later, the maturity was extended to 720 days as it became clear that the maturity of loans was shifting to avoid the higher IOF tax. For domestic banks, this measure complemented the reserve requirement on short foreign currency positions adopted in early January 2011, effectively restricting their ability to raise foreign currency borrowing and participate in the carry trade via the derivatives market.
April 2011	On April 4, the National Monetary Council mandated that any changes in foreign exchange loans/bonds (that is, renovation, rollover, restructuring, or transfer) had to be registered as a new foreign exchange operation. This was intended to close another potential loophole as corporations and banks could modify initial longer-term agreements (exempt from IOF) into short-term loans that should have paid the IOF.

Sources: Central Bank of Brazil; and press reports.
Note: IOF = Imposto sobre Operações Financeiras.

This was not the first time Brazil had employed CFMs on portfolio inflows—up until October 2008, it had levied a 1½ percent tax on bond (but not equity) inflows, but the authorities had eliminated the tax in response to the financial crisis. But the experience with capital controls subsequent to October 2009 stands out for the frequency and scope of the interventions as the authorities used an adaptive strategy to adjust to financial market creativity in bypassing the controls.

CFMs: ROLE AND EFFECTIVENESS

Many researchers have examined the impact of capital controls on capital flows. Interest in such research rises during periods of heavy flows into developing economies. Brazil, which has often made use of CFMs during the postwar era, has been the focus of many of these studies. Most, such as Cardoso and Goldfajn (1998), conclude that CFMs can be effective in the short term, but not over the longer term. Carvalho and Garcia (2006), who also focused on the case of Brazil, came to a similar conclusion in finding a limited and temporary impact of CFMs. Work in other Latin American countries has yielded similar conclusions. Clements and Kamil (2009), looking at the case of Colombia, find the total volume of inflows unaffected by CFMs, but exchange rate volatility reduced.

The effectiveness of CFMs during 2009–11 in Brazil needs to be assessed against the initial objectives. The Brazilian authorities stressed the negative macroeconomic effects of excessive currency appreciation. Thus, one criterion for assessing the effectiveness of the controls would be whether total capital inflows, and hence exchange rate appreciation pressures, abated. However, there may be other reasons for introducing CFMs in the face of heavy inflows. These include the desire to limit hot money inflows and the need to prevent credit bubbles that could endanger financial stability. Accordingly, a second possible criterion would be whether the composition of capital flows changed. Finally, capital controls can provide some maneuvering room for monetary policy, which can be particularly useful in a country such as Brazil with high interest rates.[6] This is a consequence of the "impossible trinity"—that a country cannot simultaneously have an independent monetary policy, a fixed exchange rate, and an open capital account.[7] Assessment of the controls' effectiveness might therefore focus on whether capital controls provided some additional room to maneuver for monetary policy. One way of testing this hypothesis is to analyze whether capital controls reduced the incentive for carry trade, as these are the types of capital inflows that more directly respond to interest rate differentials.

However, any such assessments are complicated by the difficulty of comparing the realized strategy to a counterfactual scenario without capital controls. In principle,

[6]See, for example, Herrera and Valdes (2001).

[7]Although Brazil has a flexible exchange rate, the desire to prevent excessive appreciation suggests that full FX flexibility ceases to be an option for the authorities to manage inflows in the short term. When this point is reached, the dilemmas of the impossible trinity become applicable.

econometric techniques would be able to control for other factors that could affect the dependent variables of interest (that is, exchange rate, total capital flows, and so on). However, the IOF is—to a large extent—endogenous to capital flows and to the exchange rate (that is, it is imposed when capital flows are high and the exchange rate is appreciating fast) and hence it would be difficult to assess the direction of causality. Finally, the IOF cannot be modeled as a dichotomous variable (defining an existing or absent characteristic) given frequent changes in rates and regulations affecting it, which are likely to generate problems of measurement error.

Total Capital Flows and the Exchange Rate

The pace of capital inflows remained high following the introduction of CFMs. Total net capital inflows averaged US$5.9 billion per month after their recovery from the financial crisis and before the imposition of the IOF in October 2009; they increased to a monthly average of US$8.5 billion from 2009:Q4 through 2010:Q3, when the IOF was reintroduced at a rate of 2 percent, and accelerated further to a monthly average of US$11.5 billion between 2010:Q4 and 2011:Q1, when the IOF was raised to 6 percent for flows into debt securities and several loopholes were being closed. Similarly, the average monthly pace of reserve accumulation remained on an upward trend, accelerating from US$4.2 billion during the first phase of the IOF to US$7 billion during the most recent phase of the IOF, thereby exceeding the previous record pace set before the financial crisis (Figure 4.9).

However, the average rate of currency appreciation declined. The rate of average monthly exchange rate appreciation during October 2010–March 2011 (about 0.6 percent) was less than half of that in the period before the financial crisis, when appreciation

Figure 4.9 Average Monthly Increase in Reserves (in millions of U.S. dollars)

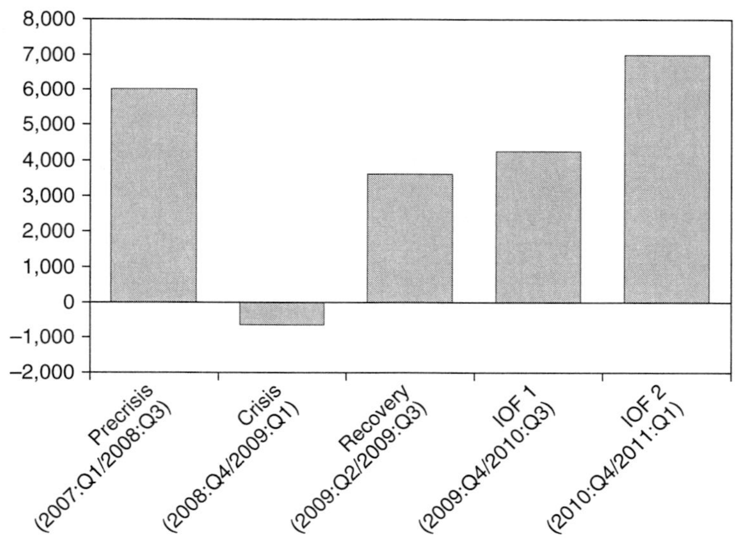

Source: IMF staff calculations.
Note: IOF = Imposto sobre Operações Financeiras.

pressures were also strong (Figure 4.10). Excluding the period of sharp depreciation during the financial crisis, and the rebound during the recovery period, it seems that the degree of exchange rate flexibility declined as the Brazilian *real* became more overvalued (Table 4.2). Given that the volume of inflows did not materially decline during this period, it may be that the slower pace of appreciation was a consequence mostly of larger intervention by the BCB.

Composition of Capital Flows

Although total flows remained high despite CFMs, the IOF seems to have affected the composition of capital inflows (Figure 4.11). Average monthly FDI following

Figure 4.10 Average Monthly Rate of *Real* Appreciation against the US Dollar (Percent)

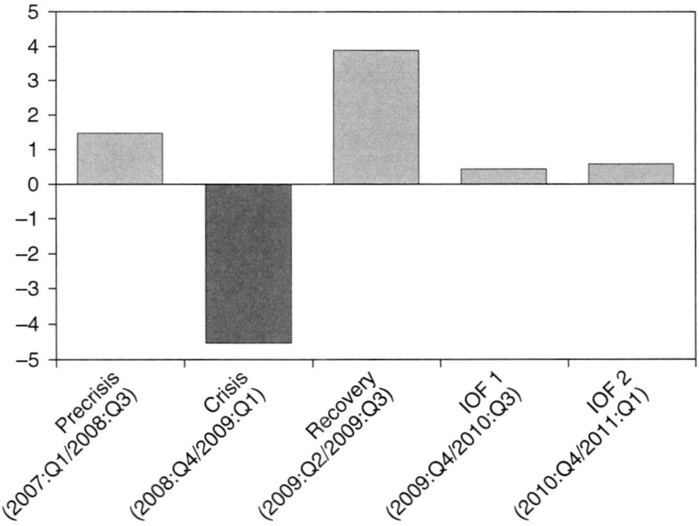

Source: IMF staff calculations.
Note: IOF = Imposto sobre Operações Financeiras.

TABLE 4.2

Average Monthly Flows, Reserves Accumulation, and Exchange Rate Dynamics

	Net Capital Flows (U.S. dollars)	Monthly Reserve Accumulation (U.S. dollars)	Average Monthly US$/*Real* Exchange Rate Appreciation (percent)
Precrisis	$5.2 billion	$1.9 billion	1.5
Crisis	$–3.5 billion	$ –0.6 billion	–4.6
Recovery	$ 5.9 billion	$ 3.6 billion	3.9
IOF 1	$ 8.7 billion	$ 4.6 billion	0.4
IOF 2	$11.5 billion	$ 7.0 billion	0.6

Sources: Central Bank of Brazil; and IMF staff calculations.
Note: The precrisis period covers 2007:Q1–2008:Q3, when capital inflows were reaching peak levels; the crisis period covers 2008:Q4 and 2009:Q1, when capital flows turned negative and GDP collapsed; the recovery period covers 2009:Q2/Q3; "IOF 1" covers 2009:Q4 through 2010:Q3, when the *Imposto sobre Operações Financeiras* (IOF) was imposed at 2 percent; and "IOF 2" covers 2010:Q4 and 2011:Q1, when the IOF was increased to 6 percent for debt securities and several loopholes were closed.

Figure 4.11 Composition of Capital Flows (Monthly Averages in millions of U.S. dollars)

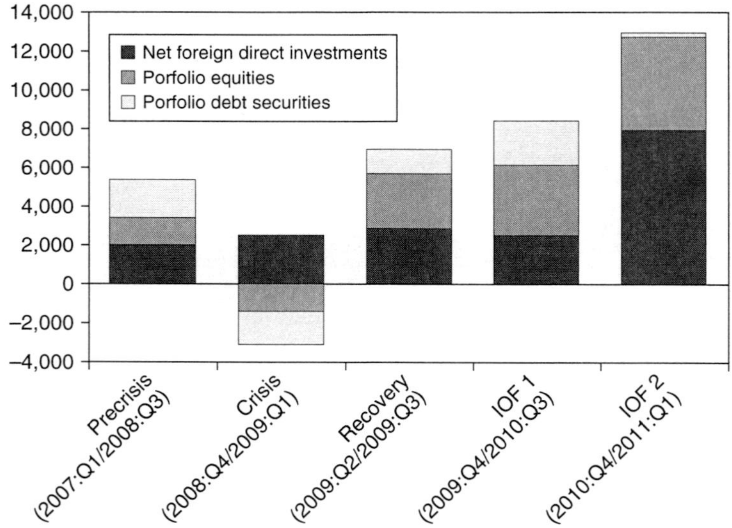

Source: IMF staff calculations.
Note: IOF = Imposto sobre Operações Financeiras.

the second round of IOF measures ("IOF 2") tripled, to almost US$8 billion compared with previous periods. Portfolio inflows into equities (which are taxed at the lower IOF of 2 percent) also continued on an upward trend.[8] Conversely, flows into domestic debt securities appeared to be strongly affected by the IOF, with a monthly average flow during the period only one-tenth of the previous rate. The IOF clearly seemed to have reduced the purchase of domestic *real*-denominated bonds by foreigners.

However, the fall in portfolio flows into domestic securities led to a large increase in external borrowing by residents. A major driver of these flows was likely the behavior of domestic banks, which substituted away from short U.S. dollar positions (subject to the new reserve requirements) and toward other forms of funding not subject to the IOF (Figure 4.12). This substitution kept FX onshore liquidity abundant and allowed the carry trade through the domestic derivatives market to continue.

The increase in FDI inflows was due in large measure to an increase in intercompany loans, whose monthly average more than doubled, reaching close to US$3 billion (Figure 4.13). This suggests that there may have been some circumvention of the IOF via FDI, which was virtually exempt from the IOF (taxed at 0.38 percent). Garcia (2007) documented that in the past it had been common practice in Brazil during previous periods of capital controls to create domestic

[8]Flows into equities were bolstered by large initial public offerings (Visa and Santander in 2009) and the recapitalization of Petrobras in 2010. Eliminating these one-off transactions, the impact of the IOF on the volume of equity inflows does not appear to have been large.

Figure 4.12 Private External Debt (Billions of U.S. dollars)

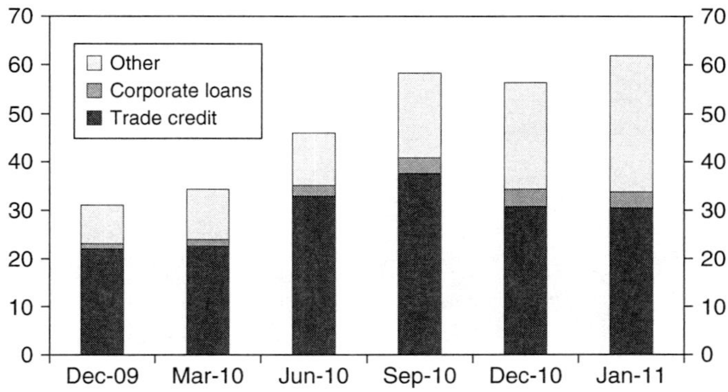

Source: IMF staff calculations.

Figure 4.13 Average Monthly Intercompany Loans (Millions of U.S. Dollars)

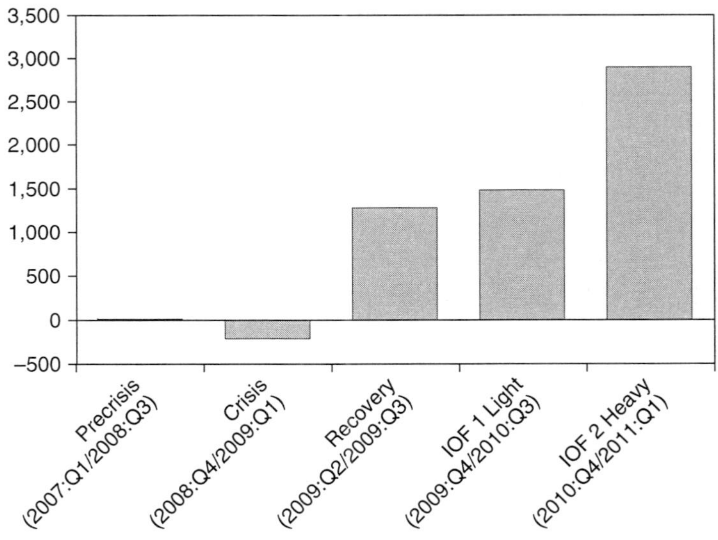

Source: IMF staff calculations.
Note: IOF = Imposto sobre Operações Financeiras.

shell companies that received an intercompany loan from a foreign party (classified in the balance of payments accounts as FDI) and use the proceeds to invest in the local equity or bond market, thereby bypassing the IOF (Table 4.3).

Despite the pickup in FDI inflows, the extension of the IOF (at 6 percent) to external borrowing appeared to reduce onshore FX liquidity substantially. Especially notable was the sudden widening of the spread between onshore U.S. dollar interest rates (the *cupom cambial*) and offshore rates, suggesting that the ability to arbitrage between onshore and offshore markets was severely curtailed (see

TABLE 4.3

Composition of Net Capital Inflows (U.S. dollars)

	Foreign Direct Investment	Portfolio into Equities	Portfolio into Debt Securities
Precrisis	1.98	1.39	1.96
Crisis	2.40	−1.43	−1.71
Recovery	2.85	2.81	1.26
IOF 1	2.48	3.65	2.28
IOF 2	7.93	4.78	0.22

Sources: Central Bank of Brazil; and IMF staff calculations.
Note: The precrisis period covers 2007:Q1–2008:Q3 when capital inflows were reaching peak levels; the crisis period covers 2008:Q4 and 2009:Q1 when capital flows turned negative and GDP collapsed; the recovery period covers 2009:Q2/Q3; "IOF 1" covers 2009:Q4 through 2010:Q3 when the Imposto sobre Operações Financeiras (IOF) was imposed at 2 percent; and "IOF 2" covers the period 2010:Q4 and 2011:Q1 when the IOF was increased to 6 percent for debt securities and several loopholes were closed.

Appendixes 4.1 and 4.2). This spread subsequently abated somewhat, though changes in other external factors (for example, global risk, commodity prices) complicate the impact assessment. However, it still appears that the expansion in the field of coverage of the IOF reduced the previous incentives for recomposition of inflows, in favor of a reduction in total flows.

Monetary Policy Independence and Incentives for Carry Trade

One useful approach to analyzing the impact of the IOF is to consider it from the perspective of a carry trade investor into Brazil.[9] Foreign investors who aim to profit from high Brazilian interest rates have several choices:

- The most straightforward approach is to invest funds directly in the domestic Brazilian bond market. Starting with a zero net position, this would be done by borrowing U.S. dollars, converting them to Brazilian currency at the spot exchange rate, and then using the proceeds to buy a Brazilian bond of a certain maturity.
- A second approach would be to borrow a smaller amount of dollars, convert the dollars to *reais*, and use the proceeds to pay the margin on a forward currency contract (buying the *real* forward against the U.S. dollar) on the domestic Brazilian futures exchange. This transaction offers the same return profile as the outright bond purchase. The IOF would apply only to the margin posted to the exchange, becoming very small.

[9]These may also be described as "carry trade" investors, to the extent that they acquire Brazilian real fixed-income assets to take advantage of the yield differential between the Brazilian currency and their home currency. This type of investment necessarily entails exposure to currency risk—effectively the investor is betting that any depreciation of the destination currency will be less than the relative interest rate differential. To be sure, the domestic currency may also appreciate against the carry trade funding currency, as is often the case during episodes of strong risk appetite in global markets.

- A third possibility, favored by investors who wish to avoid transactions onshore in Brazil, is to buy a nondeliverable forward contract (denominated in *reais* but settled in dollars) offshore (for example, in New York or London), normally from a global bank that makes a market in such contracts.

The first mechanism (direct purchase of a Brazilian bond) was immediately affected by the introduction of the IOF (as demonstrated by the reduction of flows into debt securities), but the other two were not. This left two important loopholes in the IOF. Although the purchase of domestic bonds lost attractiveness, investors flocked to the derivatives market, where the incidence of the IOF tax was minimal. A 6 percent tax on the margin (typically 10 percent or less) would reduce the IOF effective tax rate to 0.6 percent, insufficient to have any impact. The IOF's favorable treatment of positions in the futures market contributed to the buildup of large long Brazilian *real* and short U.S. dollar positions by nonresident investors. Furthermore, the rate of return from NDFs offshore was also not affected, which continued to attract carry trade flows.

The authorities moved to close the loopholes by first imposing reserve requirements on banks' short U.S. dollar positions and later by extending the IOF to foreign borrowing. The introduction of reserve requirements on short U.S. dollar positions limited the ability of banks to operate as counterparties for nonresident investors engaged in the carry trade. However, banks were able to offset their short U.S. dollar positions by borrowing abroad, and the loophole remained in place during the first quarter of 2011. But when the IOF was extended to foreign borrowing by corporations and banks in April 2011, the onshore U.S. dollar rate (*cupom cambial*) spiked to unprecedented levels and the corresponding return in Brazilian *reais* from onshore and offshore NDFs collapsed (see Figure 4.14), as banks were no longer able to conduct low-cost arbitrage between offshore U.S. dollar markets and the onshore *cupom cambial.*

Collateral Damage: Downsides of CFMs

The usefulness of CFMs needs to be assessed against their costs.

- ***Reducing desirable flows.*** Controls may end up creating barriers to the entry of all foreign savings—including for productive investments—that are needed in the context of Brazil's low domestic savings and current account deficit (for example, long-term debt or trade financing). Indeed, shortly after the IOF was raised in October 2010, domestic government bond yields started to trend upward and bid-cover ratios fell in some public debt auctions.
- ***Hampering financial sector development.*** For growing middle-income countries, capital controls may inhibit or reverse development of the domestic financial sector.
- ***Distortions.*** Controls may create distortions that shut off legitimate hedging activities, with a potentially negative impact on the real economy. This is most apparent in the spike in the onshore U.S. dollar rate. For example, the effective

Figure 4.14 Brazil—Domestic and Futures-Implied Interest Rates

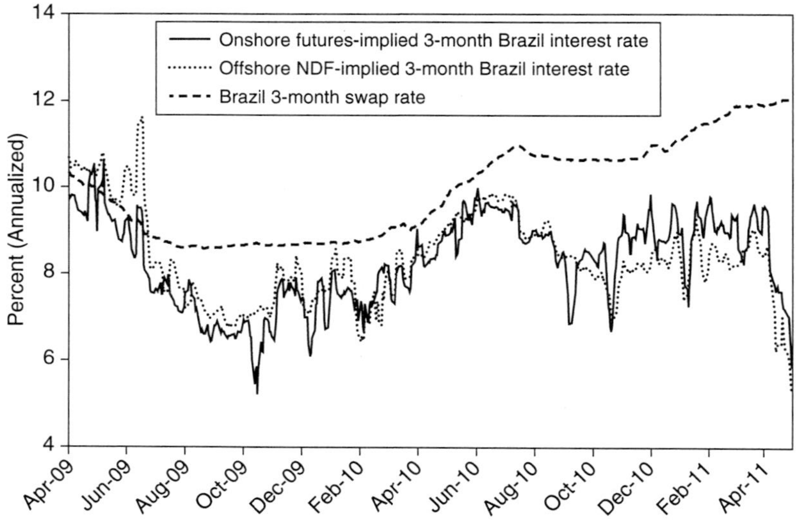

Source: Bloomberg, L.P.; and IMF staff calculations.
Note: NDF = nondeliverable currency forwards.

interest rate charged to an importer wanting to buy U.S. dollars forward as part of normal hedging operations rises as a result of these distortions. That higher cost could induce the would-be hedger to incur greater exchange rate risk, which could amplify the magnitude of unexpected shocks.

- ***Stability risks.*** Although capital controls are intended to stabilize or reduce inflows, making them less risky, they might in fact force capital to go through channels that are actually more destabilizing. Some examples include forcing inflows through derivatives markets rather than spot markets, diverting inflows through nonfinancial firms, and (possibly) through trade finance flows.

CONCLUSION

The usual policy prerequisites for the application of CFMs in Brazil were broadly met. The exchange rate had become overvalued on a multilateral basis. Fiscal policy was being tightened. Sterilized intervention had been undertaken to slow the pace of appreciation. Moreover, the authorities supported these steps with prudential measures to contain credit and funding risks.

Nonetheless, the Brazilian experience with capital controls provides a mixed picture of their usefulness. Effectiveness has to be defined relative to a specific policy goal, and the study considers three—restricting capital inflows, containing exchange rate appreciation, and carving out space for the autonomous working of monetary policy. The overall level of flows remained high despite the introduction of CFMs, but their composition changed, suggesting a number of channels for circumvention (derivatives market, intercompany loans, and so on). However, the last stage of tightening of the IOF seems to have been effective at curtailing onshore U.S. dollar liquidity, indicating that the tax may become more effective at insulating onshore from offshore markets. This could allow more room for monetary policy to react without attracting additional flows.

APPENDIX 4.1. MECHANISMS OF THE CARRY TRADE IN THE FUTURES MARKET

This appendix describes the steps involved in a nonresident investor's carry trade into the domestic futures market, and the related hedging operations by a resident counterparty. To the extent that this counterparty, typically a resident bank, hedges its currency risk in the underlying cash market, this trade results in the same balance of payments pressure that would arise if the carry trade were conducted directly in the cash market (for example, by purchasing domestic bonds). This mechanism relies critically on the resident counterparty's ability to take the nonresident's opposite position in the domestic futures market and hedge the resulting currency risk via FX borrowing (not subject to the IOF). The resident counterparty thereby provides liquidity to the nonresident investor's trade and earns a (risk-free) arbitrage profit proportional to the spread between the domestic U.S. dollar rate implied by the domestic futures market (the *cupom cambial*) and the offshore U.S. dollar rate paid on external borrowing (typically, the London interbank offered rate plus a spread). The detailed steps are described below and depicted in Figure A4.1.

- The chain of trades is initiated by a nonresident investor who buys a *real* futures contract in the domestic futures market (step 1 in Figure A4.1). That is, at maturity, the nonresident investor receives the agreed price in *reais* per U.S. dollar (settlement in the futures market takes place in local currency).
- The nonresident investor's counterparty is a resident investor, that is, a local bank that agrees to receive the value of the U.S. dollar at maturity against a payment in Brazilian *reais* (step 2).
- The local bank could choose to maintain its short Brazilian *real* position, or could choose to hedge its currency exposure. This could be done by borrowing U.S. dollars offshore (step 3); for example, by drawing on its available credit lines. Because the resulting U.S. dollar liability at maturity matches the claim to receive U.S. dollars on the U.S. dollar futures contract, the bank is hedged against currency risk (that is, a zero net position).
- External borrowing by the bank is recorded in the balance of payments as a capital inflow (step 4). If the central bank chooses to intervene, then the bank sells the proceeds from external borrowing into the spot FX market.
- By investing the Brazilian *reais* proceeds from the sale of U.S. dollars on the spot market at the domestic interest rate, the bank is able to earn an arbitrage profit whenever the *cupom cambial* is higher than the interest rate paid on its external borrowing (step 5). The only risk that is potentially left for the bank is counterparty risk on the futures contract.

Figure A4.1 Carry Trade via the U.S. Dollar Futures Market[1]

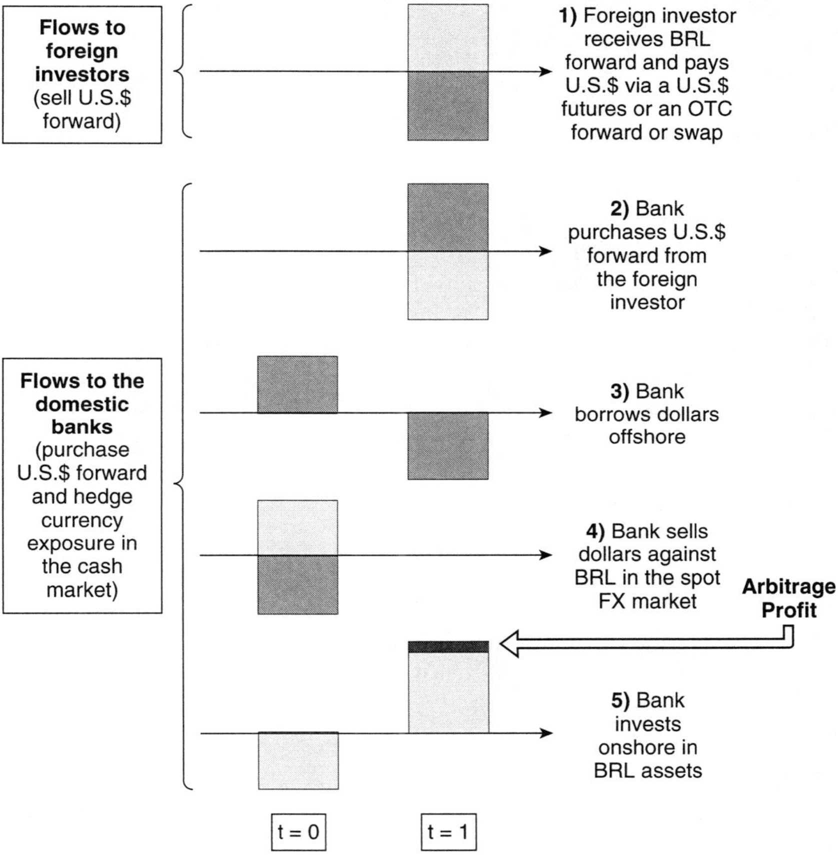

Source: IMF staff calculations.

Note: BRL = Brazilian real; FX = foreign exchange; OTC = over the counter.

[1]The horizontal line denotes the time line. Rectangles above (below) the line denote positive (negative) cash flows; rectangles shaded dark gray (light gray) denote payoffs in U.S. dollars and local currency, respectively.

APPENDIX 4.2. USING FORWARD PRICES AND SPREADS TO TEST THE EFFECTIVENESS OF CAPITAL FLOW MANAGEMENT MEASURES

This appendix describes a method for using forward prices in offshore markets to test the effectiveness of capital control measures. This method is especially useful for a currency such as the Brazilian *real*, for which forward contracts are heavily traded in both onshore and offshore markets.

The cleanest test for the impact of the IOF on foreign access to the Brazilian market makes use of offshore nondeliverable currency forward (NDF) prices. This is not the usual measure for testing or gauging the effectiveness of capital controls, but has some important advantages over alternative approaches. The usual tests for the effectiveness of capital controls are based on flows and movements in the exchange rate and reserves. These are useful but they suffer from the fact that the degree of the response cannot, in general, be used to infer the relative effectiveness of the measure. Forward or "basis" spreads, at least in principle, can be used to gauge the implied arbitrage costs that a particular measure inserts into the market.

Futures-implied interest rates can be constructed, and compared with actual interest rates. An offshore forward-implied interest rate can be calculated as:

$$i_{BRL,off} = (1 + i_{S})\ (f_{90,off}\,|e)^4 - 1.$$

where interest rates are annualized three-month rates, $i_{\$}$ is the U.S. dollar interest rate (90-day Libor), e is the spot exchange rate, and $f_{90,}$ on is the 90-day NDF, quoted in *reais* per U.S. dollar. An alternative measure is the onshore future-implied interest rate in Brazilian *reais*, based on the onshore futures contract, $f_{90,\mathrm{on}}$. This implied rate is calculated as:

$$i_{BRL,on} = (1 + i_{S})\ (f_{90,on}|e)^4 - 1.$$

Either of these can be compared with the onshore Brazilian three-month interest rate:

$$i_{BRL} = 90\text{-}day\ interest\ rate\ future\ rate.$$

These measures can be used to determine "basis spreads," as either $BS_{off} = (i_{BRL,off} - i_{BRL})$, or $BS_{on} = (i_{BRL,on} - i_{BRL})$. Full covered interest parity would entail that both of these measures be zero. For most emerging market economies, however, basis spreads are not zero, even under normal market conditions. The departure from covered interest parity, and the existence of a negative basis spread, typically reflects the effects of counterparty credit concerns, global interbank stresses, and transaction costs, possibly including costs induced by capital controls.[10] For this discussion, the issue is whether the change in regulations induces a change in basis spreads and, if so, how large a change and in what direction.

[10]See, for example, Baba and Packer (2008).

Figure A4.2 Expected Change in Relative Interest Rates if IOF Is Fully Binding

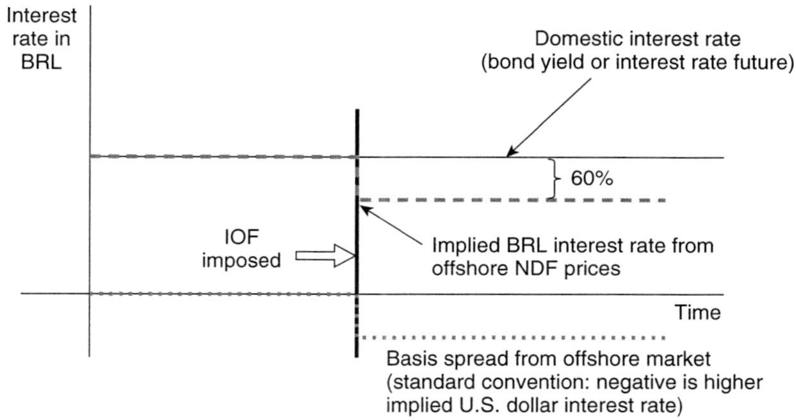

Source: IMF staff.
Note: BRL = Brazilian real; IOF = Imposto sobre Operações Financeiras; NDF = nondeliverable currency forward.

If the IOF is effective in breaking the link between domestic and foreign fixed-income markets, or in inserting a wedge between the two, this should be evident in interest rate spreads. If the new regulations eliminate arbitrage, or impose a cost of arbitrage between domestic and offshore markets, then there should be a difference between the implied interest rate in *reais* available offshore through the NDF market and the interest rate in *reais* available onshore in Brazil. The implied interest rate in *reais* should be lower offshore, where the IOF cannot be collected. The basis spread derived from NDF trading should become negative, entailing a lower-than-market interest rate in *reais*. If the 6 percent IOF is fully binding on all domestic instruments in Brazil, and if there had been full arbitrage before it was imposed, then the basis spread should widen by 2 percent on instruments with a one-year maturity.

In April 2011, both measures of the futures-implied Brazilian interest rate diverged significantly from the onshore rates available in Brazil (Figure A4.2). This divergence, which was widely noted by market participants, indicated that the returns to the carry trade from the U.S. dollar into Brazilian fixed-income markets had been significantly restricted. Based on the timing of the divergence, and the major role played by banks in arbitraging between the spot and futures markets, it appeared that the restrictions placed on bank short U.S. dollar positions in March 2011 had been at least partly responsible for the shift.

REFERENCES

Baba, Naohiko, and Frank Packer, 2008, "Interpreting Deviations from Covered Interest Parity during the Financial Market Turmoil of 2007–08," BIS Working Paper 267 (Basel: Bank for International Settlements).

Cardoso, Eliana, and Ilan Goldfajn, 1998, "Capital Flows to Brazil: The Endogeneity of Capital Controls," IMF Staff Papers Vol. 45, No. 1.

Carvalho, Bernardo, and Marcio Garcia, 2006, "Ineffective Controls on Capital Inflows Under Sophisticated Financial Markets: Brazil in the Nineties," NBER Working Paper 12283 (Cambridge, Massachusetts: National Bureau of Economic Research).

Clements, Benedict, and Magda Kamil, 2009, "Are Capital Controls Effective in the 21st Century? The Recent Experience of Colombia," IMF Working Paper 09/30 (Washington: International Monetary Fund).

Herrera, Luis Oscar, and Rodrigo Valdes, 2001, "The Effect of Capital Controls on Interest Rate Differentials," *Journal of International Economics*, Vol. 53, pp. 385–98.

Ostry, Jonathan D., Atish R. Ghosh, Karl Habermeier, Luc Laeven, Marcos Chamon, Mahvash S. Qureshi, and Annamaria Kokenyne, 2011, "Managing Capital Inflows: What Tools to Use?" IMF Staff Discussion Note No. 11/06 (Washington: International Monetary Fund).

CHAPTER 5

The Impact of External Developments on Emerging Market and Developing Economies: The Role of Exchange Rate Flexibility

JORGE IVÁN CANALES-KRILJENKO

External macroeconomic and financial conditions significantly affect domestic macroeconomic and financial outcomes in emerging market and developing economies. These external conditions go through cyclical movements that filter into domestic cycles. This should not be surprising because most emerging market and developing economies are small open economies. Exchange rate flexibility seems to have helped diffuse the transmission of the cycles originated from abroad. For example, it appears to have contained growth in domestic demand associated with easy external financial conditions. It also may have reduced the intensity of capital flows and current account deterioration, which often raise macroeconomic and financial vulnerabilities.

This chapter presents evidence of the impact of external developments in emerging market and developing economies and explores whether exchange rate flexibility makes a difference.

EXTERNAL AND DOMESTIC DEVELOPMENTS IN EMERGING MARKET AND DEVELOPING ECONOMIES: 1990–2009

The last two decades witnessed at least two full global macroeconomic cycles that can help shed light on the effect of external conditions on emerging market and developing economies and the role that exchange rate flexibility played.

External Environment

The external environment for emerging market and developing economies during the last two decades was favorable up to the Lehman events in late 2008. The cyclical swings in economic activity were mild, and world GDP grew on average about 3 percent.[1] Deviations from the average were relatively small as world growth ranged between 2 percent and 5 percent before contracting by 1 percent in 2009. World growth was on the high side during the 2004–07 easy external financial conditions (Figure 5.1).

External financial conditions shifted from easy to tight several times in the last two decades. Financial conditions are easy when both global real interest rates and risk aversion are low (Canales-Kriljenko, 2010). On these occasions, emerging market and developing economies tend to take advantage of low interest rates and investors are willing to take the risk. Using the Chicago Board Options Exchange Volatility Index (VIX) as a proxy for global risk aversion, financial conditions were easy during 1991–96 and 2004–07 (Figure 5.2).

For the median country, terms of trade showed cycles similar to those in economic activity and risk aversion, with persistent improvements between 1994–96 and 2003–08 (Figure 5.3). The terms of trade improvement during the cycle of the 2000s was larger and more persistent than during the 1990s (Figure 5.4). Yet the cross-country variation in each cycle was large. The terms of trade for individual countries did not change at the same time or in the same direction for all countries in the sample. At any moment, the terms of trade improved for some countries and worsened for other emerging market and developing economies. Yet the terms of trade for net commodity exporters clearly improved sharply during 2004–08, while that of net commodity importers weakened.

Figure 5.1 World Growth (Percent a year)

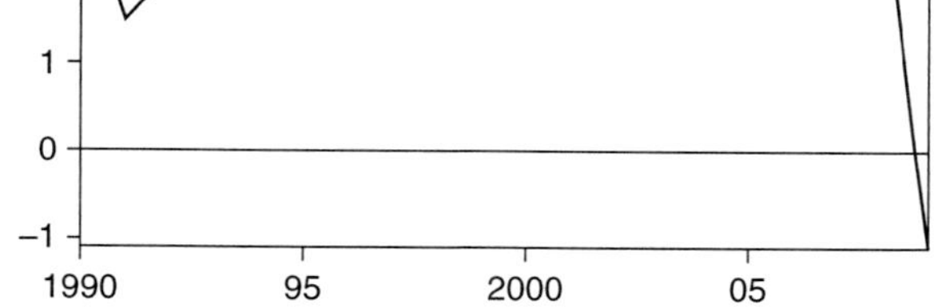

Source: IMF, World Economic Outlook database.

[1]The countries in the sample comprise Argentina, Brazil, Bulgaria, Chile, Colombia, Czech Republic, Dominican Republic, Ecuador, Egypt, El Salvador, Estonia, Indonesia, Israel, Latvia, Lithuania, Malaysia, Mexico, Pakistan, Panama, Peru, Philippines, Poland, Russia, South Africa, Tunisia, Turkey, Ukraine, Uruguay, and Venezuela. China is explicitly excluded given its size.

Figure 5.2 Chicago Board Options Exchange Volatility Index

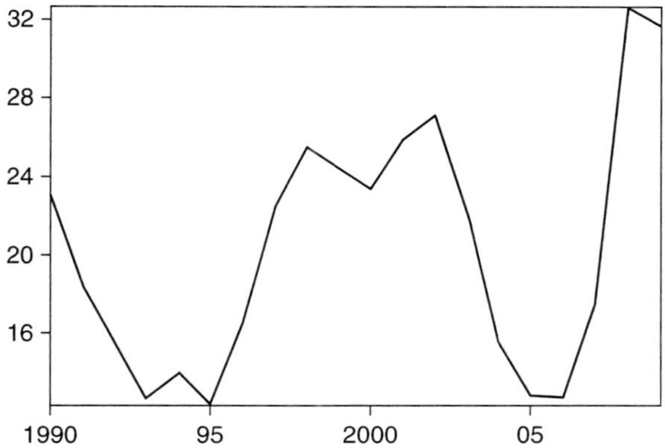

Source: Chicago Board Options Exchange.

Figure 5.3 Terms of Trade (Percent a year; median)

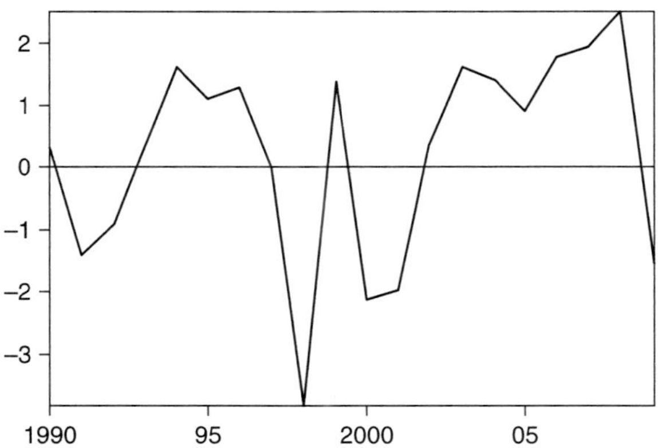

Source: IMF, World Economic Outlook database.

Domestic Impact

The median emerging market and developing economy in the sample also experienced cycles in its macroeconomic variables. Domestic demand, GDP, and credit growth arguably went through two full cycles in the last two decades. The amplitude of the cycle was larger for credit than for domestic demand and GDP growth. External trade activity was more intense in the second cycle, with similar patterns in the growth rates of real exports and imports. Real exports, however, increased more, and the current account moved from a deficit to a surplus in the median country. The improved current account balance also reflected the

Figure 5.4 Terms of Trade (Percent a year)

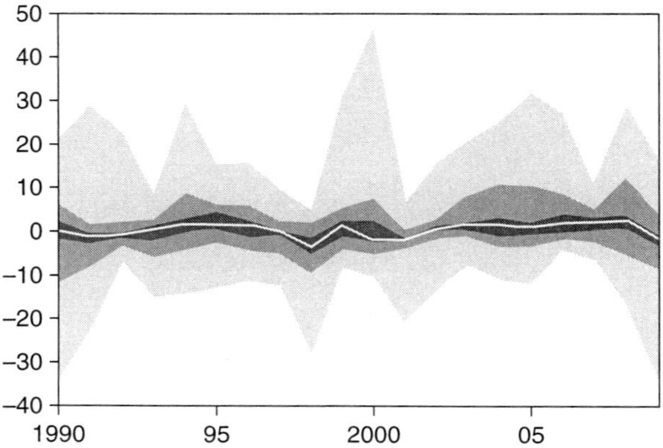

Source: IMF, World Economic Outlook database.

persistent terms-of-trade improvement in the second third of the last decade. Important differences in macroeconomic developments across countries took place (Figures 5.5 and 5.6).

Econometric Regression

To incorporate the diversity of country experiences during the period 1990–2009, the following sections include an analysis based on multivariate pooled regressions for the 29 emerging market economies in the sample. The analysis uses annual data mainly from the IMF's World Economic Outlook database, complemented with information from JPMorgan and country authorities as compiled by Haver Analytics, Inc. The Monetary and Capital Markets Department of the IMF provided the data on exchange rate regimes.

Domestic demand growth in emerging market and developing economies increases with faster world growth, better terms of trade, and more tolerance for risk (as proxied by a decline in the VIX). It often grows faster than world GDP during upswings and falls more sharply during downturns. The sensitivity to external conditions, however, is not uniform across demand components. Private investment reacts much more than private consumption to each external factor. In turn, government consumption does not react systematically to external conditions in the sample. The effect on GDP growth is qualitatively the same as that on domestic demand, but milder (Table 5.1).

Real credit growth responds to external financial conditions. In particular, real credit increases with declines in the VIX—in other words, with increases in risk tolerance or declines in risk aversion. Thus, easy external financial conditions increase the risk of credit booms and could call for policy action depending on the country's position in the cycle. Real credit does not respond strongly to either

Figure 5.5 Selected Emerging Market Macroeconomic Indicators (Percent a year; median)

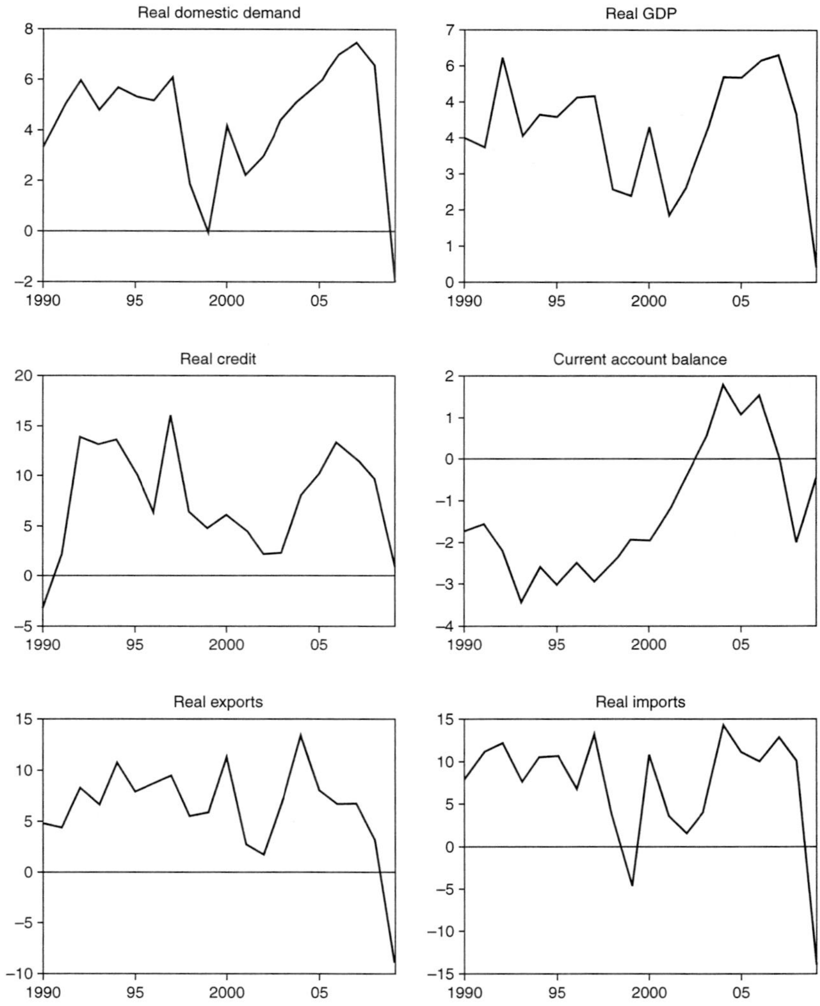

Source: IMF, World Economic Outlook database.

changes in world growth or the terms of trade: the latter has the right sign but is not statistically significant.

External conditions directly affect a country's balance of payments (Table 5.2). The current account balance in percent of GDP improves with better terms of trade and lower risk tolerance. The income effect compensates for the effect from developments in the real trade balance. In particular, better terms of trade have often lowered real export growth and increased real import growth. Lower risk tolerance (increases in the VIX) reduces both real exports and imports, but has a

Figure 5.6 Selected Emerging Market Macroeconomic Indicators (Percent a year; distribution)[1]

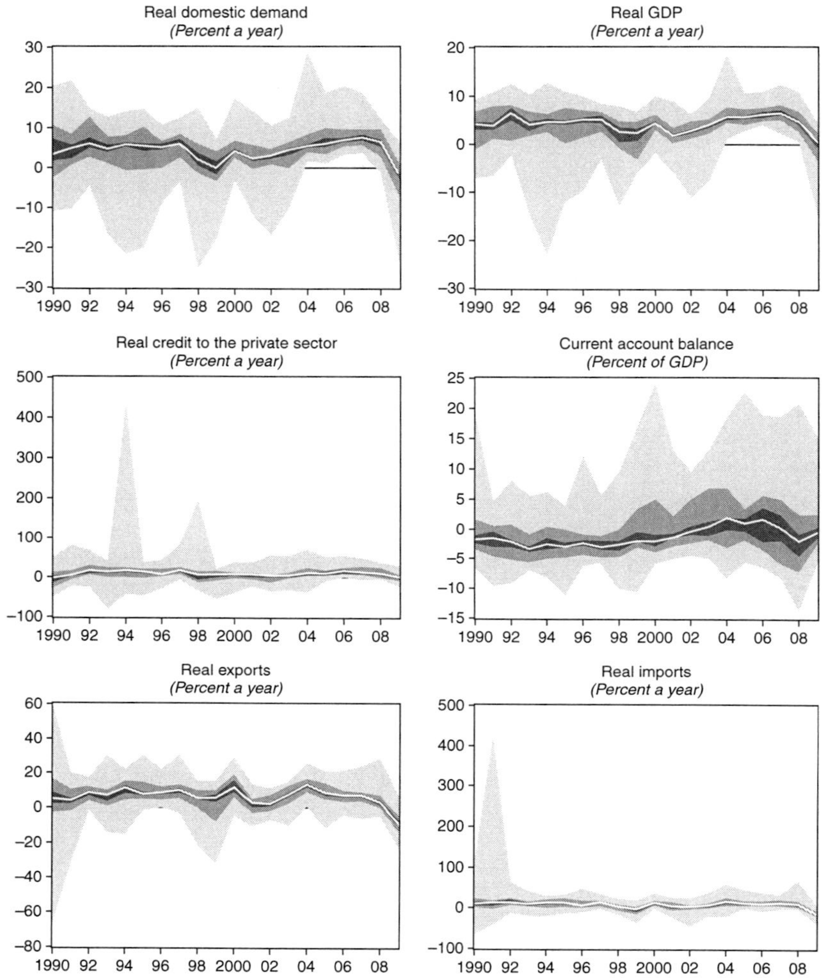

Source: IMF, World Economic Outlook database.
[1]Shaded areas represent the quintiles of the distribution. The white line represents the median.

stronger effect on the latter. Thus, it often improves the trade balance and the current account. Faster world growth increases both real exports and imports, and although the effect on real exports appears larger, the improvement in the current account is not statistically significant. On the financial side of the balance of payments, faster world growth has been associated with higher capital inflows—both gross and net. In turn, higher risk aversion has come with lower gross inflows, whereas the link to net inflows is not statistically significant.

External financial conditions have an important effect on the real exchange rate and reserve buildup for the whole country sample. In particular, periods of easy external financial conditions associated with a decline in the VIX have often led to real exchange rate appreciation and reserve buildup. In turn, periods of tight external conditions often result in real exchange rate depreciation and drops in international reserve coverage. Figures 5.7 and 5.8 show changes in the real

TABLE 5.1

Pool Regressions: Effect of External Variables on Domestic Demand, GDP, and Credit Growth[1]

	Domestic Demand	Consumption Total	Consumption Private	Consumption Government	Investment	GDP	Real Private Credit
VIX (index)	–0.16***	–0.05	–0.09**	0.05	–0.19**	–0.09***	–0.57***
Terms of trade (growth rate)	0.14***	0.12***	0.15***	0.04	0.09	0.06***	–0.01
World growth	1.28***	0.86***	1.02***	0.34	–0.47	1.01***	0.67
Adjusted R-squared	0.17	0.14	0.15	0.05	–0.01	0.23	0.11
Observations	535	525	535	539	545	544	522

Sources: IMF, World Economic Outlook database; Chicago Board Options Exchange; and Haver Analytics.
[1]The sample includes Argentina, Brazil, Bulgaria, Chile, Colombia, Czech Republic, Dominican Republic, Ecuador, Egypt, El Salvador, Estonia, Indonesia, Israel, Latvia, Lithuania, Malaysia, Mexico, Pakistan, Panama, Peru, Philippines, Poland, Russia, South Africa, Tunisia, Turkey, Ukraine, Uruguay, and Venezuela.

TABLE 5.2

Pool Regressions: Effect of External Variables on the Balance of Payments

	Real Exports[1]	Real Imports[1]	Current Accounts[2]	Gross Inflows[2]	Net Inflows[2]	Reserve Buildup[3]	Real Exchange Rate[1]
VIX	–0.26***	–0.62***	0.09**	–0.23***	–0.20**	–0.09***	–0.19**
Terms of trade	–0.09*	0.62***	0.12***	–0.06	–0.03	0.03	0.09
World growth	2.32***	1.18	0.10	1.30***	2.43***	0.16	–0.47
Adjusted R-squared	0.22	0.11	0.46	0.34	0.34	0.12	–0.01
Observations	539	539	547	520	476	545	545

Sources: IMF, World Economic Outlook database; Chicago Board Options Exchange; and Haver Analytics.
[1]Percent a year.
[2]Annual flow over U.S. dollar GDP of the earlier year.
[3]Annual change in stock over U.S. dollar GDP of the earlier year.

Figure 5.7 Real Effective Exchange Rate (Percent a year; median)

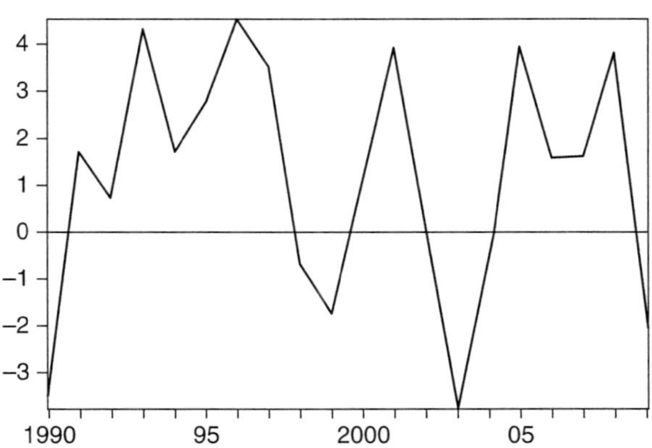

Source: IMF, Information Notice System database.
Note: Increase means appreciation.

Figure 5.8 International Reserve Buildup (Flow over earlier period GDP; median)

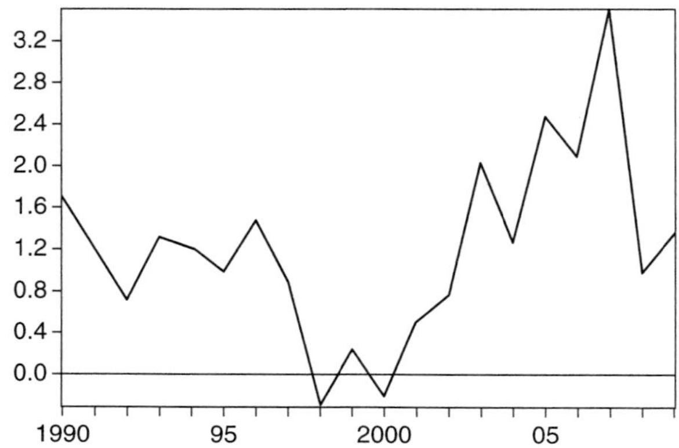

Source: IMF, International Financial Statistics and World Economic Outlook database.

Figure 5.9 Flexible Exchange Rate Regimes (Percent of total regimes)

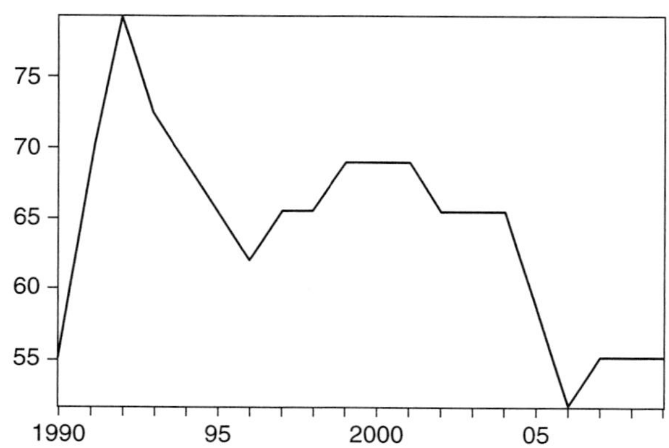

Source: IMF, Annual Report on Exchange Arrangements and Exchange Restrictions database.

exchange rate and reserve buildup for the median country, which is consistent with this interpretation. One question that comes up is whether there are systematic differences across exchange rate regimes.

EVOLUTION OF EXCHANGE RATE REGIMES: 1990–2009

Did exchange rate flexibility matter? If so, how did it make a difference? The question warrants answers from different points of view and methods. The evidence presented here suggests that it matters and that more flexible exchange rate regimes help isolate the domestic economy from external developments.

The IMF's de facto exchange rate regime classification database suggests that more emerging market and developing economies have flexible exchange rate regimes than do not. However, it also suggests that the number of countries following flexible exchange rate regimes has decreased over the last two decades (Figure 5.9). In this exercise, the cutoff exchange rate regime is a crawling peg. In other words, for the following exercises, flexible regimes are crawling pegs and all other exchange rate regimes that allow more exchange rate flexibility.

EMPIRICAL ANALYSIS

The econometric strategy consists of three tactics. First, divide the sample into observations of flexible exchange rate regimes and observations of those that are not. Second, test if each external variable matters for each subsample in a single panel regression. Finally, test if the parameters for each external variable differ in the two subsamples. This can be achieved by interacting each of the external variables with a dummy of flexible regimes and another for those that are not flexible (1 – the flexible dummy) in a pooled regression.

The analysis suggests that exchange rate flexibility shields domestic demand from external developments. The effect of the three external variables on domestic demand growth is larger for less flexible exchange rate regimes than it is for more flexible regimes. Also, the difference is statistically significant under a Wald test. The effect results mainly from the behavior of the private agents, as government consumption does not react as much to external variables, except perhaps to world growth under less flexible exchange rate regimes. As expected, the effect on investment is stronger than for other components of domestic demand. These qualitative results on domestic demand carry onto GDP growth (Table 5.3).

Exchange rate flexibility also matters for the balance of payments (Table 5.4). Gross and net capital inflows respond more to external financial developments and world growth in less flexible exchange rate regimes. Capital flows do not respond as much to terms-of-trade changes, except perhaps for gross inflows for less flexible exchange rate regimes. The results of net inflows carry through to the current account balance, although the effect of world growth on the current account is not strong. The impact on real imports of external financial conditions is strong under all exchange rate regimes, and this exercise cannot detect statistically significant differences in the parameters across regimes. Real exports also respond to external conditions under both regimes, but the effect of external financial conditions is stronger under less flexible regimes. In particular, a decline in risk aversion increases real exports more under less flexible exchange regimes than under more flexible ones.

Do more flexible exchange rate regimes end up with less reserve buildup and more real exchange appreciation during favorable external conditions? They arguably do in response to external financial conditions. When external financial conditions are easy, countries with more flexible exchange rate regimes end up with a more appreciated currency in real terms than those with lower exchange rate flexibility. The sensitivity of reserve buildup to the VIX is also lower in more

TABLE 5.3

Pool Regressions: Effect of External Variables on Domestic Demand, GDP, and Real Credit[1]

	Domestic Demand	Consumption			Investment	GDP	Real Credit
		Total	Private	Government			
VIX * flexible dummy[2]	–0.11**	–0.03	–0.05	0.03	–0.25***	–0.07**	–0.61***
Terms of trade * flexible dummy	0.05	0.07**	0.09***	0.00	0.12*	0.02	–0.19
World growth * flexible dummy	0.84***	0.61***	0.68***	0.18	–0.20	0.81***	0.57
VIX * (1–flexible dummy)	–0.22***	–0.08*	–0.16***	0.11*	–0.10	–0.12***	–0.49*
Terms of trade (1 – flexible dummy)	0.37***	0.25***	0.30***	0.09	0.02	0.15***	0.31
World growth * (1 – flexible dummy)	1.84***	1.24***	1.44***	0.65**	–0.82*	1.28***	0.74
Adjusted R-squared	0.23	0.18	0.18	0.07	0.00	0.25	0.11
Observations	535	525	535	539	545	544	522
Wald test of equal coefficients across regimes							
VIX	**		**		*	*	
Terms of trade	***	***	***			***	*
World growth	***	***	***			**	

Sources: IMF, World Economic Outlook database; Chicago Board Options Exchange; and Haver Analytics.
[1]The sample includes Argentina, Brazil, Bulgaria, Chile, Colombia, Czech Republic, Dominican Republic, Ecuador, Egypt, El Salvador, Estonia, Indonesia, Israel, Latvia, Lithuania, Malaysia, Mexico, Pakistan, Panama, Peru, Philippines, Poland, Russia, South Africa, Tunisia, Turkey, Ukraine, Uruguay, and Venezuela.
[2]The flexible dummy takes a value of 1 for the more flexible exchange regimes under the IMF classification, defined as crawling pegs and above.

TABLE 5.4

Pool Regressions: Effects of External Variables on the Balance of Payments

	Real Exports[1]	Real Imports[1]	Current Account[2]	Gross Inflows[2]	Net Inflows[2]	Reserve Buildup[3]	Real Exchange Rate[1]
VIX * flexible dummy[2]	–0.20***	–0 55***	0.06	–0.12*	–0.06	–0.08***	–0.25***
Terms of trade * flexible dummy	–0.10*	0.65***	0.13***	–0.03	0.00	0.04*	0.12*
World growth * flexible dummy	2.37***	0.59	0.28	0.59*	1.41***	0.02	–0.20
VIX * (1 – flexible dummy)	–0.38***	–0.72***	0.13***	–0.37***	–0.37***	–0.11***	–0.10
Terms of trade (1 – flexible dummy)	–0.02	0.55**	0.11**	–0.15**	–0.11	0.00	0.02
World growth * (1 – flexible dummy)	2.09***	2.07**	–0.15	2.57***	4.23***	0.38***	–0.82*
Adjusted R-squared	0.24	0.11	0.46	0.38	0.37	0.13	0.00
Observations	539	539	547	520	476	545	545
Wald test of equal coefficients for							
VIX	***		*	***	***		*
Terms of trade							
World growth			**	***	***	**	

Sources: IMF, World Economic Outlook database; Chicago Board Options Exchange; and Haver Analytics.
[1]Percent a year.
[2]Annual flow divided by U.S. dollar GDP of the earlier year.
[3]Annual change in stock divided by U.S. dollar GDP of the earlier year.

flexible regimes, but the differences are not statistically significant. The answer is less clear when other external variables change independently. An increase in world growth increases reserve buildup in less flexible exchange rate regimes and depreciates the currency in real effective terms. Better terms of trade increase reserve buildup and real appreciation in more flexible regimes.

There is some evidence that the systematic differences across regimes can be credited to the regimes themselves. Crediting the empirical differences found across regimes to the regimes themselves assumes that other policies, such as fiscal measures, have not differed substantially across regimes. Otherwise, one could be crediting the insulation from external developments to exchange rate flexibility, when in reality the difference was a response to the fiscal policies in place in more flexible exchange rate regimes. The data suggest that this is not the case. Pooled regressions suggest that fiscal policies have not significantly varied across exchange rate regimes. Therefore, it would seem safe to credit the systematic differences in behavior of real and financial variables to the exchange rate regimes themselves.

At least in this sample, fiscal balances systematically responded to external developments, but in roughly the same way across exchange rate regimes (Table 5.5).

TABLE 5.5

Pool Regressions: Effect of External Variables on Fiscal Accounts[1]

	Revenue		Spending			
	Total	Taxes	Total	Goods and Services	Interest Bill	Overall Balance
1. Total impact						
VIX	0.00	0.02	0.01	–0.01	–0.26*	–0.04
Terms of trade	0.05***	–0.01	–0.01	–0.01	0.28***	0.09***
World growth	0.08	0.11	–0.26**	–0.07*	3.17***	0.41***
Adjusted R-squared	0.92	0.57	0.92	0.99	0.22	0.41
Observations	418	446	354	220	352	224
2. Impact by regime						
VIX * flexible dummy[2]	–0.02	0.04**	–0.01	–0.01	–0.16	–0.03
Terms of trade * flexible dummy	0.04**	0.00	–0.02	0.00	0.24**	0.09***
World growth * flexible dummy	0.12	0.14*	–0.31**	–0.09**	2.46***	0.47***
VIX * (1 – flexible dummy)	0.03	0.01	0.05	0.00	–0.43***	–0.04
Terms of trade (1 – flexible dummy)	0.06***	–0.03*	0.01	–0.02*	0.36**	0.10***
World growth * (1 – flexible dummy)	0.03	0.07	–0.20	–0.01	4.25***	0.33**
Adjusted R-squared	0.92	0.58	0.93	0.99	0.23	0.41
Observations	418	446	354	220	352	224
Wald test of equal coefficients across regimes						
VIX	**	**	**		**	
Terms of trade						
World growth						

Sources: IMF, World Economic Outlook database; Chicago Board Options Exchange; and Haver Analytics.

[1]The sample includes Argentina, Brazil, Bulgaria, Chile, Colombia, Czech Republic, Dominican Republic, Ecuador, Egypt, El Salvador, Estonia, Indonesia, Israel, Latvia, Lithuania, Malaysia, Mexico, Pakistan, Panama, Peru, Philippines, Poland, Russia, South Africa, Tunisia, Turkey, Ukraine, Uruguay, and Venezuela.

[2]The flexible dummy takes a value of 1 for the more flexible exchange regimes under the IMF classification, defined as crawling pegs and above.

Overall balances in percent of GDP improved with terms-of-trade gains and increases in world growth. No systematic change in overall balances in percent of GDP took place in response to changes in the VIX. Fiscal revenue improved with terms-of-trade gains in the sample, while fiscal spending remained unaffected. Thus, fiscal authorities have systematically saved part of the bonanza arising from favorable external prices. In turn, world growth had no systematic relationship with fiscal revenue, but significantly increased the interest rate bill and reduced fiscal spending, resulting in an improvement in overall balances.

CONCLUSION AND POLICY IMPLICATIONS

The experience of emerging market and developing economies during 1990–2009 suggests that external developments have played an important role in determining their macroeconomic conditions. In particular, domestic demand, GDP, and current account balances in individual emerging market and developing economies have responded to changes in world GDP, global risk tolerance, and the terms of trade.

Exchange rate flexibility has helped insulate countries from external developments. The pickup in domestic demand has usually been smaller in countries with more flexible exchange rate regimes during periods of easy global money. Conversely, domestic demand growth has fallen less in more flexible regimes during periods of tight external liquidity.

Domestic demand growth is often less volatile in more flexible exchange rate regimes. Analysis based on multivariate pooled regressions for 29 emerging and advanced economies shows that domestic demand rises when (1) global risk aversion (VIX) falls; (2) terms of trade improve; and (3) world growth increases. The effects of external developments, however, are often milder in more flexible exchange rate regimes.

Although exchange rate flexibility could help smooth economic cycles that originated abroad, it requires a monetary anchor not based on exchange rate management. Setting up a monetary policy framework that provides an alternative to exchange rate management could take time and requires investment in operational expertise.

REFERENCE

Canales-Kriljenko, Jorge Iván, 2010, "Challenges Arising from Easy External Financial Conditions," in *Regional Economic Outlook: Western Hemisphere—Crisis Averted—What's Next?* (Washington: International Monetary Fund, May).

PART IV

Fiscal Policy

CHAPTER 6

Public Debt Targeting: An Application to Caribbean Countries

ALEJANDRO GUERSON AND GIOVANNI MELINA

It is a well-established fact in the international finance literature that developments in international financial markets can be a source of instability, and can amplify real shocks (see, for example, Kaminsky, Reinhart, and Vegh, 2004). The channels include the direct impact of capital flows on aggregate demand, including through domestic financial markets, and also the multiplication effect from the impact of capital flows on government access to financing and borrowing costs. In countries with high public debt, negative real or financial shocks can undermine creditworthiness, perhaps to the point at which the sovereign's ability to honor its debt obligations is perceived to be at risk. At that point, a second round of indirect effects can sink an economy into a negative spiral of high interest rates, credit crunch, and recession.

According to the logic above, the stock of public debt is a critical *state variable* of the economy, not just in terms of determining its sustainable level of consumption and public sector spending in the long term, but also in terms of affecting the business cycle dynamics in the short term. A sovereign debtor subject to financial markets' swings might (1) be forced into procyclical expenditures, if access to financing becomes too costly or just unavailable in low states of the cycle, further amplifying business cycle fluctuations, and (2) need additional self-insurance against loss of access to financing, as opposed to using public debt and access to financing as a source of insurance against macroeconomic shocks. Moreover, the financial contagion literature indicates that the negative dynamics described above can take place even if direct channels and change in fundamentals do not necessarily warrant the financial markets' reaction outlined (see, for example, Kaminsky and Reinhart, 2000). Points (1) and (2) above imply that keeping public debt at sufficiently low levels is a form of self-insurance, as it allows expenditure smoothing over the business cycle by permitting access to financing without jeopardizing creditors' perceptions about a sovereign's ability to honor debt commitments.

This chapter proposes a fiscal framework that, based on the reasoning above, seeks to smooth primary expenditures over the business cycle by providing financial creditors sufficient assurance of a high probability that public debt obligations will remain within a preannounced band. The use of a public debt band is critical, as it allows for primary balance flexibility and, as a result, avoids the need for large fiscal consolidations in bad states of the cycle, which would undermine credibility. Operationally, the fiscal framework proposal consists of the announcement of four intermediate parameters that pin down the primary expenditure envelope for the next budget cycle, which is set so that public debt remains below a preannounced threshold in the medium term with a specified probability. Empirical simulations for a sample of Caribbean countries show that allowing debt to move within a relatively narrow band allows for large improvements in terms of primary expenditure smoothing in the business cycle. The simulations in this chapter indicate that expenditure smoothing can be better than under a structural balance rule. This is a tough test for the proposal, as the Caribbean economies are typically highly indebted, very open, undiversified, and subject to significant real and financial shocks.

The proposed framework has the following desirable features: (1) it balances the direct impact of countercyclical government spending on aggregate demand vis-à-vis the indirect feedback effect of excess public sector deficit and public debt accumulation, as these can affect sovereign risk and interest rates; (2) it can enhance credibility as reputation builds over time; (3) it does not need a potential output estimation for the current year; (4) it is state-contingent, therefore permitting some overall balance flexibility; and (5) it forces the use of a consistent medium-term macroeconomic framework for budgeting. As anticipated, the framework is applied to Caribbean economies, which, in general show high levels of public debt and procyclical primary expenditure, as will be shown in the section on Application to Caribbean Countries. Details on the computation of debt dynamics are provided in Appendix 6.1.

THE PROPOSAL: PUBLIC DEBT TARGETING

We propose a fiscal framework under which a government commits to a high probability of keeping debt within a specified band. The policy entails two main parameter announcements: a trajectory of public debt and its probabilistic band, and a primary expenditure budget envelope for the next budget cycle. The two main announcements are linked by four intermediate technical parameters, which are also announced: (1) a medium-term horizon in years; (2) a public debt upper threshold at the end of the medium-term horizon; (3) a notional spending trajectory that maps the next year's primary expenditure announcements to debt trajectories over the medium term; and (4) a probability value attached to debt remaining below the upper threshold.

Operationally, under the public debt targeting framework, a government is asked to set primary spending budget envelopes for the next year according to probabilistic public debt outcomes over the medium term. Concretely, in year t, a government would announce a primary spending budget for the year, $S(t)$ (budget envelope), such that if primary spending for the following T years (medium-term horizon) were to remain at the same level in real per capita terms (spending trajectory), public debt would take a level $D(t+T)$ percent of GDP or lower (debt upper threshold) with probability $P(t+T)$ (probability). In year $t+1$, the government would repeat the same announcement, choosing a level of spending $S(t+1)$ such that after T years, public debt takes at most a level of $D(t+T+1)$ with probability $P(t+T+1)$, and so on.

The proposed framework is recursive in nature. Budgets are adjusted every year for a given choice of targets and thresholds after the impact of shocks on the previous year's deficit and public debt has been observed. For example, if a negative shock results in lower revenues in year t compared with the budget projection, then, for a given $S(t)$ budget, the deficit and the amount of debt accumulation would be higher than originally expected. All else being equal, this would result in a lower $S(t+1)$ budget envelope relative to the one that would have been determined by the framework without the negative shock, for a given set of medium-term debt target threshold, probability value, and horizon length. In this way, the proposal explicitly tackles the issue of the trade-off between expenditure smoothing over the business cycle and the need to avoid sharp increases in public debt, as the need for expenditure adjustment is averaged away over a sequence of periods.

The proposal can, more generally, be expanded to accommodate a preannounced degree of discretionary expenditure. The spending trajectory can be set up in terms of an acyclical notional trajectory, as in the example above, or expanded with additional procyclical or countercyclical impulses around the primary spending level in real per capita terms. The simulations to be presented below show an example in this regard.[1] In the example, we simulate a discretionary spending space such that, if real GDP growth is higher (lower) than population growth, a specified share can be spent (saved) in the current budget period. This discretionary stimulus or expenditure impulse can be set to be countercyclical or procyclical, as deemed appropriate.[2]

The proposal has several desirable properties in terms of fiscal policy management:

Credibility

Commitment to a public debt band is anchored on a specific framework that sets government spending according to projected debt trajectories—this is a critical feature in terms of building credibility. For example, negative shocks that reduce GDP and revenues and result in a larger deficit and public debt relative to budget projections would be less likely to trigger expectations of public debt entering an unsustainable path, as a strategy for a compensating

[1]Note that as the framework is set in terms of primary spending, automatic stabilizers on revenues and interest expenditures are allowed to play in full.

[2]The possibility of a countercyclical impulse would find its rationale in Keynesian arguments for aggregate demand smoothing, such as from nominal rigidities. However, a procyclical discretionary impulse could in some cases be appropriate if it helps to contain the non-Keynesian effects of public debt accumulation.

consolidation is automatically in place. Budget announcements acknowledge up-front the possibility of shocks and the resulting deviations, but at the same time they are clear about the mechanism by which public debt will be brought back on track. As a government abides by its policy framework announcements, reputation can build up, making access to financing in bad times more fluid and on better terms. In addition, the framework proposal sets primary spending on a smooth trajectory, which also contributes to increasing the credibility of the debt band announcement. This is because it significantly reduces the need for unrealistically large primary spending consolidation in bad times, as government deficits and debt accumulation are averaged away over a sequence of budget cycles.

Primary Expenditure Smoothing

Because debt thresholds are set according to medium-term economic paths, deficits can be larger than budgeted if revenues turn out lower than projected while primary expenditures remain at the budget level. The focus on primary spending, as opposed to total expenditures, is not a shortcoming of public debt targeting. First, for a given tax framework in place, primary expenditures are the relevant expenditure aggregate in terms of assessing debt sustainability. And second, interest expenditures tend to be largely predetermined. Excluding interest expenditures from the spending announcement implies that shocks to interest costs (for example, from interest rates or exchange rates) are accommodated.

Flexibility

The proposed framework is not a spending rule. Under public debt targeting, the government is not committing to keep primary spending constant in real per capita terms. That is a notional spending trajectory used as an intermediate technical parameter to pin down primary expenditures for the next budget, jointly with the other intermediate technical parameters outlined above. Each year, primary spending is recalculated recursively, as explained above. The framework is set in terms of primary expenditures, which implies that automatic stabilizers on revenues are allowed to play in full, while unanticipated changes in interest expenditures are accommodated.

Medium-Term Macroeconomic Framework

Public debt targeting requires fiscal projections over the medium term, as determined by its various parameter choices. Probabilistic projections need to be determined according to a relatively agnostic representation of the economy (a "model"), which is fully disclosed and can therefore be subject to scrutiny. This implies that public debt targeting forces medium-term budget planning. Institutional mechanisms to ensure independence from political influence and stability of the representation are likely needed. At a minimum, the framework requires minimizing the space for arbitrary and unreasonable macroeconomic parameters in the budget and in medium-term projections.

A key input is therefore an economic model that can be used to produce consistent macroeconomic forecasts incorporating the possibility of shocks. The model should be capable of providing stochastic forecasts for the variables relevant to make probabilistic public debt projections, although other variables considered important determinants of the business cycle should also be included.

PUBLIC DEBT TARGETING AND STRUCTURAL BALANCE RULES

Kopits and Symansky (1998) define fiscal rules as numerical constraints set on the budget on a permanent basis. If we take this definition, then the proposal in this chapter is not a rule: what is stable over time is the framework, as determined by the choices of the four intermediate medium-term parameters involved and the economic model of choice, but not the actual numerical targets. Under public debt targeting, primary expenditure and debt levels change in every budget cycle, as the budget envelope for the following year is recalculated after observing the impact of shocks on public debt.[3]

Besides definitional issues, the framework compares favorably with some alternatives. Numerical constraints, particularly on the fiscal balance—as in the Maastricht Treaty signed by the European Union—have the advantage of simplicity. This could be argued as being important if public scrutiny is considered necessary when special interests or other political economy pressures for spending are strong. However, by their nature, such constraints would not necessarily suffice to avoid procyclical spending or excessive debt accumulation—the two main objectives typically sought.[4]

This is why proponents of fiscal rules prefer to focus on the structural or cyclically adjusted balance rules. These are based on measures of the structural or noncyclical components of revenues and expenditures, and therefore account for the transitory impact of business cycle fluctuations on the budget and other transitory or one-off factors. By their nature, provided structural balance targets are set at an appropriate level, these should be consistent with both debt sustainability and a nonprocyclical stance. However, there are disadvantages or limitations often attached to these rules: (1) difficulty in discriminating permanent versus transitory changes in revenues and expenditures, which can undermine transparency and credibility; (2) insufficiency of GDP to assess in full the state of the cycle; and (3) inability to allow space for discretionary fiscal policy.

These limitations are not necessarily fair, as refinements can be introduced to improve structural balance rules' application in practice.[5] Regardless, public

---

[3]However, if rules are more generally defined as institutional mechanisms aimed at supporting fiscal credibility and discipline, then the proposed framework could be considered a rule.

[4]Balassone and Kumar (2007) show, for a sample of developed and developing economies, that the overall balance behavior over the business cycle is asymmetric, as these tend to be relatively more negative in bad times than they are positive in good times.

[5]For example, mechanisms can be introduced for an ex post compensation for miscalculations about the state of the cycle, as, for example, in Switzerland. Also, a broader set of variables could be used to

debt targeting would not have these limitations. First, the identification of permanent and transitory output components is not necessary.[6] Instead, spending levels are determined based on projected public debt dynamics, which is simpler and more transparent as these are anchored around the debt accumulation identity. Second, given the wider set of indicators needed to produce debt projections, the methodology forces the use of a broader set of variables to determine appropriate primary spending levels, which are also crucial in determining the state of the business cycle, such as interest rates and real exchange rates.[7] Third, the proposed framework tackles the impact of debt sustainability concerns on the business cycle in the most direct way possible, given the commitment to public debt thresholds and the announcement of a debt trajectory band. Fourth, as explained above, the framework can be designed to allow for cyclical space for discretionary primary spending, possibly including a state-contingent additional primary expenditure component (set to be either procyclical or countercyclical, as deemed appropriate), but without necessarily allowing full discretion.

In our view, however, the most promising application of public debt targeting is as a transition framework toward the adoption of a structural balance rule when public debt is high and marginal deficits and public debt accumulation can impact sovereign spreads. Expenditure smoothing over the business cycle requires the ability to finance fiscal deficits, and therefore relies on the assumption that markets would tolerate deterioration in creditworthiness in bad times. To the extent that public debt targeting is an intermediate step that seeks to reduce debt within certain bounds consistent also with expenditure smoothing, it can then be a suitable framework for a transition toward lower indebtedness. The use of a debt band, as it results from the framework proposal in this chapter, balances out the objective to smooth primary expenditures over the business cycle with the need to avoid sharp increases in public debt.[8]

---

determine structural versus cyclical components of revenues or expenditures in addition to GDP. Discretionary expenditures could also be included, provided this introduction is attached to an over-the-cycle compensatory mechanism. See Bornhorst and others (2011).

[6]This is not referring to the technical aspects and multiple methodologies available to identify cycle and trend. It refers to available methodologies that are weak in identifying the trend position at end-sample points, which results in large practical miscalculations that can undermine credibility, even when the methodology remains unchanged. See Bornhorst and others (2011).

[7]For example, the IMF's 1998 *World Economic Outlook* shows that, for a sample of Asian countries, exchange rates and commodity prices are more important in assessing the cyclical components of revenues and expenditures than GDP fluctuations.

[8]At the other extreme of the spectrum, simple debt rules may not be credible either, as they might be difficult to comply with under tail risks. For example, a simple commitment to reduce public debt within a specified deterministic path (for example, a debt ceiling) might prove politically and socially difficult as it implies a commitment to adjust negative shocks in full within the current year, forcing a strongly procyclical fiscal stance. This difficulty can undermine their credibility.

APPLICATION TO CARIBBEAN COUNTRIES

The Caribbean economies are good candidates for our proposal in this chapter, given their high public debt levels and procyclical primary expenditure. The empirical evidence presented below is indicative of financial developments associated with this behavior.

The Conduct of Fiscal Policy in Caribbean Countries: Some Stylized Facts

We start by establishing some stylized facts that are indicative of the relevance of the policy proposal for Caribbean countries.

High public-debt-to-GDP ratios. Since 2009, the median public-debt-to-GDP ratio has remained at about 90 percent of GDP, and about four times the size of total revenues (Figure 6.1, panel a). Most countries show very high public debt ratios, and also in almost all cases, debt-to-GDP ratios are increasing or persistently high (Figure 6.1, panel b).

Procyclical primary expenditures. The median cyclical components of real output, primary expenditures, and total revenues show positive co-movement over the last 15 years (Figure 6.1, panel c). The cyclical components' median correlation of primary expenditures with both total revenues and real GDP is about 50 percent. This is a general pattern across the developing world.

Strong cross-country synchronization of GDP, government revenues, and primary expenditures, suggesting that common external factors are important. Virtually all countries show a positive correlation of the output, total revenue, and primary expenditure cycles with cross-country median fluctuations (Figure 6.1, panel d).

Strong cross-country correlation of domestic financial and foreign exchange markets, possibly corresponding to the state of the U.S. business cycle. Every country's GDP cycle is positively correlated with that of the United States; there is also evidence of cross-country correlation in interest rates, real exchange rates, and net capital inflows (Figure 6.1, panel e). This suggests that external financial developments are an important channel of transmission of external real and financial shocks.

Financial variables explain a substantial share of the variation in primary expenditures. Net capital inflows, real exchange rate depreciation, and interest rates jointly explain one-half of the average forecast-error variance of primary expenditures (Figure 6.1, panel f).[9] The statement assumes that a significant share of variation in financial indicators has an external (exogenous) source, as suggested by the real and financial cross-country correlations.

[9]Individual-country forecast variance decompositions are derived from a two-lag six-variable vector autoregression featuring annual observations of the output growth rate, a short-term interest rate, the growth rate of the real exchange rate, the change in net capital inflows, the total revenue growth, and the primary expenditure growth, respectively.

Figure 6.1 Fiscal Behavior and the Business Cycle

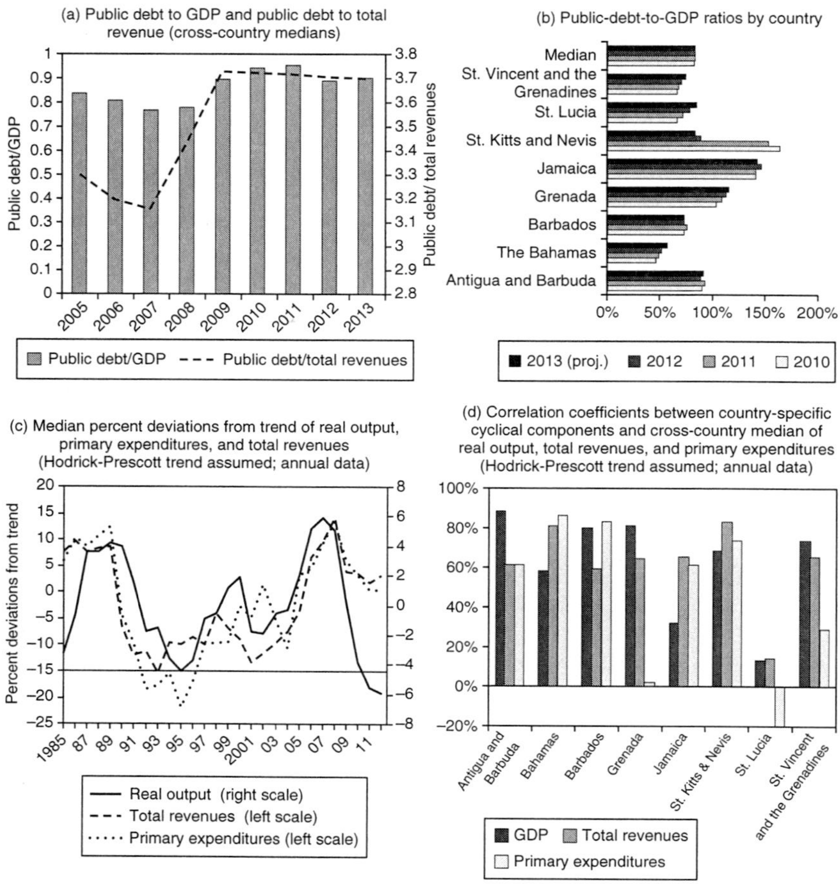

(e) Correlation coefficients between country-specific financial variables and cross-country medians (in percent)

	Net Capital Inflows	Real Exchange Rate Depreciation	Interest Rate	U.S. GDP
Antigua and Barbuda	19.4	38.9	74.6	49.9
Bahamas	48.9	32.1	58.9	70.3
Barbados	35.2	46.8	59.7	67.5
Grenada	49.0	61.2	26.1	39.8
Jamaica	45.1	6.2	29.0	78.4
St. Kitts & Nevis	67.0	15.9	38.0	46.2
St. Lucia	−18.8	49.6	62.5	28.6
St. Vincent and the Grenadines	35.7	68.9	61.3	78.1

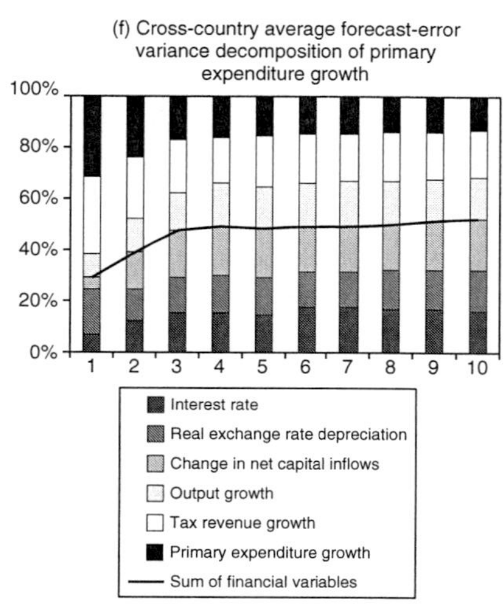

Source: IMF staff calculations.

Simulation

The starting point of the simulation is the public debt accumulation identity. We decompose public debt to GDP into: (1) the commercial component denominated in the domestic currency; (2) the commercial component denominated in foreign currency;[10] and (3) the official bilateral/multilateral fraction of public debt (usually denominated in U.S. dollars). Let d_t^j be the annual public-debt-to-GDP component of type j (for example, the component denominated in local currency). d_t^j evolves according to the following:

$$d_t^j = \frac{(1+i_t^j)}{(1+g_t)(1+\pi_t)} d_{t-1}^j - \alpha_t^j b_t, \tag{6.1}$$

where i_t^j, g_t, π_t, α_t^j, and b_t represent the interest rate paid on a government debt of type j, the real GDP growth rate, the annual inflation rate, the share of primary balance servicing public debt of type j, and the primary-balance-to-GDP ratio, respectively. b_t is given by the difference between total revenues and primary (non-interest) expenditures divided by GDP. The sum of all types of public debt to GDP must yield the total debt-to-GDP ratio for a given year:

$$d_t = \sum_j d_t^j . \tag{6.2}$$

Appendix 6.1 provides a full description of how we computed and decomposed public debt to GDP in the simulations.

This decomposition allows a more realistic evaluation of the sensitivity of debt indicators to interest rate and exchange rate shocks than simply maintaining the assumption of fixed shares, which implies that debt is continuously rebalanced by recurrent debt repurchase and reissuance. The interest rate specification used in Equation (6.1) is the implicit or average rate for the debt category, and not the marginal rate. These are approximated by taking the moving average of the marginal interest rate in year t and the previous $M-1$ years, where M is the average maturity of the debt category measured in years.

Model and Estimation

The inputs to produce debt simulations according to Equations (6.1) and (6.2) are obtained from stochastic simulations that capture the volatility, correlation, and persistence of the required inputs and other variables considered important to determine the state of the business cycle.

Simulations are produced by fitting historical data to a vector autoregression (VAR) model, and then using the coefficients to produce a large number of stochastic projections. We specify the VAR as follows:

---

[10]We abstract from cross-foreign-currency-parity changes. This is not a significant simplification, as most countries' foreign currency debt used in the sample is denominated in U.S. dollars, if not exclusively so.

$$X_t = A(L)X_{t-1} + Bi_t^* + \varepsilon_{t,} \tag{6.3}$$

where $X_t = \left(g_t\ i_t^d\ \eta_t\ m_t\ \tau_t\ s_t\right)^T$ is a (6 × 1) vector of endogenous variables containing real output growth, a short-term market-determined domestic interest rate, the change in the bilateral real exchange rate (versus the U.S. dollar), the change in real net capital inflows, the percent change in total revenues, and the percent change in primary expenditures, respectively. i_t^* is the U.S. federal funds rate; $A(L)$ is a polynomial in the lag operator of degree ranging from 1 to 4, depending on the country estimation output. B is a vector of coefficients; and ε_t is a vector of well-behaved error terms: $\varepsilon_t \sim N(0, \Omega)$. Employing growth rates has the advantage of dealing with stationary variables and avoiding any explicit assumption on trends.

VAR models for stochastic simulations of debt-to-GDP dynamics have already been adopted in the literature.[11] The main differences in our specification relative to previous work are (1) the explicit introduction of financial variables—such as net capital inflows and the foreign interest rate—that play a substantial role in explaining the volatility in Caribbean countries; and (2) the distinct treatment of total revenues and primary expenditures. In fact, in the stochastic simulations, the primary balance is computed as a second step starting from the simulated growth rates of total revenues and primary expenditures. Keeping revenues and expenditures separated allows us to simulate the feedback effects of expenditure-smoothing policies.[12]

Monte Carlo Simulation

We use the fitted VAR model to simulate the effect of expenditure-smoothing fiscal policies (active). For comparison, we also simulate primary expenditures using the VAR-fitted equation for primary expenditures (passive). The passive simulations provide an agnostic diagnosis of the prevailing public debt sustainability conditions.

The simulations are computed by generating a sequence of random vectors $\hat{\varepsilon}_{t+1}, \ldots, \hat{\varepsilon}_T$ such that $\forall\ \omega \in [t+1, T]$, $\hat{\varepsilon}_\omega = W\upsilon_\tau$, where $\upsilon_\omega \sim N(0,1)$ and W is the Choleski factorization of $\Omega = W'W$. At every forecast period, we draw 2,000 random vectors $\hat{\varepsilon}_\omega$, while the VAR produces joint dynamic responses of all elements in X.[13] As noted in Garcia and Rigobon (2005), in the passive simulation, the method is not sensitive to the ordering of variables in the VAR, as stochastic

---

[11]Examples of works along these lines are, among others, Garcia and Rigobon (2005); Celasun, Debrun, and Ostry (2007); Penalver and Thwaites (2006); and Tanner and Samake (2008).

[12]The simulation results need to be taken with caution. Any VAR approach to policy simulation is inherently subject to the Lucas critique. In fact, when policies change, the behavior of market participants might change as well, possibly affecting the estimated coefficients. This limitation can be addressed using a general equilibrium model.

[13]For the purposes of the simulations, we also use assumptions on the U.S. federal funds rate, the London interbank offered rate on the U.S. dollar, and U.S. inflation in line with the *World Economic Outlook* (IMF, 2010), and we fit the domestic consumer price index to a simple pass-through equation to project the domestic inflation rate.

simulation results are shaped by the variance-covariance matrix of reduced-form errors Ω, which is unique. However, the active simulations are sensitive to ordering. By setting primary expenditures last in order, we minimize the contemporaneous (within-year) feedback from primary expenditures to the rest of the economy.

Computing the simulations for the fiscal policy framework proposed in this chapter requires two inputs. The first is the starting point of the primary expenditure path. The resulting level of primary expenditure represents the primary expenditure envelope for the next budget cycle. Second, a specification of the primary expenditure pattern in the future is necessary to calculate public debt projections over the medium term. For this, we use the assumption that primary expenditure remains constant in real per capita terms (see Equation (6.4) below). This exercise is performed for each of the 2,000 random draws using the debt accumulation identity, which results in a distribution of public debt outcomes at each projected horizon. The starting level of primary expenditure is then pinned down iteratively by backward induction, after the desired debt upper threshold, horizon length, and probability have been chosen. In this way, the next budget's primary expenditure envelope is consistent with a debt-to-GDP upper threshold $\bar{d}$ to be met T years ahead with probability p, where $\bar{d}$, T, and p are parameter choices of the policymaker. We denote $\tilde{s}_{t+1}$ as the primary expenditure level that is consistent with $d_{t+T} \leq \bar{d}$ with probability p.

Notice that setting $p = 0.5$ is, by construction, the level of primary expenditure that stabilizes public debt to GDP in expected terms over the medium term. A higher p implies that the policymaker is seeking additional primary expenditure consolidation and, as a result, is choosing to set public debt to GDP on a downward trend in expected terms. A higher probability is therefore a more prudent choice, as it ensures that debt will remain within low bounds with a higher probability.

The choice of the medium-term horizon length, T, is also important. In this case, for a given debt threshold and probability choices, a longer horizon (high T) increases the smoothness of the primary expenditure path, as the need for adjustment is averaged away over more years. Too long a horizon, however, could undermine the credibility of the framework.

We propose a specification for the forward-looking primary-expenditure-smoothing path according to the following:

$$s_{\omega} = \tilde{s}_{\omega} - \kappa(g_{\omega} - \bar{g}), \forall \omega \in [t+1, T], \tag{6.4}$$

where $\bar{g}$ is a "trend" growth rate of real GDP, which we set equal to the average population growth rate; g_{ω} is the simulated growth rate of real GDP; κ is a parameter representing the responsiveness of the primary expenditure growth rate to deviations of real GDP growth from trend growth; $\tilde{s}_{t+1}$ represents the consolidation (if $\tilde{s}_{t+1} < 0$) of primary expenditures at time $t + 1$; while $\tilde{s}_{\omega} = \bar{g}$, $\forall\ \omega \in [t + 2, T]$.

Setting $\kappa = 0$ corresponds to running no discretionary expenditure impulse: it implies that primary expenditure is projected to remain constant in real per capita terms after the initial consolidation occurring in year t+1. In other words, for κ = 0, the primary expenditure level at t+1 is set so that, if primary expenditure remains constant in real per capita terms for T years, public debt will remain below the chosen upper threshold $\bar{d}$ with probability p in year t+T. A positive κ represents a countercyclical fiscal policy impulse, as it would result in additional primary expenditure growth opposite to that of real per capita GDP growth. Analogously, we take a negative κ to represent a procyclical fiscal policy impulse.

Results

Table 6.1 shows the results of our simulation exercises for a sample of Caribbean economies. For illustrative purposes, we set the proposal to a medium-term horizon of five years. Maximum debt threshold announcements for 2015 are purely illustrative. In the last three columns, we show the primary expenditure consolidation in the 2011 budget in percentage points of GDP that would be necessary to maintain the debt-to-GDP ratio below the illustrative threshold with probabilities of 50 percent and 70 percent.

Among the countries reported, Jamaica is the only one that does not show a particular need for further consolidation in 2011. This is probably the result of the consolidation program that the government has undertaken since 2009. In fact, under the passive behavior, debt to GDP is predicted to decline from 139 percent

TABLE 6.1

Fiscal Framework Proposal Simulation for Caribbean Countries (Percent)

						Required Consolidation of Primary Expenditures in 2011		
	Estimated Debt/GDP in 2010	Estimated Primary Balance/ GDP in 2010	Expected Debt/GDP in 2015 under "Passive" Behavior	Illustrative Debt/GDP Threshold in 2015	Probability Debt/GDP < Threshold	Acyclical (k = 0)	Countercyclical (k = 0.5)	Procyclical (k = –0.5)
						(Percentage points of GDP)		
Antigua and Barbuda	119	–1.8	160	120	0.5	8.3	9.1	7.6
					0.7	10.3	11.1	9.4
Bahamas	65	-3.9	79	60	0.5	0.8	1.1	0.4
					0.7	1.9	2.4	1.3
Barbados	122	–1.2	137	130	0.5	7.8	7.6	7.9
					0.7	10.3	10.4	10.2
Grenada	116	0.3	135	110	0.5	1.3	0.7	1.4
					0.7	3.7	3.2	3.7
Jamaica	139	7.6	117	100	0.5	–4.2	–4.0	–4.4
					0.7	–0.7	–0.7	–0.7
St. Kitts and Nevis	184	–1.9	205	180	0.5	11.1	11.7	10.5
					0.7	13.6	14.3	13.1
St. Lucia	80	–3.2	87	70	0.5	0.7	1.3	0.1
					0.7	2.5	3.4	1.7
St. Vincent and the Grenadines	91	–1.4	115	90	0.5	6.1	5.8	6.4
					0.7	7.7	7.5	7.9

Sources: Country authorities; and authors' estimates and projections.

in 2010 to 117 percent in 2015. In 70 percent of the simulated cases, Jamaica meets the target of a debt-to-GDP ratio below 100 percent if it follows acyclical (primary expenditure constant in real per capita terms) or moderately procyclical or countercyclical rules even in the case of a small expenditure increase in 2011.

For the remaining countries, our simulations predict an upward trend for debt-to-GDP ratios in the next five years under the passive primary expenditure behavior. For the Bahamas, Grenada, and St. Lucia, a primary expenditure consolidation of about 2 percentage points of GDP to 3 percentage points of GDP in 2011—together with acyclical or moderately procyclical or countercyclical primary expenditure rules—would be enough to maintain debt to GDP in 2015 below the level predicted for 2010 in 70 percent of the simulated cases. For Antigua and Barbuda, Barbados, St. Kitts and Nevis, and St. Vincent and the Grenadines, the framework signals a significant need for consolidation in the 2011 budget, in excess of 7 percentage points of GDP.

Figure 6.2 provides a series of public debt fan charts that underlie the results explained above, based on the simulation exercise. In particular, we proceed to simulate

Figure 6.2 Fan Charts of Public-Debt-to-GDP Ratios under "Passive" and Public Debt Targeting

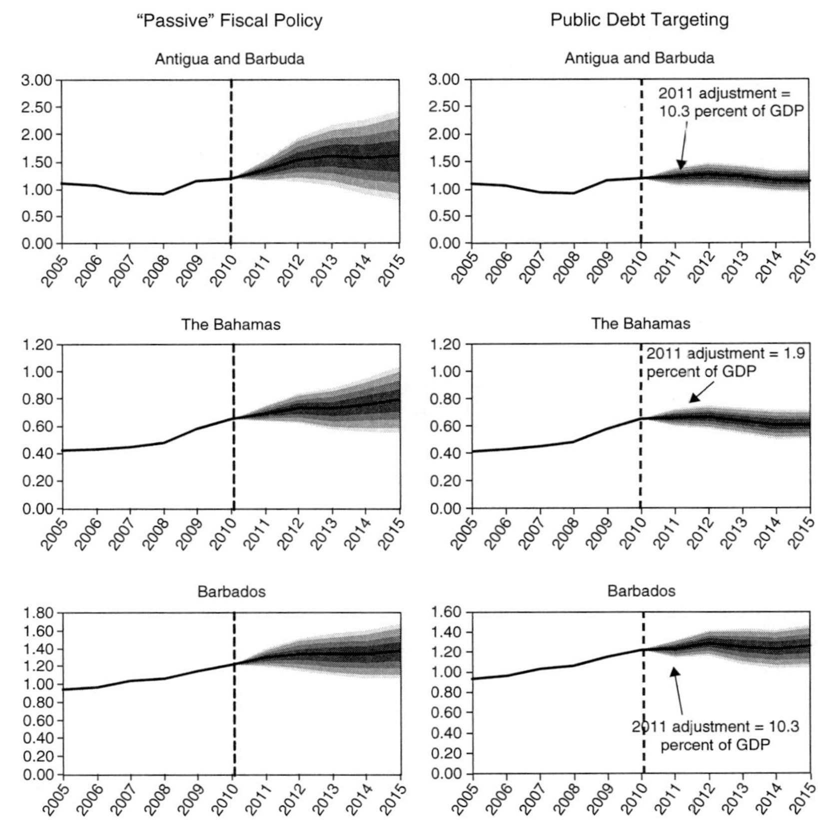

(continued)

Figure 6.2 (continued)

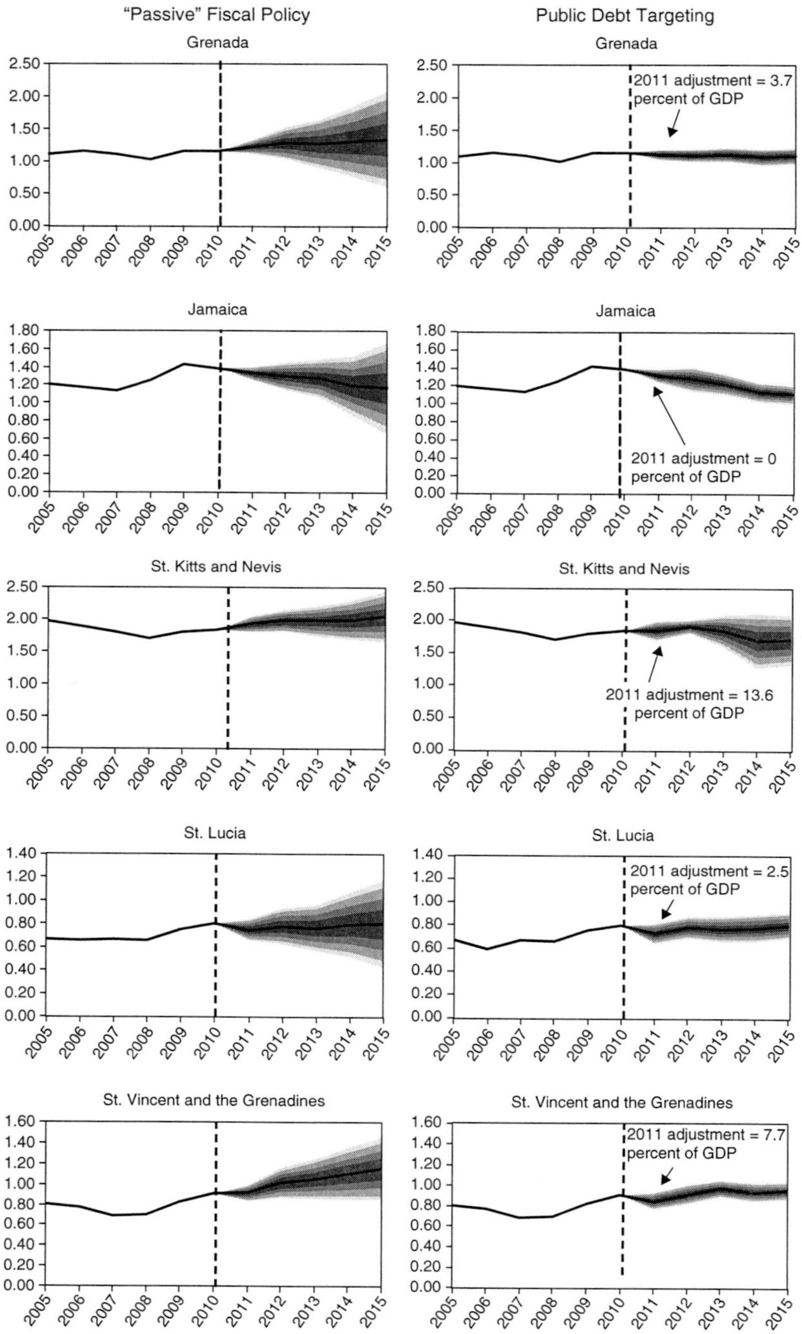

Source: IMF staff calculations.

Note: Variations in shading correspond to 50, 75, 90, and 95 percent confidence intervals.

the proposed policy for a sequence of periods. The parameter choices remain the same as in previous sections. To this end, we perform recursive simulations, mimicking what would happen in practice as the public debt targeting framework is applied over subsequent annual budget cycles. First, we calculate the primary expenditure envelope for the next budget cycle (2011) using the same parameter choices as in Table 6.1, while allowing the VAR to generate the remaining vector variables for 2011. With the simulations for 2011, we compute the implied end-2011 public debt stock using the debt accumulation identity (Equation (6.1)). Notice that as each of the 2,000 simulations in the Monte Carlo experiment is subject to a random shock, the deficits and debt stocks for the period will vary across simulations, despite the use of the same framework for all of them. Then, for each simulation, we recalculate the primary expenditure for the 2012 budget period consistent with the same proposed framework parameters, allow the VAR to simulate the remaining variables, and calculate the public debt stock as of end-2012. We proceed in this way until the 2015 budget period.

PUBLIC DEBT TARGETING IN THE BUSINESS CYCLE: A QUANTITATIVE ASSESSMENT

For reference, we compare the results outlined in the previous section with the following two alternatives: (1) primary expenditure trajectory under the historical behavior, as obtained from the unrestricted VAR, and (2) for the structural primary balance rule that targets the same public-debt-to-GDP ratio for comparability,[14] with elasticities of real levels of revenues and primary expenditures to the output gap of 1 and 0, respectively.[15] GDP gaps are estimated using the Hodrick-Prescott filter trend as a measure of potential GDP. We obtain quantitative measures for three different sets of results considered of interest: (1) the degree of primary expenditure smoothing; (2) the cyclical properties of primary expenditure vis-à-vis GDP and revenues; and (3) the public debt-smoothing properties.

Primary Expenditure Smoothing

The simulations show that the primary expenditure smoothing properties of public debt targeting compare favorably relative to a structural balance rule for this sample of countries. As an indicator of variability over time, we compute the growth rate of simulated real primary expenditures over the simulation years (2011–15) and the standard deviation of these growth rates for each of the 2,000 simulations. Then we calculate the coefficient of variation (CV) as the standard deviation scaled by the average growth rate over 2011–15, and average it over the 2,000 simulations. The results are presented in Table 6.2. The coefficient of variation of the growth rate of primary expenditures under public debt targeting is in

---

[14]Also, the simulations under the structural balance rule are based on the same long-term GDP growth and real interest rate assumptions.

[15]The primary expenditure under a structural balance rule is calculated as structural revenues minus the primary surplus that targets the same public-debt-to-GDP target as in the framework proposal, for comparability. Structural revenues are calculated as the simulated revenues times the output gap (computed as the ratio of the GDP trend using the Hodrick-Prescott filter with $\lambda = 100$ divided by the GDP level).

TABLE 6.2

Smoothing Properties of Public Debt Targeting (Coefficient of variation of simulated real growth rates of primary expenditures)[1]

	Historical Behavior[2]	Structural Balance Rule[3]	Public Debt Targeting[4]
Antigua and Barbuda	25.7	17.6	3.4
Bahamas	1.5	1.3	2.3
Barbados	3.3	1.3	1.9
Grenada	91.9	5.8	2.7
Jamaica	2.3	2.2	1.7
St. Kitts and Nevis	1.5	3.0	2.7
St. Lucia	3.5	2.2	1.5
St. Vincent and the Grenadines	6.1	2.4	1.8

Sources: Country authorities; and authors' estimates and projections.
[1]Ratio of the standard deviation to the mean of the average real growth rate of simulated primary expenditures. Mean and standard deviation computed from a Monte Carlo experiment based on the VAR simulation. The simulations for the structural balance rule and the policy framework proposal are based on the same parameters and public debt target levels. In absolute terms.
[2]Primary expenditure simulations based on the estimated VAR coefficients.
[3]Primary expenditure simulations based on a structural primary balance with output gap elasticities of revenues and primary expenditures of 1 and 0, respectively.
[4]Primary expenditure simulations based on the policy proposal. All parameters are set as in Table 6.1.

general lower than under a structural balance rule.[16] Under this particular parameter choice, only for two out of eight country cases, the CV under the public debt targeting framework proposal is higher than under a comparable structural balance rule, but not significantly so.[17]

Cyclically adjusted primary balances also show that the cycle-smoothing properties of the debt targeting proposal are comparable with those of a structural balance rule. Table 6.3 reports the CV of cyclically adjusted primary balances, both for the structural balance rule and public debt targeting. The CV is computed as the standard deviation of the cyclically adjusted primary balances across the 2,000 simulations, and then scaled by the year average for each year of the simulation period 2011–15. The results show that for five out of eight cases, the structural balance rule has more variability in cyclically adjusted primary balances under a structural balance rule, in principle signaling more shock-absorbing capacity compared with public debt targeting.

However, notice that these calculations are based on the same simulations as in Table 6.2, which in general showed a more stable primary expenditure pattern for the public debt targeting framework. This means that, from consolidating the results in Tables 6.2 and 6.3, it is possible to conclude that (1) revenues are, in general, also more stable under public debt targeting (numerator of the CV effect), and/or (2) average (or trend) real growth rates of revenues, GDP, and primary expenditures are also higher under debt targeting (denominator of the CV effect),

[16]The calculations of the CV reported in Table 6.3 exclude the growth rate of primary expenditures in 2011 because for both fiscal policy choices, it captures the initial consolidation required to set public debt on a sustainable path.

[17]Notice that this is not a horse race between the two methodologies, as the results are conditional on the set of parameter choices for each.

TABLE 6.3

Coefficient of Variation of Cyclically Adjusted Primary Balances (Monte Carlo-based simulations, 2011–15)[1]

	2011	2012	2013	2014	2015	Average 2011–2015
Antigua and Barbuda						
Structural balance rule[2]	0.65	1.61	0.56	0.27	0.34	0.69
Public debt targeting[3]	0.41	0.53	0.55	0.40	0.62	0.50
The Bahamas						
Structural balance rule[2]	7.26	2.83	2.82	0.76	1.32	3.00
Public debt targeting[3]	1.32	1.53	0.79	0.59	1.20	1.09
Barbados						
Structural balance rule[2]	0.86	0.94	4.37	0.64	0.72	1.51
Public debt targeting[3]	0.34	3.52	0.90	2.27	9.12	3.23
Grenada						
Structural balance rule[2]	0.24	0.24	0.24	0.22	0.30	0.25
Public debt targeting[3]	0.35	0.20	0.21	0.30	0.39	0.29
Jamaica						
Structural balance rule[2]	0.53	0.71	0.58	0.20	0.28	0.46
Public debt targeting[3]	0.18	0.10	0.32	0.19	0.37	0.23
St. Kitts and Nevis						
Structural balance rule[2]	0.35	1.26	0.69	0.25	0.33	0.58
Public debt targeting[3]	0.82	0.91	1.02	1.26	6.52	2.10
St. Lucia						
Structural balance rule[2]	0.56	3.22	2.73	6.88	13.24	4.94
Public debt targeting[3]	0.41	0.94	0.38	0.74	1.80	0.85
St. Vincent and the Grenadines						
Structural balance rule[2]	1.15	0.66	0.61	1.47	3.23	1.43
Public debt targeting[3]	0.33	0.34	0.67	0.60	2.31	0.85

Sources: Country authorities; and authors' estimates and projections.

[1] The cyclically adjusted primary balances are calculated as revenues scaled by the output gap, minus primary expenditures, and then the difference is divided by potential GDP. The potential GDP and the output gap calculations are based on the HP filter. The coefficients of variation are calculated as the standard deviation of the cyclically adjusted primary balances over the 2,000 simulated series, divided by the average.

[2] Primary expenditure simulations based on a structural primary balance with output gap elasticities of revenues and primary expenditures of 1 and 0, respectively.

[3] All parameters are set as in Table 6.1.

resulting in lower coefficients of variation. This means that the stabilization impact of accounting for the indirect effects under public debt targeting appears to more than offset the direct impact of a structural expenditure rule, which allows more primary balance variability to cushion shocks.

The simulation results on expenditure smoothing confirm the key conceptual difference between public debt targeting and structural balance rules. A structural balance rule does not take into account the indirect non-Keynesian feedback to the rest of the economy. In other words, it implicitly assumes that fiscal policy credibility is high, in the sense that sovereign spreads, interest rates, foreign exchange markets, and capital flows are not perturbed by deficits and debt accumulation. It therefore remains appropriate for countries with full credibility (not countries included in this chapter), or for cases in which credibility problems are resolved solely by the implementation of a structural balance rule consistent with debt sustainability.

Cyclical Properties of Primary Expenditures

Primary expenditures show, in general, a similar degree of co-movement with GDP as a structural balance rule for the set of parameter choices in this experiment. We illustrate this point by computing the correlations of the real growth rates of primary expenditures with the real growth rates of GDP and government revenues for each of the 2,000 simulations. The average correlation is then displayed in Table 6.4. The correlations with GDP of both the structural balance rule and the framework proposal are, as expected, significantly lower than under the historical behavior. Moreover, the correlations with GDP of public debt targeting are higher than under the structural balance rule for five out of eight country cases, but in three of the five cases the difference in correlation is small.[18]

The correlation between the real growth rates of primary expenditures and revenues under public debt targeting is high, however. The average correlation for the country sample is 52 percent for the parameter choice explained. This is not necessarily a limitation of the proposal, as the framework parameters can be set to increase the smoothness of spending (for example, by extending the medium-term horizon beyond five years). In fact, a positive correlation between revenues and expenditures implies that there is a need for a degree of procyclical adjustment, which prevents public debt from growing above the markets' comfort zone. This is, therefore, a concrete feature of the framework proposal, as it forces the

TABLE 6.4

Cyclical Properties of Primary Expenditures (Correlation of growth rates of primary expenditures with GDP and revenues)[1]

	Correlations of Real Growth Rates of Primary Expenditures and GDP			Correlations of Real Growth Rates of Primary Expenditures and Revenues		
	Historical Behavior[2]	Structural Balance Rule[3]	Public Debt Targeting[4]	Historical Behavior[2]	Structural Balance Rule[3]	Public Debt Targeting[4]
Antigua and Barbuda	–0.01	0.12	0.28	0.09	0.87	0.70
Bahamas	0.36	–0.45	0.29	–0.15	0.64	0.37
Barbados	0.33	0.04	0.17	0.03	0.84	0.32
Grenada	0.15	0.01	–0.08	0.65	0.96	0.46
Jamaica	0.08	0.08	0.44	0.30	0.94	0.56
St. Kitts and Nevis	0.78	0.00	0.02	0.49	0.94	0.66
St. Lucia	0.70	–0.41	–0.43	–0.14	0.94	0.77
St. Vincent and the Grenadines	0.25	–0.05	–0.16	0.52	0.94	0.32

Sources: Country authorities; and authors' estimates and projections.
[1]Correlation within each simulation's real growth rates of primary expenditure with GDP and revenues, then averaged for the 2000 simulations.
[2]Primary expenditure simulations based on the estimated VAR coefficients.
[3]Primary expenditure simulations based on a structural primary balance with output gap elasticities of revenues and primary expenditures of 1 and 0, respectively.
[4]Primary expenditure simulations based on the policy proposal in this paper. All parameters are set as in Table 6.1.

[18]These correlations include the initial adjustment for the 2011 budgets reported in Table 2.

policymaker to acknowledge and to make a choice on the trade-off between some degree of procyclical expenditure consolidation (so as to avoid too large a deficit and debt accumulation in bad states of the cycle) and public debt volatility.[19]

Public Debt Smoothing

The points made above raise the issue of the volatility of public debt outcomes when the proposed framework is applied in practice, as an indicator of the change in the sovereign's creditworthiness. To illustrate the quantitative implications in terms of debt smoothing, we compute the dispersion of debt outcomes out of the simulation exercise when the policy framework is applied over a sequence of periods. The results are summarized in Table 6.5. The first observation is that the volatility of the debt-to-GDP ratio by 2015 under the framework proposal appears to be less than one-half of that under historical behavior. In addition, the parameter choice also implies lower average volatility in debt outcomes than under a structural balance rule, with the coefficient of variation being on average about three-fourths of that for the structural balance rule.

Notice that there are two opposite forces at play behind this result. On the one hand, smoother expenditures can result in larger fiscal imbalances and, therefore, higher public debt volatility, for a given pattern of revenues (direct or Keynesian effect). On the other hand, if expenditure smoothing results in smoother macroeconomic outcomes, including not only GDP but also other critical variables

TABLE 6.5

Expected Public Debt Level and Dispersion (Based on simulations for 2015)[1]

	Historical Behavior[2]			Structural Balance Rule[3]			Public Debt Targeting[4]		
	Expected	Std. Dev.	CV	Expected	Std. Dev.	CV	Expected	Std. Dev.	CV
Antigua and Barbuda	160.4	42.3	0.26	120.9	18.0	0.15	114.3	11.0	0.10
Bahamas	79.4	12.5	0.16	64.3	6.7	0.10	60.9	5.3	0.09
Barbados	136.8	15.9	0.12	125.6	12.8	0.10	125.3	10.8	0.09
Grenada	134.6	37.9	0.28	108.9	7.9	0.07	111.3	6.4	0.06
Jamaica	116.9	26.0	0.22	139.1	11.3	0.08	110.9	5.4	0.05
St. Kitts and Nevis	205.3	19.9	0.10	174.7	12.7	0.07	170.7	19.7	0.12
St. Lucia	87.1	21.1	0.24	84.0	8.4	0.10	79.8	5.7	0.07
St. Vincent and the Grenadines	115.0	15.7	0.14	105.2	6.5	0.06	94.9	4.3	0.05

Sources: Country authorities; and authors' estimates and projections.

[1]Public debt and standard deviation of public debt are presented in percent of GDP. Calculated based on a Monte Carlo experiment with 2,000 simulations. CV is the coefficient of variation, calculated as the standard deviation of the debt-to-GDP ratio divided by the mean.

[2]Primary expenditure simulations based on the estimated VAR coefficients.

[3]Primary expenditure simulations based on a structural primary balance with output gap elasticities of revenues and primary expenditures of 1 and 0, respectively.

[4]Primary expenditure simulations based on the policy proposal in this chapter. All parameters are set as in Table 6.1.

---

[19]Notice that the simulation experiment also shows that the average correlation between revenue and GDP growth rates for this sample of countries is 88 percent under a structural balance rule, which is very high. However, this is only the result of a simplistic identification strategy of cyclical revenues, based only on output gap measures with unit revenue elasticity as explained above.

such as real exchange rates and interest rates, the volatility of the debt-to-GDP ratio might actually be lower (indirect or non-Keynesian effect). The simulation results appear to indicate that, as per the parameter estimates in the VAR, the second effect is relatively stronger: the proposed framework generates both smoother primary expenditures and lower volatility of public debt (Figure 6.2).

The fan charts in Figure 6.2 illustrate the main policy announcement under public debt targeting, together with the primary expenditure budget envelope for the next budget cycle. They show the projected trajectory of public debt and its potential dispersion from economic shocks.

This analysis emphasizes the importance of including a measure of debt volatility under public debt targeting. It is possible to develop a similar framework without the use of probabilistic outcomes to assess public debt dynamics (including, if necessary, an additional primary balance surplus amount for prudential purposes). However, such a framework would not capture the impact of shocks on debt dynamics in an appropriate way. This is because, under public debt targeting, the degree of primary surplus reset required after every year's observed shocks is a function not only of the parameter choice but also of the sensitivity of public debt dynamics to shocks, and also of the volatility, persistence, and correlation of the main variables affecting debt dynamics. Furthermore, the trade-offs in terms of debt structure play a critical role in determining the appropriate fiscal stance (for example, all else being equal, requiring more expenditure consolidation if a large share of public debt is denominated in foreign currency). This implies that the economic consideration that is at the heart of the proposal, namely the trade-off between expenditure smoothing and debt smoothing, would not be accounted for appropriately without some measure of dispersion in public debt outcomes.

LIMITATIONS

The main limitation of the public debt targeting proposal is that it requires a sufficiently strong political and societal commitment to fiscal prudence. This limitation extends to fiscal rules and numerical constraints as well. Without a strong willingness and capacity to contain special interests, distributional conflicts, or other political economy pressures, the mere adoption of the framework cannot be expected to deliver the intended results. In other words, we take the view that the causality goes from societal commitment to the adoption of a fiscal framework or rule—either the one proposed here or any other—and not the other way around.

Moreover, even if such societal agreement exists, the framework application requires some more technical preconditions. Fiscal institutions need to be sufficiently developed to appropriately monitor and control the budget (budget processes, fiscal accounting and auditing practices, public financial management, and so on). In particular, it is critical that public debt creation outside the government level used in the framework formulation be addressed for the policy to be credible. For example, the observed changes in central government debt can be significantly larger than accounted for by the reported central government deficit, change in government deposits, prefinancing operations, and valuation changes. This suggests that other sources of debt creation, typically from public entities and other quasi-fiscal bodies, can be important. Ideally, and unlike the examples in this chapter, the framework should be applied to the consolidated government finances, or at least to the most aggregated government definition possible. The budget process and institutions would need to be effective limiting factors to the universe of public entities and bodies, particularly when they can be sources of public debt and contingent liabilities.

In addition, budgets would need to include sufficient provisions for unforeseen spending. For example, in the case of Caribbean countries, natural disasters—such as hurricanes and flooding—usually damage public infrastructure and private property, and typically require government expenditures in excess of the budget. For the framework to work in such an environment, budgeted primary expenditures should include allocations for such contingencies. Otherwise, the framework's objective of enhancing credibility would be weakened, as would result from the need to compensate for additional spending needs with lower current or capital spending in other areas. Expanding the proposal with a specific countercyclical component in case of natural shocks could be a possibility in this regard.

The technical complexity of public debt targeting could be considered a limitation. It could be argued that market participants would need to be sufficiently sophisticated to affect the formation of expectations sought in the proposal. However, we do not believe that this is a major limitation. Indeed, the two main announcements are clear, easy to understand, objective, and practical operationally: a debt trajectory within narrow probabilistic bands and next years' primary expenditure budget envelope. The four intermediate technical parameters, which play the role of mapping the two main announcements, are the complicated part. The need is therefore not necessarily for a framework that allows every taxpayer or bondholder to understand the mechanics of the framework, but for independent and technically able institutions (private and public) that can assess the consistency of the announcement and inform the public.

This is why an independent institutional body (such as a "Fiscal Council") could be an important complement to a debt targeting framework. It could assess consistency and keep the public informed. External institutions could play a role in assisting with the assessment when deemed necessary. In addition, institutional arrangements would need to be set up so that the framework is stable over time, in the sense that changes in the key framework parameters—such as the horizon, the debt threshold level, and probability—do not change from one budget cycle to the next arbitrarily.

DISCUSSION

Public debt targeting can be used as a transitional framework toward the adoption of a structural balance rule. Implicitly, a structural balance rule assumes that there are no significant sovereign debt or credibility problems that can trigger the non-Keynesian effects: expenditures are determined in relation to potential GDP and structural government revenues (consistent with public debt sustainability targets over the long term). The cyclical movements in revenues are not considered critical, and any resulting cyclical deficits can be covered with debt issuance. Implicitly, this assumes that a government is fully credible, in the sense that it can commit not to default on public debt regardless of the circumstances, and therefore faces an infinitely elastic financing supply at low risk premiums regardless of the fiscal deficit and the stock of public debt. As this is not a realistic assumption for many countries, a fiscal policy framework that seeks to smooth the business cycle needs to incorporate the indirect effects from deterioration of the sovereign's creditworthiness in bad states of the cycle.

If public debt is high, access to financing may be too costly at the time it is needed the most (or just unavailable), and could have destabilizing indirect effects on the rest of the economy through increases in sovereign interest premiums and on credit and foreign exchange markets more generally. In the public debt targeting framework, these indirect effects are accounted for explicitly, and the choice of technical intermediate parameters allows the best compromise between avoiding sharp changes in government expenditure and avoiding sharp changes in public debt. As public debt targeting is consistently applied over time and public debt declines to sufficiently low levels, indirect effects would eventually become less important and countries could adopt structural balance rules.

The proposal also is consistent with political economy constraints on fiscal policy decisions. First, although the proposal finds its rationale in the constraints imposed by financial markets, it does not imply that the impact of political economy factors on fiscal performance is minimized in any way. On the contrary, the proposal takes as a fact the possibility of the existence of political economy factors as a reason for fiscal sustainability problems and excessive debt accumulation. If so, financial markets may end up setting the limit eventually. And second, a sufficiently high level of political and social consensus on the value of a sustainable fiscal stance is a core precondition if this proposal is expected to be effective. Moreover, even if social consensus is already sufficiently high, institutional (formal or informal) incentives might distort decisions away from the desired collective objective.

CONCLUSION

Avoiding the procyclical fiscal policy bias observed in most of the developing world has a direct impact on smoothing aggregate demand (Keynesian effects). However, eliminating altogether the procyclical fiscal policy bias may not always be optimal in terms of smoothing aggregate demand. This is because countries with sufficiently high public debt (those with marginal increases in public debt that have a first-order impact ON investors' perception of sovereign risk) might find it optimal to pursue some degree of fiscal consolidation during recessions to minimize the resulting deterioration in creditworthiness. This can result in an increase in sovereign spreads and domestic interest rates, and all the associated collateral damage, including crowding out of private investment and consumption (non-Keynesian effects). If public debt is already sufficiently high, excessive deficit and debt accumulation in low states can drag an economy into a negative spiral of high interest rates, credit crunch, and output decline.

This chapter has proposed a fiscal policy framework that balances out these two opposite effects, based on setting primary expenditure budget envelopes consistent with probabilistic debt sustainability outcomes. The proposal is based on policymakers' announcement of two main indicators: a medium-term debt trajectory with the corresponding probability bands and a budget envelope for primary expenditures in the next budget cycle. These two announcements are easy to communicate and simple to understand for the general public, which is critical in order to anchor expectations on a sovereign's fiscally sustainable path (implied by a declining debt trajectory that is resilient to shocks) while also avoiding the need for sharp expenditure consolidation during bad periods of the cycle (which could also undermine fiscal sustainability prospects given possible social and political resistance). Overall, the framework proposal puts a premium on the need to assure financial markets of fiscal sustainability as key to smoothing the business cycle by taking into account the indirect (non-Keynesian) effects from deterioration in a government's creditworthiness in lieu of focusing only on the direct impact of fiscal policy on aggregate demand.

Monte Carlo simulations for a sample of highly-indebted Caribbean economies show that, for a set of plausible parameter choices, the public debt targeting framework can reduce primary expenditure's procyclical bias while reducing the volatility of public debt. Empirically, it is shown that for the Caribbean countries in the sample and within a VAR methodology, these indirect effects more than offset the direct impact of procyclical adjustments required to avoid excessive debt accumulation on aggregate demand.

The proposal has some operational advantages. First, possible transparency issues related to distinguishing permanent from transitory shocks (for example, as in structural balance rules) are eliminated. Instead, spending levels are determined based on projected public debt dynamics, which is simpler and more transparent, as these are anchored around the debt accumulation identity. Second, the methodology forces the use of a broad set of variables to determine appropriate primary spending levels that capture the state of the business cycle, given the wide set of indicators needed to produce debt projections (including interest rates and real exchange rates). Third, it tackles the impact of debt sustainability concerns on the business cycle directly, given the explicit commitment to public debt thresholds and a debt trajectory band. And fourth, the framework can be designed to allow for a cyclical space for discretionary primary spending, possibly including a state-contingent additional primary expenditure component, but without necessarily allowing full discretion.

APPENDIX 6.1. SOVEREIGN DEBT DYNAMICS

Debt-to-GDP dynamics takes into account that the government issues both bonds denominated in local currency and bonds denominated in foreign currency, as well as borrows from bilateral and/or multilateral lenders (which we call, for simplicity, "official debt"). Thus, the stock of debt at the end of period t, denoted by D_t equals the sum of the debt denominated in domestic currency, D_t^d; the debt denominated in foreign currency (typically U.S. dollars), D_t^f, converted to domestic currency at the existing nominal exchange rate, e_t (units of domestic currency per unit of foreign currency); and the official debt (also denominated in U.S. dollars) $D_t^o : D_t = D_t^d + e_t D_t^f + e_t D_t^o$. This relationship can be converted in terms of ratios to GDP by dividing both sides by nominal GDP (expressed in local currency), Y_t:

$$d_t = d_t^d + d_t^f + d_t^o, \tag{A1}$$

where $d_t^d = \dfrac{D_t^d}{Y_t}, d_t^f = \dfrac{e_t D_t^f}{Y_t}, d_t^o = \dfrac{e_t D_t^o}{Y_t}$.

The dynamics of the domestic-currency-denominated debt is described by the government's flow budget identity $D_t^d = (1+i_t)D_{t-1}^d - \alpha_t \beta_t$, where i_t is the interest rate on local-currency-denominated government debt whose maturity is at time t, B_t is the primary balance, and $\alpha_t \in [0,1]$ is the fraction of primary balance used to service the domestic debt exposure. The primary balance is defined as $B_t = T_t - G_t$, where T_t is the revenue collected and G_t represents the non-interest public spending. The budget identity can be expressed in terms of ratios to GDP by dividing both sides by Y_t:

$$\frac{D_t^d}{Y_t} = \frac{Y_{t-1}}{Y_t}\frac{D_{t-1}^d}{Y_{t-1}}(1+i_t) - \alpha_t \frac{B_t}{Y_t},$$

$$d_t^d = \frac{1+i_t}{1+y_t} d_{t-1} - \alpha_t b_t,$$

where y_t is the growth rate of nominal GDP and b_t is the ratio of primary balance to GDP. Deflating the nominal growth rate by the inflation rate, π_t, the flow of budget identity can be expressed in the terms below, for real growth rate, g_t:

$$d_t^d = \frac{(1+i_t)}{(1+\pi_t)(1+g_t)} d_{t-1} - \alpha_t. \tag{A2}$$

Analogously, the dynamics of the foreign-currency-denominated debt is described by the following first-order difference equation:

$$D_t^f = (1+i_t^f)D_{t-1}^d - \beta_t \frac{B_t}{e_t},$$

where i_t^f is the nominal interest rate paid on government bonds denominated in foreign currency whose maturity is at time t, and $\beta_t \in [0,1]$ is the fraction of primary balance used to service the foreign commercial debt exposure. Multiplying both sides by e_t and dividing through by Y_t yields the following:

$$\frac{e_t D_t^f}{Y_t} = \frac{e_t}{e_{t-1}} \frac{Y_{t-1}}{Y_t} \frac{e_{t-1} D_{t-1}^f}{Y_{t-1}} \left(1 + i_t^f\right) - \beta_t \frac{B_t}{Y_t},$$

$$d_t^f = \frac{(1+\in_t)(1+i_t^f)}{(1+y_t)} d_{t-1}^f - \beta_t b_t,$$

where $\in_t$ represents the nominal exchange rate depreciation. By deflating both the nominal growth factor and the nominal exchange rate factor by the domestic inflation rate, the above expression can be expressed in terms of the real growth rate g_t, the real exchange rate depreciation η_t, and the real interest rate paid on foreign commercial debt $(1+i_t^f)/(1+\pi_t^*)$:

$$d_t^f = \frac{\left(1+\eta_t\right)\left(1+i_t^f\right)}{\left(1+g_t\right)\left(1+\pi_t^*\right)} d_{t-1}^f - \beta_t b_t. \tag{A3}$$

The dynamics of the official debt-to-GDP ratio is analogous to the one above. A substantial difference is that typically the interest rate applied by bilateral or multilateral lenders, i_t^o, is lower than the market rate:

$$d_t^o = \frac{\left(1+\eta_t\right)\left(1+i_t^o\right)}{\left(1+g_t\right)\left(1+\pi_t^*\right)} d_{t-1}^o - \left(1-\alpha_t-\beta_t\right) b_t. \tag{A4}$$

Another difference across various components of sovereign debt is that the average maturity of each class of debt differs. We take these differences into account when we compute the interest rate paid in every period. Let m^d, m^f, and m^o be the average maturities of domestic, foreign, and official debt, respectively, and ι_t^d, ι_t^f, and ι_t^o be the one-period government bond rate for the afore-mentioned classes of sovereign debt. Then:

$$i_t^d = \frac{1}{m^d} \sum_{n=1}^{m^d} \iota_{t-n}^d, \qquad i_t^f = \frac{1}{m^f} \sum_{n=1}^{m^f} \iota_{t-n}^f, \qquad i_t^o = \frac{1}{m^o} \sum_{n=1}^{m^o} \iota_{t-n}^o.$$

The nominal interest rate paid on one-period commercial bonds denominated in foreign currency, ι_t^f, can be computed as the sum of an international risk-free rate, i_t^*, and a spread σ_t^f representing the country's sovereign risk: $\iota_t^f = i_t^* + \sigma_t^f$. Similarly, $\iota_t^o = i_t^* + \sigma_t^o$, where typically the spread paid to multilateral and bilateral lenders, σ_t^o, is lower than that paid to international financial markets, σ_t^f.

Finally, as information on the fraction of primary balance servicing each component of debt is not available, we assume that at time t, the fraction of primary balance that services a certain component of debt is proportional to the existing share of debt of a particular type over the total:

$$\alpha_t = \frac{d_{t-1}^d}{d_{t-1}}, \quad \beta_t = \frac{d_{t-1}^f}{d_{t-1}}.$$

Summing up Equations (A2) to (A4) yields the initial Equation (A1).

REFERENCES

Aizenman, J., M. Gavin, and R. Haussman, 1996, "Optimal Tax Policy with Endogenous Borrowing Constraint," NBER Working Paper No. 5338 (Cambridge, Massachusetts: National Bureau of Economic Research).

Alesina, A., and R. Perotti, 1994, "The Political Economy of Budget Deficits," NBER Working Paper No. 4637 (Cambridge, Massachusetts: National Bureau of Economic Research).

Atkeson, A., 1991, "International Lending with Moral Hazard and Risk of Repudiation," *Econometrica*, Vol. 59 (4), pp. 1069–89.

Backus, D., P. Kehoe, and F. Kydland, 1992, "International Real Business Cycles," *Journal of Political Economy,* No. 100, pp. 745–75.

Balassone, F., and M. Kumar, 2007, "Cyclicality of Fiscal Policy," in *Promoting Fiscal Discipline*, Chapter 3 (Washington: International Monetary Fund).

Berg, A., and J. Sachs, 1988, "The Debt Crisis, Structural Explanations of Country Performance," *Journal of Development Economics,* No. 29, pp. 271–306.

Blanchard, O., 1985, "Debt, Deficits, and Finite Horizons," *Journal of Political Economy*, No. 93 (April), pp. 223–47.

Bornhorst, F., G. Dobrescu, A. Fedelino, J. Gottschalk, and T. Nakata, 2011, "When and How to Adjust Beyond the Business Cycle? A Guide to Structural Fiscal Balances," *IMF Technical Note and Manuals 11/02* (Washington: International Monetary Fund).

Bulow, J., and K. Rogoff, 1989a, "Sovereign Debt: Is to Forgive to Forget?" *American Economic Review,* No. 79, pp. 43–50.

Catao, L., and B. Sutton, 2002, "Sovereign Defaults: The Role of Volatility," IMF Working Paper 02/149 (Washington: International Monetary Fund).

Celasun, O., X. Debrun, and J. Ostry, 2007, "Primary Surplus Behavior and Risks to Fiscal Sustainability in Emerging Market Countries: A 'Fan-Chart' Approach," *IMF Staff Papers*, Vol. 53, No. 3.

Chari, V., and H. Cole, 1995, "A Contribution to the Theory of Pork Barrel Spending," Federal Reserve Bank of Minneapolis.

Chuhan, P., S. Claessens, and N. Mamingi, 1998, "Equity and Bond Flows to Latin America and Asia: The Role of Global and Country Factors," *Journal of Development Economics,* No. 55 (April), pp. 439–63.

Cline, W., and K. Barnes, 1997, "Spreads and Risk in Emerging Markets Lending," *Institute of International Finance*, Institute of International Finance Research Paper No. 97–1 (Washington).

Edwards, S., 1986, "The Pricing of Bonds and Bank Loans in International Markets. An Empirical Analysis of Developing Countries' Foreign Borrowing," *European Economic Review,* No. 30, pp. 565–89.

Eichengreen, B., and A. Mody, 1998, "What Explains Changing Spreads on Emerging Market Debt: Fundamentals or Market Sentiment?" NBER Working Paper No. 6408 (Cambridge, Massachusetts: National Bureau of Economic Research).

Garcia, M., and R. Rigobon, 2005, "A Risk Management Approach to Emerging Market's Sovereign Debt Sustainability with an Application to Brazilian Data," NBER Working Paper No. 10336 (Cambridge, Massachusetts: National Bureau of Economic Research).

Gavin, M., R. Haussman, R. Perotti, and E. Talvi, 1996, "Managing Fiscal Policy in Latin America," Working Paper No. 325, Office of the Chief Economist (Washington: Inter-American Development Bank).

Gavin, M., and R. Perotti, 1997, "Fiscal Policy in Latin America," in NBER *Macroeconomics Annual 1997* (Cambridge, Massachusetts: MIT Press).

International Monetary Fund, 2010, *World Economic Outlook: Recovery, Risk, and Rebalancing*, World Economic and Financial Surveys (Washington, October).

Kaminsky, G., and C. Reinhart, 2000, "On Crises, Contagion and Confusion," *Journal of International Economics*, Vol. 51 (June), pp. 145–68.

———, and C. Vegh, 2004, "When It Rains It Pours: Procyclical Capital Flows and Macroeconomic Policies," NBER Working Paper No. 10780 (Cambridge, Massachusetts: National Bureau of Economic Research).

Kopits, G., and S. Symansky, 1998, *Fiscal Policy Rules,* IMF Occasional Paper No. 162 (Washington: International Monetary Fund).
Masson, P., 1985, "The Sustainability of Fiscal Deficits," *IMF Staff Papers,* Vol. 32 (August), pp. 577–605 (Washington: International Monetary Fund).
Min, H., 1998, "Determinants of Emerging Market Bond Spread: Do Economic Fundamentals Matter?" Policy Research Paper No. 1899 (Washington: World Bank).
Penalver, A., and G. Thwaites, 2006, "Fiscal Rules for Debt Sustainability in Emerging Markets: The Impact of Volatility and Default Risk," Bank of England Working Paper No. 307 (London). http://papers.ssrn.com/sol3/papers.cfm?abstract_id=933299.
Perotti, R., 1997b, "Fiscal Policy and Saving in Good Times and Bad Times," in *Promoting Savings in Latin America,* ed. by Ricardo Haussman and Helmut Reisen.
Reinhart, C., K. Rogoff, and M. Savastano, 2002, "Debt Intolerance," unpublished (Washington: International Monetary Fund).
Talvi, E., and C. Vegh, 2000, "Tax Base Variability and Procyclical Fiscal Policy," NBER Working Paper No. 7499 (Cambridge, Massachusetts: National Bureau of Economic Research).
Tanner, E., 2003, "Fiscal Rules and Countercyclical Policy, Frank Ramsey Meets Gramm-Rudman-Hollings," IMF Working Paper 03/220 (Washington: International Monetary Fund).
Tanner, E., and I. Samake, 2008, "Probabilistic Sustainability of Public Debt: A Vector Autoregression Approach for Brazil, Mexico, and Turkey," *IMF Staff Papers,* Vol. 55, No. 1.

PART V

Monetary Policy and Dedollarization

CHAPTER 7

What Is Driving Financial Dedollarization in Latin America?

MERCEDES GARCÍA-ESCRIBANO AND SEBASTIÁN SOSA

Financial dollarization—the process in which a large share of residents' assets and liabilities are denominated in U.S. dollars—has been a distinguishing feature of the banking sector of many countries in Latin America, making it one of the most dollarized regions in the world. Financial dollarization is typically a consequence of past episodes of severe economic crisis and high inflation that made the U.S. dollar the preferred currency to minimize risks for both savers and lenders. When economic stability was restored and inflation declined, dollarization ratios of deposits and loans have usually remained high. Hence, financial dollarization continues to be a source of concern for policymakers because it contributes to the vulnerability of the banking system to exchange rate fluctuations.

During the past decade, some Latin American countries with high dollarization ratios in the early 2000s experienced a gradual and sustained decline in financial dollarization. Prominent examples of successful market-friendly dedollarization processes include Bolivia, Paraguay, Peru, and Uruguay (Figure 7.1).

What explains dedollarization? What could countries do to overcome dollarization hysteresis? A great deal of work exists on the causes of financial dollarization, yet the empirical literature on the causes of dedollarization is scant. Although financial dollarization is widely accepted at least in part as an optimal response to periods of particular uncertainty that undermined confidence in the local currency, the persistence of high dollarization ratios after periods in which inflation fell substantially is still a puzzle. One explanation, introduced by Ize and Levy-Yeyati (2003), argues that price instability is not enough to explain financial dollarization. They developed a model of optimal portfolio choice of risk-averse borrowers and lenders in which the equilibrium level of deposit dollarization depends on the relative price and real exchange rate volatility.[1] Another strand of the

[1]Specifically, their minimum variance portfolio (MVP) model implies that if real exchange depreciation is less volatile than inflation, then consumers would prefer to hold U.S. dollar deposits, as it is less risky. The authors test the model using cross-sectional data on deposit dollarization for 23 countries. De Nicolõ, Honokan, and Ize (2005) and Rennhack and Nozaki (2006) provide evidence supporting the MVP hypothesis.

Figure 7.1 Financial Dollarization in Selected Latin American Countries

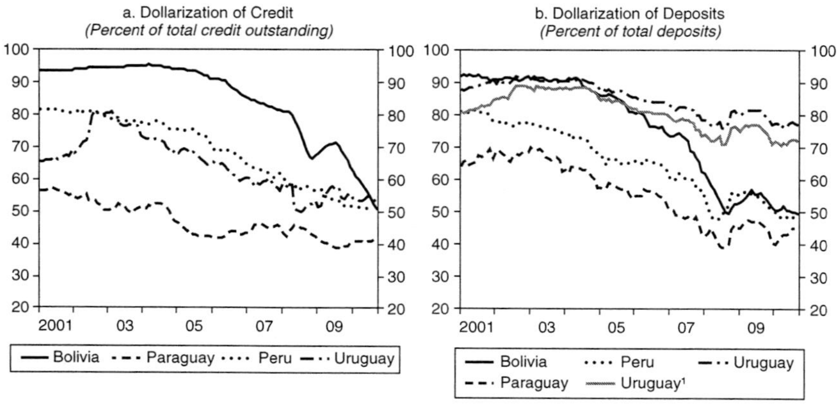

Source: IMF staff calculations.
[1] Excludes foreign currency deposits for nonresidents.

literature highlights the role of currency-blind regulatory frameworks—for example, Broda and Levy-Yeyati (2003) argue that explicit deposit insurance that applies uniformly across all deposits exacerbates deposit dollarization.

Reinhart, Rogoff, and Savastano (2003), Galindo and Leiderman (2005), and Erasmus, Leichter, and Menkulasi (2009) review the international experience on dedollarization. They highlight that dollarization persists after periods of substantial decline in inflation and after macroeconomic stability has been restored. Cases of forced dedollarization—for example, Bolivia and Peru in the 1980s—have entailed high macroeconomic costs, and dollarization quickly returned.[2] On the contrary, successful cases have been market based and combined macroeconomic stability with other policies (such as capital market development in local currency).[3] Kokenyne, Ley, and Veyrune (2010), using data on deposit and credit dollarization for a sample of 32 emerging markets between 2001 and 2009, find that higher exchange rate volatility coupled with stable inflation fosters dedollarization. García-Escribano (2010) analyzes dedollarization across categories of loans and deposits in Peru and finds that dedollarization has been driven by macroeconomic stability, the introduction of prudential policies (such as an active management of reserve requirements) to better reflect currency risk, and the

[2]In the 1980s, Bolivia and Peru forced the conversion of foreign currency deposits to local currency, resulting in capital flight and financial disintermediation. When the restriction on foreign currency deposits was lifted, redollarization was rapid.

[3]Reinhart, Rogoff, and Savastano (2003) identify only four successful cases (Israel, Mexico, Pakistan, and Poland), among a group of 86 countries, of significant and persistent deposit dedollarization. Galindo and Leiderman (2005) identify the cases of Chile, Israel, and Poland as successful.

development of the capital market in local currency (for example, through the issuance of long-term treasuries in Peruvian soles) that facilitated bank funding and pricing of long-term loans in domestic currency.

The main purpose of this chapter is to explore the short-term drivers of financial dedollarization in Bolivia, Paraguay, Peru, and Uruguay. A standard unrestricted vector autoregression (VAR) is used to examine the role of three sets of factors—macroeconomic variables, prudential regulations, and the development of the capital market in domestic currency—as drivers of dedollarization of both credit and deposits in these countries.

The main results are as follows:

- Drivers of deposit dedollarization are different from those of credit dedollarization.
- The appreciation trends experienced during the last decade have been key for deposit dedollarization in these countries.
- Active management of reserve requirement differentials has contributed to credit dedollarization.
- The introduction of other prudential measures to create incentives to internalize the risks of dollarization (such as higher provision requirements for foreign currency loans and tighter limits on banks' net open position) has also fostered credit dedollarization.
- The extension of the domestic currency yield curve has facilitated credit dedollarization.
- Dedollarization of deposits has also contributed to credit dedollarization.

DEDOLLARIZATION TREND—STYLIZED FACTS

Dedollarization has gradually declined in Bolivia, Paraguay, Peru, and Uruguay following the successful implementation of macroeconomic stabilization policies. Figure 7.2 shows the evolution of dollarization, with deposits and credits in foreign currency evaluated at a constant exchange rate to exclude changes in dollarization owing to valuation effects. Deposit dollarization in Bolivia and Peru sharply increased following the collapse of Lehman Brothers, but quickly reversed thereafter.

Deposit dollarization declined (on average) by 27 percentage points between 2001:Q1 and 2010:Q3 (Table 7.1). But there are cross-country differences: although deposit dollarization fell by 42 percentage points in Bolivia, it only declined by 10½ percentage points in Uruguay. The average decline in credit dollarization has been similar, amounting to 26 percent, with falls ranging from 41 percentage points in Bolivia to 15 percentage points in Paraguay. The decline in deposit dollarization matched the decline in credit dollarization in Bolivia and Peru, although the reduction in the share of foreign currency deposits was larger in Paraguay and smaller in Uruguay.

Figure 7.2 Financial Dollarization in Selected Latin American Countries

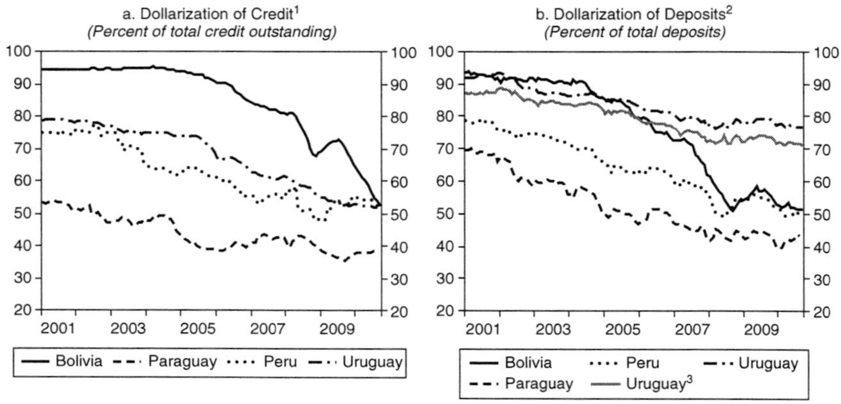

Source: IMF staff calculations.
[1] Foreign currency credit evaluated at constant exchange rate.
[2] Foreign currency deposits evaluated at constant exchange rate.
[3] Excludes nonresident foreign currency deposits.

TABLE 7.1

Dedollarization 2001–10[1] (Percent)

		Dollarization		Dedollarization
		2001:Q1	2010:Q3	2001–2010
Bolivia	Deposits	93.2	51.4	–41.8
	Credit	94.4	53.8	–40.7
Paraguay	Deposits	69.7	43.5	–26.1
	Credit	53.3	38.6	–14.7
Peru	Deposits	78.5	49.7	–28.7
	Credit	78.9	52.1	–26.8
Uruguay	Deposits[2]	87.0	76.6	–10.4
	Credit	75.1	52.5	–22.6
Average	Deposits	82.1	55.3	–26.8
	Credit	75.4	49.2	–26.2

Source: authors' calculations.
[1]Foreign currency deposits and credit evaluated at constant exchange rate.
[2]Excludes nonresident foreign currency deposits.

Dollarization is higher for less liquid deposits. Despite the differences in dollarization across deposits of different maturities, dollarization declined for all types of deposits (Figure 7.3). In other words, the decline in deposit dollarization reflects a dollarization decline within deposit maturities and not just compositional changes between deposits of different maturity structure. Similarly, dollarization differs across types of credit, and it is higher for loans with longer maturities (that is, mortgages and commercial credit). All credit sectors

Figure 7.3 Deposit Dollarization by Maturity

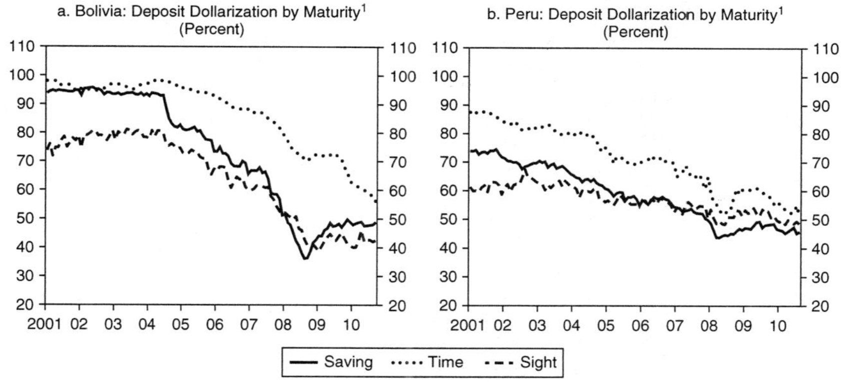

Source: IMF staff calculations.
[1] Foreign currency deposits evaluated at constant exchange rate.

Figure 7.4 Credit Dollarization by Category

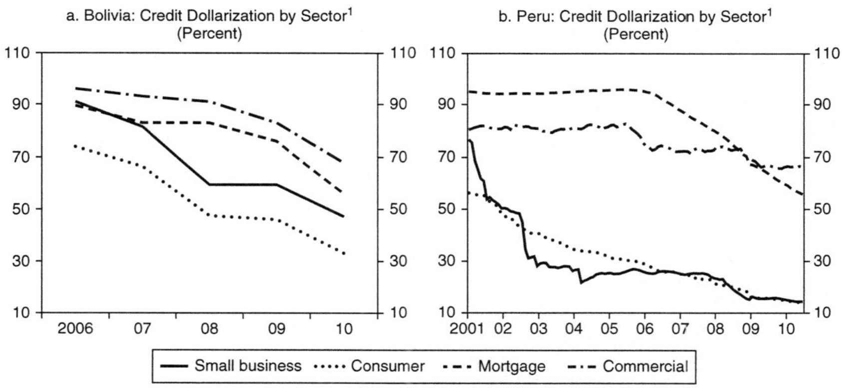

Source: IMF staff calculations.
[1] Foreign currency credit evaluated at constant exchange rate.

exhibited a decline in dollarization during the past decade (Figure 7.4).[4] Hence, dedollarization of credit has been driven mainly by dedollarization changes within each type of credit and not only by compositional changes in credit between sectors. Following García-Escribano (2010), Table 7.2 decomposes the

[4]Figures 7.3 and 7.4 illustrate the evolution of dollarization for each category of deposit and credit in Bolivia and Peru, where data with this breakdown are available.

TABLE 7.2

Peru: Decomposition of Dedollarization—Within and Between Components

a. Credit[1]

	Dollarization		Share in Total Credit (Percent)		2001–2010		
Sectors	**2001**	**2010**	**2001**	**2010**	**Between Effect**	**Within Effect**	**Total Effect**
Commercial	80.8	66.4	79.0	63.1	−10.5	−11.4	−21.9
Small business	50.3	14.4	2.6	6.0	0.5	−0.9	−0.4
Consumer	47.8	14.0	9.0	17.0	1.1	−3.0	−1.9
Mortgage	94.1	55.8	9.4	13.9	2.5	−3.6	−1.1
Total	**78.3**	**52.9**	**100**	**100**	**−6.4**	**−18.9**	**−25.4**

b. Deposits[1]

	Dollarization		Share in Total Deposits (Percent)		2001–2010		
Maturities	**2001**	**2010**	**2001**	**2010**	**Between Effect**	**Within Effect**	**Total Effect**
Sight	58.7	48.4	19.1	30.1	5.3	−2.0	3.4
Saving	71.7	45.7	32.1	26.8	−2.4	−8.3	−10.8
Time	84.6	50.8	48.9	43.1	−2.9	−16.5	−19.4
Total	**75.5**	**48.7**	**100**	**100**	**0.0**	**−26.8**	**−26.8**

Sources: Banco Central de Reserva del Pteru (BCRP); Superintendencia de Banca, Seguros y Administradoras Privadas de Fondos de Pensiones (SBS); and IMF staff calculations.

[1] Credit and deposits in foreign currency are evaluated at a constant nominal exchange rate. Data for credit (deposits) extend until June (August) 2010.

changes in credit and deposit dollarization for Peru into a "within" and "between" component.[5]

EXPLAINING DEDOLLARIZATION: EMPIRICAL APPROACH

This section describes the methodology and the three groups of factors—specifically, macroeconomic conditions, prudential policy measures, and the development of a capital market in domestic currency—that could have affected banks' and agents' preferences for borrowing and lending in domestic and foreign currency.

[5]Changes in credit dollarization through time can be decomposed as:

$$d_t - d_\tau = \sum_{i=1}^{I} d_{it}\frac{c_{it}}{c_t} - \sum_{i=1}^{I} d_{i\tau}\frac{c_{i\tau}}{c_\tau} = \sum_{i=1}^{I}(d_{it} - d_{i\tau})\frac{c_{it}}{c_t} + \sum_{i=1}^{I} d_{i\tau}\left(\frac{c_{it}}{c_t} - \frac{c_{i\tau}}{c_\tau}\right),$$

where d_{it} is dollarization of credit in sector i in year t, and c_{it} is the total credit extended to sector i in year t. The first term captures the time-series changes in dollarization within sectors. The second term captures the effect of changes in credit composition. A similar decomposition can be done for deposits.

Methodology

The empirical approach used to examine the drivers of short-term variations in both deposit and credit dollarization is a standard country-specific unrestricted VAR model. In addition to changes in credit and deposit dollarization, the model also includes three sets of variables:

1. Macroeconomic variables,
2. Introduction of prudential measures to create incentives for agents to internalize the risks of financial dollarization, and
3. Development of a capital market in domestic currency.

The variables included in each of these groups are defined in Table 7.3. The selection of these variables is mainly driven by the existing literature.

The identification strategy used is a standard Choleski decomposition, and the selected ordering is as follows: (1) introduction of prudential measures in the financial sector; (2) extension of the yield curve for public bonds in local currency; (3) macroeconomic variables; (4) change in deposit dollarization; and (5) change in credit dollarization. The main results, however, are robust to different ordering of the variables in the model.

The model is estimated with three lags (and six lags in an alternative specification, to check robustness), using monthly data from January 2001 through September 2010 (starting in 2003 and 2004 for Bolivia and Uruguay, respectively, to exclude the financial crises in these countries from the sample).

TABLE 7.3

Definition of Variables in the Vector Autoregression

Macroeconomic variables	
$Inflation_t$	Sum over t and $t-1$ of the monthly percent change of the consumer price index
e_t	Sum over t and $t-1$ of the monthly percent change of the nominal exchange rate
s_t	Standard deviation of the daily percent change of the nominal exchange rate over 90 days
$\Delta embi_t$	First-difference of the EMBI spread, divided by 100
Prudential measures	
ΔRR_t	Difference over t and $t-2$ of the spread between the required reserve rate on foreign currency deposits and the rate on domestic currency deposits (in percent)
d_t	Dummy equal to 1 (for three months) after the introduction of prudential measures (other than changes in reserve requirements); zero otherwise
Development of domestic capital market	
d_t^{10-30}	Dummy equal to 1 if medium- to long-term bonds (between 10 and 30 years, depending on the country) were issued in that month; zero otherwise
Financial dollarization	
ΔDL_t	Change over t and $t-1$ of the deposit dollarization ratio
ΔCL_t	Change over t and $t-1$ of the credit dollarization ratio

Note: EMBI = JPMorgan's Emerging Market Bond Index. Deposit and credit dollarization are computed at a constant exchange rate. In Peru, where data are available, dollarization ratios are computed using December 2008 weights; hence changes in dollarization do not reflect composition changes between categories of credit and deposits.

Macroeconomic Variables—Role of Exchange Rate Trend and Volatility

Dedollarization has followed the successful implementation of macroeconomic stabilization policies, which have resulted in low inflation, anchored inflation expectations, gradual appreciation of currencies, and generally stronger fundamentals. Figure 7.5 shows that, unlike during the previous decades, which were characterized by high inflation, these four countries have successfully contained inflation during the period of analysis.

The decline in dollarization during the past decade in these four countries has been accompanied by an exchange rate appreciation trend (Figures 7.6 and 7.7). The empirical analysis in the next section examines whether this appreciation trend has been an important factor explaining dedollarization by testing if months with greater appreciation led to a faster decline in deposit dollarization.

As dollarization rates declined (and hence, vulnerabilities associated with financial dollarization were contained) and preconditions for macroeconomic stability were in place, monetary authorities seem to have had a greater tolerance for exchange rate volatility in some of these countries. A strand of the literature looks at the opposite direction of causality, suggesting that financial dollarization is influenced by exchange rate volatility. However, the evidence of this relationship is mixed. Kokenyne, Ley, and Veyrune (2010) show that "two-way" exchange rate volatility fosters dedollarization by rendering foreign exchange risk more apparent. Barajas and Morales (2003) provide evidence that greater exchange rate volatility reduces credit dollarization in a sample of Latin American countries. García-Escribano (2010) and Luca and Petrova (2008) find similar results for Peru and a sample of transition economies, respectively. In contrast, Berkmen and Cavallo (2010), Rennhack and Nozaki (2006), and Neanidis and Savva (2009) do not find evidence that a more flexible exchange rate regime, by itself, promotes

Figure 7.5 Inflation (Average annual inflation; percent)

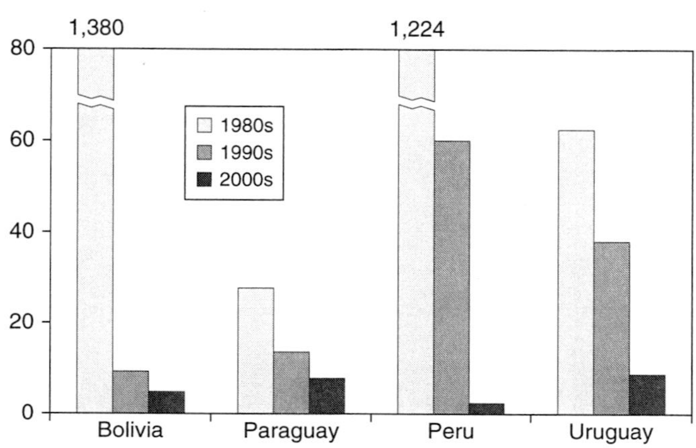

Source: IMF staff calculations.

Figure 7.6 Changes in the Exchange Rate and Dollarization Ratios, 2003–10[1,2]

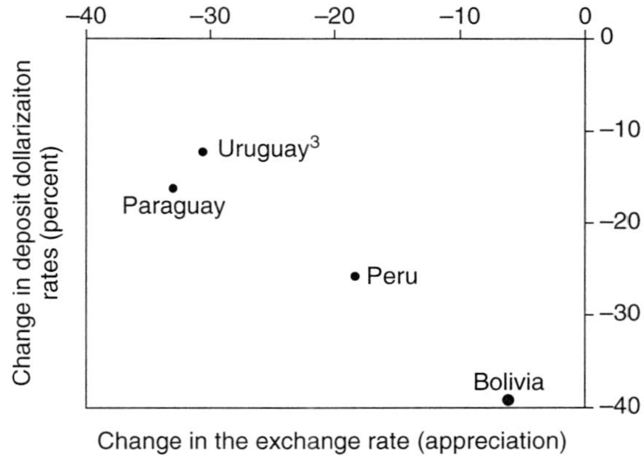

Source: IMF staff calculations.
[1]Nominal exchange rate (domestic currency/U.S. dollar). Data extend until August 2010. Data for Uruguay start in January 2004.
[2]Foreign currency deposits evaluated at constant exchange rate.
[3]Excludes foreign currency deposits for nonresidents.

Figure 7.7 Nominal Exchange Rate and Dollarization[1]

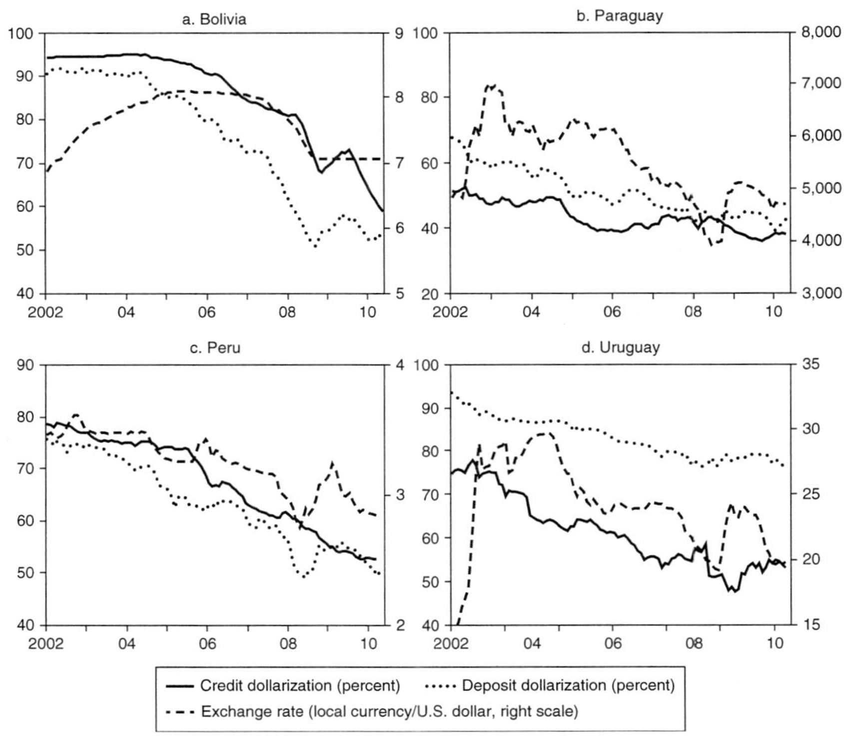

Source: IMF staff calculations.
[1]Foreign currency deposits and credit evaluated at constant exchange rate.

Figure 7.8 Exchange Rate Volatility and Changes in Dollarization[1]

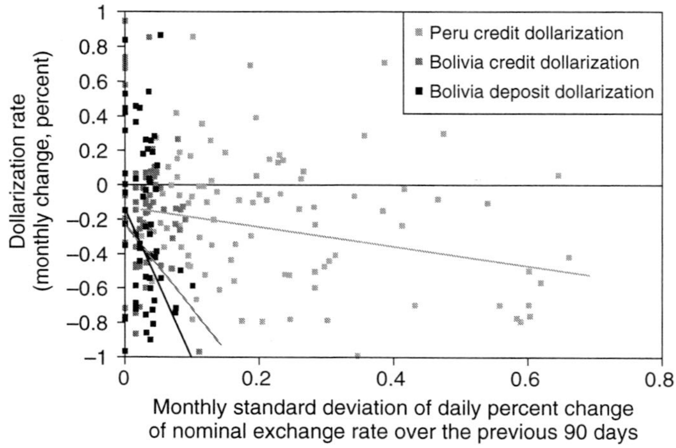

Source: IMF staff calculations.
[1]Foreign currency credit and deposits evaluated at constant exchange rate.

dedollarization. Arteta (2005) finds that more flexibility is actually associated with higher dollarization, especially in the case of deposits. Figure 7.8 shows that higher exchange rate volatility associated with an appreciation trend has been accompanied by a fall in dollarization in the case of credit in Bolivia and Peru, and deposits in Bolivia.

Introduction of Prudential Measures

During the past decade, Bolivia, Paraguay, Peru, and Uruguay introduced different prudential measures to lower banks' incentives to borrow and lend in foreign currency, as well as to diminish agents' preferences for using foreign currency as a means of payment.

Bolivia and Peru have raised provisions for foreign currency loans.[6] Bolivia, Paraguay, Peru, and Uruguay have tightened capital requirements against open foreign exchange positions.[7] Uruguay has required differentiated capital risk weights on foreign currency loans since mid-2006. Bolivia introduced a financial

[6]Since early 2009, Bolivian banks are required to constitute an additional provision of up to 1.5 percent for foreign-currency-denominated loans classified as "A" (best quality). Since mid-2006, Peruvian banks have to carry out a routine evaluation of currency risks or, alternatively, set up an additional reserve ranging from 0.25 percent to 1 percent for credit in foreign currency that has not been evaluated.

[7]Bolivia reduced the limit for a bank's long open position to 60 percent, from 70 percent, in late 2009. Paraguay introduced a net open position limit of 50 percent of capital in mid-2007, and reduced the limit on the long position to 30 percent in late 2008. Peru changed the limit to banks' long (short) open position to 75 (15) percent of capital in early 2010, from a previous limit of 100 (10) percent

transaction tax on foreign currency debits and credits, but exempted transactions in bolivianos (mid-2006).

Moreover, these four countries have implemented active management of their reserve requirements.[8] In particular, increases in the spread between the required reserve requirement ratios on foreign currency deposits and domestic currency deposits seem to have fostered dedollarization of deposits and credits. Following changes in reserve requirement ratios, the remuneration rates have been modified.[9]

In addition to the financial prudential measures listed above, the regulatory framework of these countries includes other measures—such as asymmetric liquidity requirements for foreign and domestic currency liabilities in Peru—with an impact on banking dollarization, but because these were not modified or introduced during the period of analysis, they are not considered in the empirical analysis.

Capital Market Development in Local Currency

Credit dedollarization seems to have been facilitated by the development of the capital market in local currency, in particular through the issuance of long-term public bonds in domestic currency. With the exception of Paraguay, these countries have been actively developing their public debt market in domestic currency in recent years (Figure 7.9). Bolivia, Peru, and Uruguay have issued public bonds in domestic currency with maturities exceeding 10 years, resulting in a considerable extension of the domestic yield curve, which in turn has facilitated bank funding and pricing of long-term loans in domestic currency. The longest maturity of fixed-rate government paper in domestic currency in Peru is 32 years, whereas it was 5 years in 2003.[10] The curve also extends now up to 30 years in Bolivia and 15 years in Uruguay.

---

of capital. Uruguay set a net open position limit of 150 percent of minimum required regulatory capital in late 2003.

[8]In December 2008, Bolivia raised the marginal cash reserve requirement for deposits in foreign currency above the level observed in September to 30 percent (the measure was effective in January 2009). In June 2009, Bolivia established that the marginal reserve requirement in domestic currency could be reduced by an amount equivalent to the increase in domestic currency credit relative to the stock of June 30, 2009—up to the equivalent of 100 percent of the cash reserve requirement (2 percent) and 40 percent of the reserve requirement in securities (10 percent). Hence, the reserve requirements associated with deposits in bolivianos and Unidades de Fomento de Vivienda could decline by half in practice (from 12 percent of deposits to 6 percent).

[9]Changes in remuneration rates are not considered in the empirical analysis below, but further work could usefully focus on this variable.

[10]The inflation-adjusted "VAC" curve extends up to 39-year tenors, but has limited liquidity, as they represent only 10 percent of the domestic public bonds in Peru. The rest of the domestic public bonds are the fixed-coupon "Tasa Fija" bonds.

Figure 7.9 Development of Debt Market in Domestic Currency and Dollarization[1]

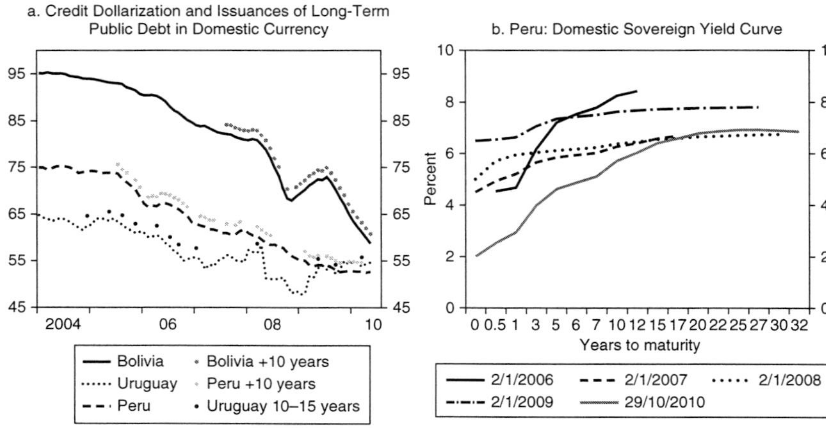

Source: IMF staff calculations.
[1]Foreign currency credit evaluated at constant exchange rate.

EMPIRICAL RESULTS

This chapter's main objectives are achieved through two standard tools of VAR analysis: impulse response functions and variance decomposition. Impulse responses constitute a practical way to identify the dynamic responses of changes in deposit and credit dollarization to shocks to the rest of the variables in the model, taking into account not only the direct effects of disturbances, but also the indirect effects through reactions of other variables in the model. In this section, we present impulse responses showing the effects at each month, and not the cumulative—and typically larger—effects over time. Variance decomposition provides a quantification of the relative importance of each of the shocks as sources of variations in dollarization levels.

Active management of reserve requirement differentials—in particular by increasing the spread between reserve requirement ratios on foreign and local currency deposits—seems to have contributed to dedollarization (Figure 7.10). In fact, an increase in the ratio of foreign-to-local-currency reserve requirement rates has helped to foster credit dedollarization in Paraguay and Peru, and deposit dedollarization in Bolivia and Paraguay. The impact is quite rapid, with significant effects only one month after the shock.

The introduction of other prudential measures creating incentives to internalize the risks of financial dollarization has also tended to help credit dedollarization in Bolivia, Paraguay, and Uruguay by discouraging lending in foreign currency to unhedged borrowers (Figure 7.11). These measures include raising provision requirements for foreign-currency-denominated loans, introducing differentiated capital risk weights on foreign currency loans, and tightening capital requirements against open foreign exchange positions. These measures typically affect changes

Figure 7.10 Response of Dollarization to a Shock to Differential Reserve Requirement Ratios[1]

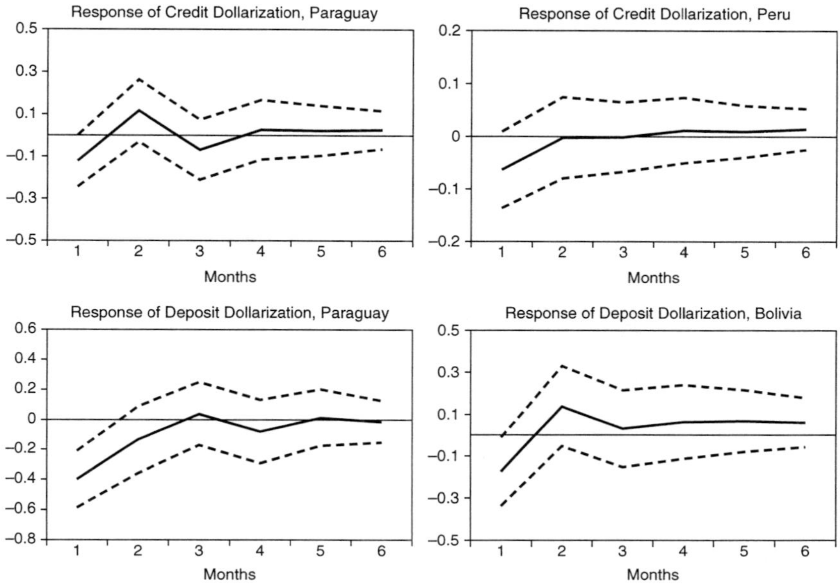

Source: authors' calculations.
[1]One standard deviation shock ±2 standard errors.

in credit dollarization on impact, with effects lasting up to two months. The impact on deposit dollarization, in contrast, is not statistically significant.

The extension of the yield curve of local currency public bonds has also contributed to credit dedollarization in these countries (Figure 7.12). Bolivia, Peru, and Uruguay have recently issued public bonds in domestic currency with maturities exceeding 10 years, but Paraguay has not yet started to issue long-term public debt in local currency. The existence of a benchmark for long-term domestic currency debt has facilitated the pricing of private instruments in local currency at longer maturities. The effects of issuance of domestic currency long-term public bonds on deposit dedollarization, however, are not significant.

The exchange rate appreciation trend observed in the past decade has been important in explaining deposit dedollarization in Bolivia, Peru, and Uruguay (Figure 7.13). The impact of an exchange rate shock is typically rapid and significant. Expectations of further appreciation and higher returns of local currency deposits have created incentives to shift to local currency deposits. In Paraguay, however, the effects on deposit dollarization do not appear to be significant. In Bolivia, the exchange rate appreciation has also played a role in credit dedollarization, but we do not find any such effects in Paraguay, Peru, and Uruguay.

The evidence of the effects of exchange rate volatility on financial dollarization is mixed, somewhat inconclusive, and requires some interpretation. Shocks to exchange rate volatility have contributed to dedollarization of credit in Peru

Figure 7.11 Response of Dollarization to the Introduction of Prudential Measures[1]

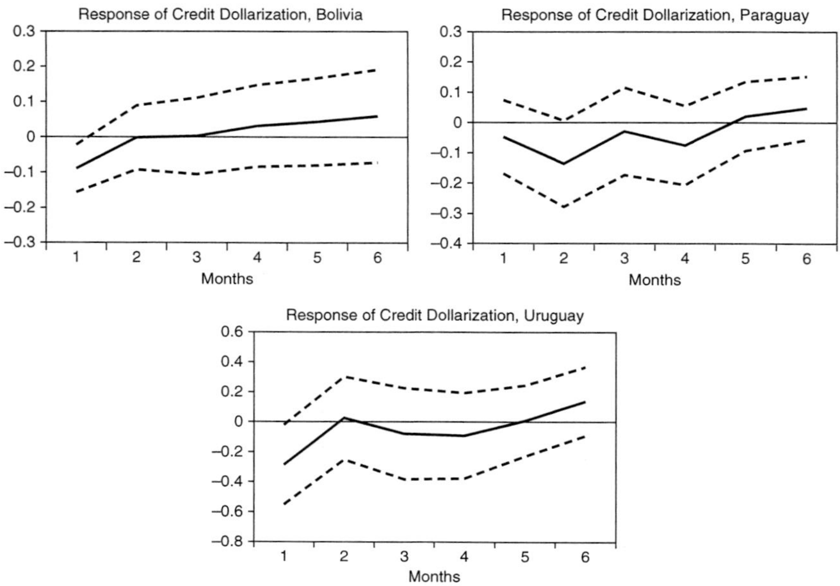

Source: authors' calculations.
[1]One standard deviation shock ±2 standard errors.

Figure 7.12 Response of Dollarization to the Issuance of Local Currency Long-Term Bonds[1]

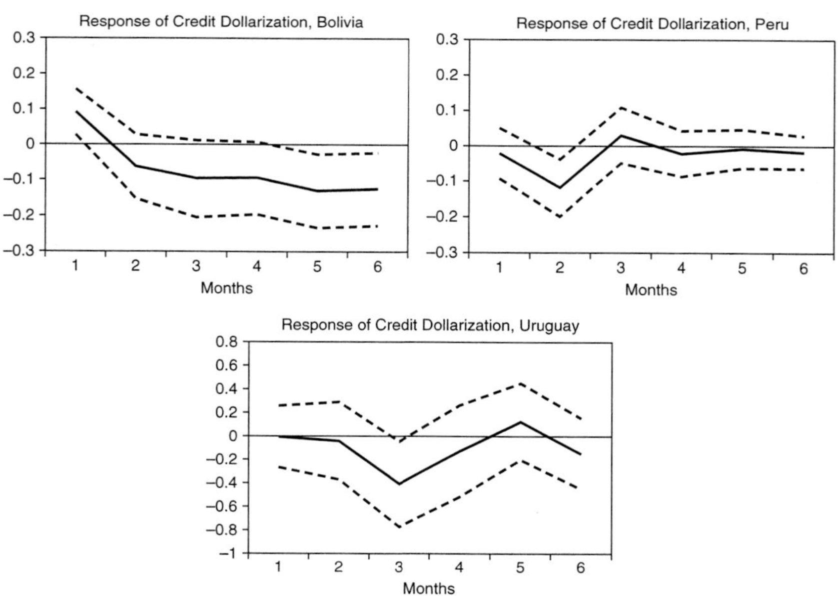

Source: authors' calculations.
[1]One standard deviation shock ±2 standard errors.

Figure 7.13 Response of Dollarization to an Exchange Rate Shock[1]

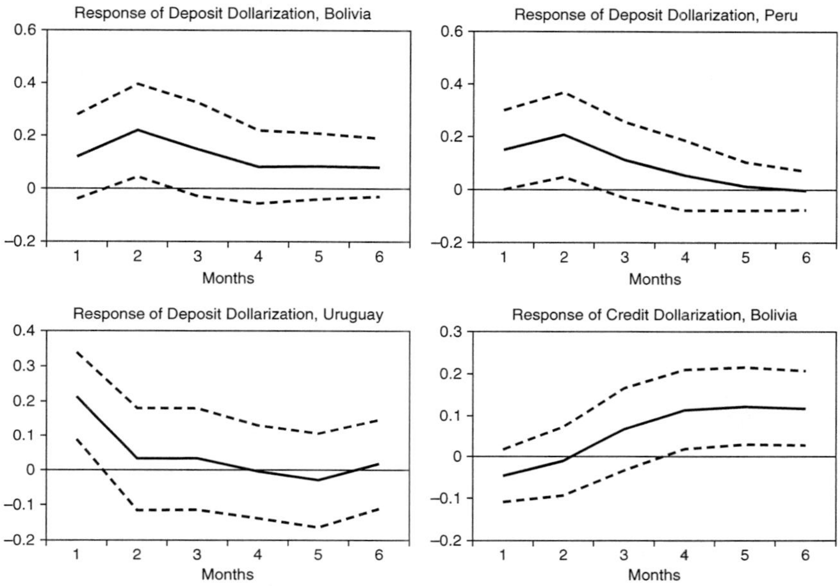

Source: authors' calculations.
[1]One standard deviation shock ±2 standard errors.

(Figure 7.14)—a result consistent with the findings of García-Escribano (2010) using a different specification of the model. Exchange rate volatility shocks seem to have helped deposit dedollarization in Paraguay, although the results are not strongly significant. In Uruguay, exchange rate volatility does not appear to have contributed to dedollarization. Interestingly, shocks to exchange rate volatility have had a positive impact on both deposit and credit dedollarization in Bolivia. This is a bit surprising at first, given that the size of these shocks in Bolivia is much smaller than in the other three countries (Table 7.4). In fact, Bolivia's exchange rate regime is a crawling peg to the U.S. dollar, with smooth exchange rate movements. During this period, the boliviano has appreciated slowly but steadily under the crawling peg since 2005, and has remained de facto pegged since October 2008. Thus, in the case of Bolivia, higher exchange rate volatility has not implied two-way volatility, but larger changes in the same direction—appreciation in most of the period of analysis. Thus, a plausible interpretation is that exchange rate volatility shocks actually reflected larger appreciation changes, fueling the perception of deposits in bolivianos as a "one-way bet," and providing stronger incentives to switch to them.[11]

In this chapter, the methodological approach used also allows for examining the existence of any relationship between changes in deposit and credit dollarization,

[11]There is an alternative interpretation of the results. The trend toward appreciation could signal in some of these countries a regime shift toward more exchange rate flexibility. This may imply that the

Figure 7.14 Response of Dollarization to an Exchange Rate Volatility Shock[1]

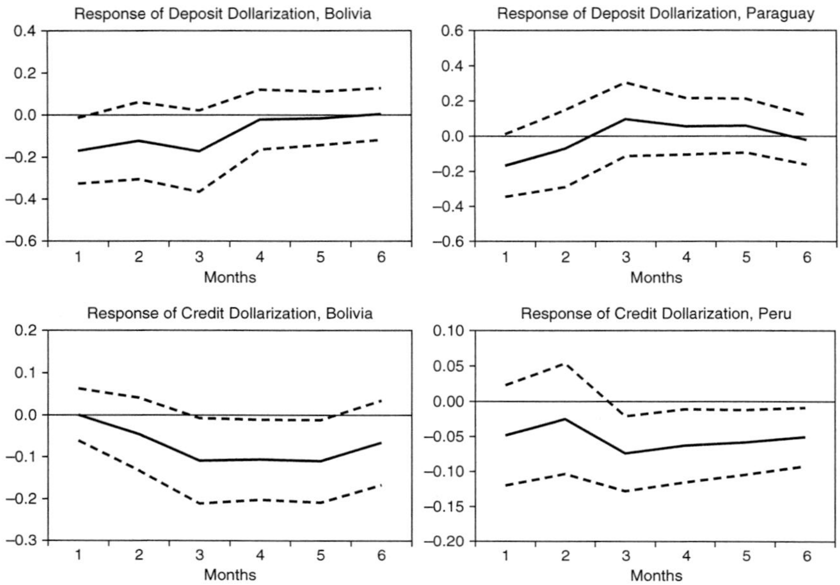

Source: authors' calculations.
[1]One standard deviation shock ±2 standard errors.

TABLE 7.4

Size of the Shock[1]

	Exchange Rate Shock	Volatility Shock
Bolivia	0.21	0.01
Paraguay	2.56	0.14
Peru	1.31	0.08
Uruguay	2.06	0.16

Source: Authors' calculations.
[1]One standard deviation shock.

and the direction of causality. Our findings show that causation goes from changes in deposit to changes in credit dollarization. In fact, changes in deposit dollarization have a strong impact on credit dollarization in the same direction in all countries in the sample (Figure 7.15). These results are expected, and mainly reflect banks' tendency to maintain matched foreign currency positions. Thus, the declining trend in deposit dollarization has also played a role in fostering dedollarization of credit during this period.

ex ante expected volatility could be higher than the ex post observed volatility, because agents would now expect that the central bank allows sharp exchange rate movements in either direction if necessary. Under this interpretation, changes in the exchange rate (in light of the appreciation trend) would to some extent capture greater flexibility, fostering dedollarization by introducing a two-way exchange rate risk.

Figure 7.15 Response of Credit Dollarization to a Shock to Deposit Dollarization[1]

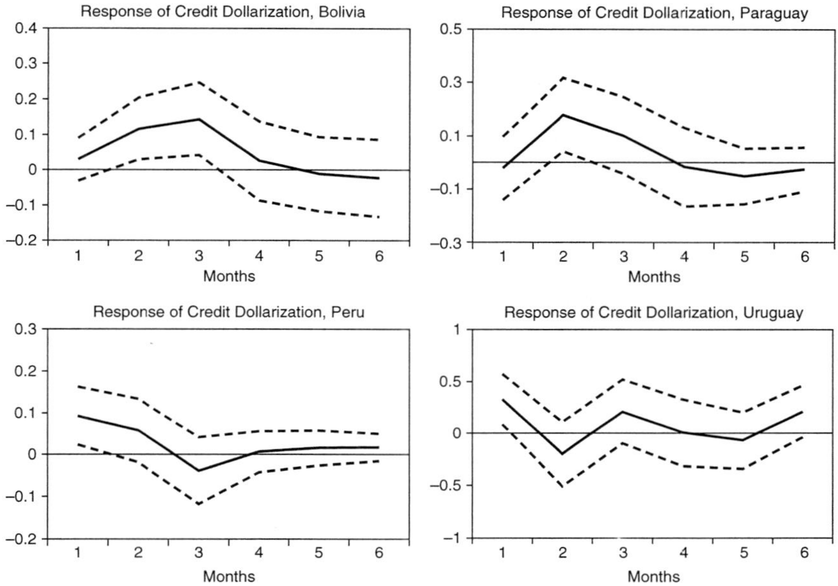

Source: authors' calculations.
[1]One standard deviation shock ±2 standard errors.

To assess the sensitivity of our results, we conduct a number of robustness tests. First, we extend the number of lags included in the model to six months. Second, we estimate the model using alternative Choleski orderings of the variables. Third, we modify the definition of deposit (and credit) dollarization, by using the ratio of foreign currency deposits (credit) to total deposits (credit) at current exchange rates instead of measuring at constant exchange rates as in the baseline specification. Finally, in the case of Uruguay, we estimate the VAR using only dollarization ratios for deposits of residents, in contrast to the baseline estimation, where we include total deposits.[12] The results of these exercises do not differ significantly from those obtained in our baseline specification.

Tables 7.5 and 7.6 show the relative importance of shocks to different variables included in the model to explain variations in deposit and credit dollarization. These tables illustrate the role played by each of the variables with an impact on dollarization, based on the impulse response functions shown above. On average, changes in prudential regulation (including changes in reserve requirement ratios) explain about 7 percent of credit dollarization variations.[13] The contribution of

[12]While nonresident deposits account for about 20 percent of deposits in Uruguay's banking system, they represented more than 40 percent in 2001—before the 2002 banking crisis.
[13]For a horizon of six months.

TABLE 7.5

Variance Decomposition of Changes in Credit Dollarization

Contribution of Shocks to Prudential Measure Variables (percent)					
Horizon (Months)	**Bolivia**	**Paraguay**	**Peru**	**Uruguay**	**Average**
1	7.9	4.0	3.7	5.8	5.3
3	4.9	9.4	3.1	4.9	5.6
6	8.4	10.6	3.1	6.8	7.2

Contribution of Shocks to Local Currency Bond Market Development (percent)				
Horizon (Months)	**Bolivia**	**Peru**	**Uruguay**	**Average**
1	7.7	0.3	0.0	2.7
3	8.8	8.1	8.3	8.4
6	15.8	7.8	9.2	10.9

Contribution of Shocks to Deposit Dollarization (percent)					
Horizon (Months)	**Bolivia**	**Paraguay**	**Peru**	**Uruguay**	**Average**
1	0.8	0.1	5.8	7.5	3.6
3	14.3	7.4	7.0	9.4	9.5
6	9.1	7.6	6.7	9.9	8.3

Source: Authors' calculations.

TABLE 7.6

Variance Decomposition of Changes in Deposit Dollarization

Contribution of Shocks to Exchange Rate Changes (percent)					
Horizon (Months)	**Bolivia**	**Paraguay**	**Peru**	**Uruguay**	**Average**
1	2.3	0.2	3.2	13.0	4.7
3	10.2	1.2	9.4	10.6	7.8
6	10.9	1.5	9.2	8.9	7.6

Source: Authors' calculations.

shocks to the development of a local currency public bond market is about 11 percent on average. Changes in deposit dollarization, in turn, account for about 8 percent of credit dollarization fluctuations. In the case of deposits, exchange rate movements explain about 8 percent of dollarization variations. The percentages explained by these variables seem to be somewhat low. This may be related to the short number of lags (three months) used in the baseline model. In fact, in the alternative specification with six lags, the fraction explained by these variables is substantially larger.

In sum, what have been the main short-term drivers of financial dedollarization in Bolivia, Peru, Paraguay, and Uruguay? Table 7.7 summarizes our findings.

- To be clear, forces driving deposit dedollarization are different from those driving credit dedollarization.
- In the case of credit, an active management of reserve requirements and the introduction of other prudential measures to internalize the risks associated

TABLE 7.7

What Drives Dedollarization?

	ΔRR	d	$d^{10\text{-}30}$	e	s	Inflation	$\Delta embi$	ΔDL
Deposit Dollarization								
Bolivia	√	n.s.	n.s.	√	√	n.s.		n.s.
Paraguay	√	n.s.		n.s.	√	n.s.		n.s.
Peru	n.s.	n.s.	n.s.	√	n.s.	n.s.	n.s.	n.s.
Uruguay	n.s.	n.s.	n.s.	√	n.s.	n.s.	n.s.	n.s.
Credit Dollarization								
Boliva	n.s.	√	√	√	√	n.s.		√
Para	√	√		n.s.	n.s.	n.s.		√
Peru	√	n.s.	√	n.s.	√	n.s.	n.s.	√
Uruguay	n.s.	√	√	n.s.	n.s.	n.s.	n.s.	√

Source: Authors' calculations.
Note: See Table 7.3 for definition of variables.

with financial dollarization have both played a role in fostering dedollarization.

- Development of a capital market in local currency by extending the yield curve of public bonds has also contributed to credit dedollarization.
- Dedollarization of deposits has also contributed to credit dedollarization given banks' matching behavior of foreign currency positions.
- In the case of deposits, the main factor behind dedollarization has been the appreciation trend observed in all these countries in recent years.
- Changes in other macroeconomic variables, such as inflation rates and EMBI spreads, do not appear to have any short-term impact on financial dedollarization. This does not mean that macroeconomic stability is not important. On the contrary, macroeconomic stability and strong fundamentals are preconditions for dedollarization. Once stability is achieved and macroeconomic fundamentals are relatively strong, changes in macroeconomic variables may not have a marginal effect on dedollarization.

CONCLUSION

Although the steady decline in financial dollarization observed in Bolivia, Paraguay, Peru, and Uruguay in recent years has been remarkable, dollarization levels remain high. This suggests that one decade of efforts may not be enough to fight a phenomenon so entrenched in these economies, and countries should continue striving to lower dollarization levels in the financial sector.

What are the main policy implications, not only for these countries to continue on the route to dedollarization but also for other countries with still high levels of financial dollarization? Our findings highlight the importance of:

- First, maintaining strong fundamentals and macroeconomic stability (for instance, keeping low and stable inflation);

- Second, ensuring that the prudential regulation framework of the financial sector (including an active management of reserve requirements) provides incentives for an appropriate internalization of currency risks by agents; and
- Third, developing further local currency capital markets. Capital markets in domestic currency in these countries are still narrow, and their continued development would help to enhance dedollarization. This implies deepening not only local currency markets for public bonds but also for private bonds.

REFERENCES

Armas, A., N. Batini, and V. Tuesta, 2007, "Peru's Experience with Partial Dollarization and Inflation Targeting," IMF Country Report 07/53 (Washington: International Monetary Fund).

Armas, A., A. Ize, and E. Levy, eds., 2006, *Financial Dollarization—The Policy Agenda* (Washington: International Monetary Fund; New York: Palgrave Macmillan).

Arteta, C., 2005, "Exchange Rate Regimes and Financial Dollarization: Does Flexibility Reduce Bank Currency Mismatches?" *Berkeley Electronic Journals in Macroeconomics*, Topics in Macroeconomics 5: Article 10.

Banco Central Reserva de Peru, 2005, "Fenómeno de la Dolarización," in *Reporte de Inflación* (May), pp. 42–6.

Barajas, A., and R.A. Morales, 2003, "Dollarization of Liabilities: Beyond the Usual Suspects," IMF Working Paper 03/11 (Washington: International Monetary Fund).

Berkmen, P., and E. Cavallo, 2010, "Exchange Rate Policy and Liability Dollarization: What Do the Data Reveal about Causality?" *Review of International Economics*, 18(5), pp. 781–95.

Broda, C., and E. Levy-Yeyati, 2003, "Endogeneous Deposit Dollarization," *Staff Report 160* (New York: Federal Reserve Bank of New York).

Castillo, P., and D. Winkelried, 2010, "Dollarization Persistence and Individual Heterogeneity," *Journal of International Money and Finance*, 29(8), pp. 1596–618.

Cayazzo, Jorge, Antonio Garcia Pascual, Eva Gutierrez, and Socorro Heysen, 2006, "Toward an Effective Supervision of Partially Dollarized Banking Systems," IMF Working Paper 06/32 (Washington: International Monetary Fund).

De Nicolõ, G., P. Honokan, and A. Ize, 2005, "Dollarization of Bank Deposits: Causes and Consequences," *Journal of Banking and Finance*, 29, pp. 1697–727.

Erasmus, L., J. Leichter, and J. Menkulasi, 2009, "Dedollarization in Liberia—Lessons from Cross-country Experience," IMF Working Paper 09/37 (Washington: International Monetary Fund).

Fernandez-Arias, E., 2005, "Financial Dollarization and Dedollarization," Inter-American Development Bank, Economic and Social Study Series (Washington: Inter-American Development Bank).

Galindo, A., and L. Leiderman, 2005, "Living with Dollarization and the Route to Dedollarization," IDB Working Paper No. 526 (Washington: Inter-American Development Bank).

García-Escribano, M., 2010, "Peru: Drivers of Dedollarization," Central Reserve Bank of Peru, Working Paper Series No. 2010–11.

———, 2010, "Peru: Drivers of Dedollarization," IMF Working Paper 10/169 (Washington: International Monetary Fund).

Ize, A., and E. Levy-Yeyati, 2003, "Financial Dollarization," *Journal of International Economics*, Vol. 59, pp. 323–47.

J.P. Morgan Securities Inc., 2009, "Local Markets Guide" (October).

Kokenyne, A., J. Ley, and R. Veyrune, 2010, "Dedollarization," IMF Working Paper 10/188 (Washington: International Monetary Fund).

Luca, A., and I. Petrova, 2008, "What Drives Credit Dollarization in Transition Economies?" *Journal of Banking and Finance*, 32 (5), pp. 858–69.

Morón, E., and J.F. Castro, 2003, "De-dollarizing the Peruvian Economy: A Portfolio Approach," Centro de Investigación de la Universidad del Pacifico, Documento de Discusión 03/01.
Neanidis, K., and C.S. Savva, 2009, "Financial Dollarization: Short-Run Determinants in Transition Economies," *Journal of Banking and Finance*, 33, pp. 1860–73.
Quispe, Z., 2000, "Política Monetaria en una Economía con Dolarización Parcial: el Caso de Perú," Banco Central Reserva de Perú, Estudios Económicos No. 6.
Reinhart, C., R. Rogoff, and M. Savastano, 2003, "Addicted to Dollars," NBER Working Paper No. 10015 (Cambridge, Massachusetts: National Bureau of Economic Research).
Rennhack, R., and M. Nozaki, 2006, "Financial Dollarization in Latin America," in *Financial Dollarization—The Policy Agenda*, ed. by A. Armas, A. Ize, and E. Levy (Washington: International Monetary Fund; New York: Palgrave Macmillan).

CHAPTER 8

Interest Rate and Exchange Rate Channels in Dollarized and Non-Dollarized Economies

SANTIAGO ACOSTA-ORMAECHEA AND DAVID COBLE

The study of the transmission of monetary policy in both advanced and developing economies has been the objective of numerous papers in recent years. This monetary transmission is broadly conceived as the analysis of how monetary policy decisions ultimately affect inflation, which is generally the primary objective of central banks.

Under an inflation targeting regime, in particular, the economic authorities conduct monetary policy by setting a reference interest rate to achieve a pre-announced inflation target, while leaving other monetary aggregates and the exchange rate to be largely determined by market forces. However, these monetary policy decisions affect inflation with a delay, as they first tend to impact on different variables and only after that, through different channels, the inflation rate.[1]

The objective of this chapter is to study the transmission of monetary policy empirically, comparing the cases of four small and open economies that operate under an inflation targeting regime and are exposed to different levels of dollarization. In particular, we aim to disentangle to what extent the degree of dollarization may help explain some key differences in the transmission of monetary policy in such countries.[2] For this we examine two countries that run well-established inflation targeting regimes and have a negligible exposure to dollarization problems: Chile and New Zealand. The cases of Peru and Uruguay are also studied, as

A version of this chapter was published in April 2013 in *Revista Economía Chilena* (Volume 16, Number 1). Available at: http://www.bcentral.cl/eng/studies/economia-chilena/articles.htm.

[1]See Mishkin (1996) for an in-depth discussion of the main channels of monetary policy transmission.

[2]Although dollarization is an endogenous phenomenon and it will ultimately depend on the credibility of monetary policy, we take it as a given in this analysis. This is also assumed, for instance, in the works of Aghion, Bacchetta, and Banerjee (2000) and Céspedes, Chang, and Velasco (2004). This assumption is justified since dollarization (or dedollarization) is a reflection of the behavior of monetary policy over the long term. Although it will ultimately change endogenously, depending on the credibility of monetary policy, the various lags observed in such changes somewhat justify taking it as a given when studying empirically the short-term effects of monetary policy shocks.

these countries also operate under IT regimes yet are exposed to a large degree of dollarization in their respective banking systems.[3,4]

To clarify the sequence through which policy decisions are transmitted to the rest of the economy, we divide the analysis into two stages. First, we examine how the policy rate affects the key interest rates of each country, notably the money market rate, the deposit rate, and the lending rate. Broadly speaking, we intend to evaluate the strength of what is in practice the first part of the transmission, which involves the pass-through from the policy rate to a number of key interest rates of each economy. In the second stage, we use a vector autoregression (VAR) model to evaluate how changes in the money market rate affect output and inflation in these economies. Our aim is to assess empirically to what extent the strength and channels of the transmission differ across countries. Finally, we evaluate through different rolling VAR models whether the degree of credit in the economy and the level of dollarization may help explain the strength of the response of inflation to policy rate innovations in these countries.

A large strand of the empirical work on monetary policy considers different VAR models applied to both advanced and emerging market economies.[5] This chapter follows a similar methodology but applies it to a different set of countries, giving rise to new challenges. We found, for example, a significant price puzzle when considering the VAR specification of Kim and Roubini (2000). To correct for this problem, we modified the specification by including a corrected measure of inflation: we eliminated the foreign component of domestic inflation in our set of variables in the VAR model. This correction is important because the strength of the monetary policy transmission should be evaluated considering only those variables that are under the effective control of the monetary authority. Since this is clearly not the case for foreign inflation, this source of variability of

[3]Uruguay does not yet have a full-fledged inflation targeting regime, as the country only recently began transitioning toward this monetary arrangement. This transition took place in early 2005, when it began to conduct monetary policy with the objective of meeting a pre-announced inflation target. In addition, after September 2007, Uruguay adopted the policy rate as the main instrument for monetary policy. Previously, monetary policy was essentially run by setting objectives on monetary aggregates to meet their inflation target.

[4]Our selection of countries is to some extent arbitrary. However, our main concern in this chapter is rather heuristic, and for this reason we decided to consider a number of cases that allow us to understand more thoroughly the monetary transmission mechanism in dollarized and non-dollarized economies. In this regard, we selected a number of countries in the Latin American region that operate under an inflation targeting regime with a similar degree of openness, which are dependent to a large extent on commodity prices and are also exposed to different levels of dollarization. With this objective in mind, we took three of the most relevant inflation targeting regimes in the region: Chile, Peru, and Uruguay. The decision to incorporate New Zealand was based on the fact that the country is a prominent benchmark in terms of running a well-established inflation targeting regime, has a strong dependence on commodity prices, and is also a small and open economy. This type of benchmarking helps assess more thoroughly the performance of the selected Latin American countries vis-à-vis key advanced economies that operate under an inflation targeting regime.

[5]See, for instance, Kim and Roubini (2000), Peersman and Smets (2001), and Leiderman, Maino, and Parrado (2006).

domestic prices should be eliminated from the model. In addition, this chapter provides a comprehensive assessment of how interest rate shocks are initially transmitted to the rest of the economy through domestic credit markets, which is unusual in this literature. Likewise, it also includes an empirical evaluation of the role of financial deepening in the transmission of monetary policy. In this regard, we show that the response of inflation to the interest rate shock does not seem to depend on the degree of development of credit markets. This finding supports the view that monetary policy can in principle be effective even in the context of relatively low levels of credit in the economy.

We also found that in Chile and New Zealand there is a significant pass-through from the policy rate to the main interest rates of the economy. Accordingly, a contractionary monetary policy shock reduces inflation and output, suggesting a strong transmission of monetary policy through the traditional interest rate channel. Conversely, in Peru and Uruguay, the interest rate pass-through is rather weak, and so is the overall transmission to output and inflation. For the latter two economies, however, evidence indicates that the exchange rate channel—rather than the interest rate channel—may play a more substantial role in curbing inflationary pressures, as indicated by the relatively larger exchange rate pass-through observed in these two economies. Finally, as indicated previously, the chapter does not find conclusive evidence regarding the role of financial deepening in the transmission of monetary policy. However, it is found that as Peru and Uruguay reduced their levels of dollarization, the effectiveness of the monetary policy transmission increased somewhat.

KEY STYLIZED FACTS

Chile, New Zealand, Peru, and Uruguay are all small open economies that currently operate under inflation targeting regimes. All have relatively similar degrees of trade openness and are important commodity exporters (Figure 8.1). One key difference is, however, the degree of banking sector dollarization. In Chile and New Zealand, almost all credit and deposits are denominated in local currency, whereas in Peru and Uruguay the share of foreign-currency-denominated credit and deposits is rather large, though on a downward path.[6]

There are also additional differences regarding the performance of key fundamentals in these countries, as indicated in Table 8.1.[7] For instance, Uruguay and Peru had a relatively low variability in both the nominal exchange rate (NER) against the U.S. dollar and the real effective exchange rate (REER). This may reflect a "fear of floating" type of behavior, which could result from their significant degree of dollarization. In addition, Uruguay experienced a higher

[6]See García-Escribano and Sosa (2011) for a discussion of the recent dedollarization trends in Peru and Uruguay.

[7]See Appendix 8.1 for details on the variables used in Table 8.1.

Figure 8.1 Selected Macroeconomic Indicators

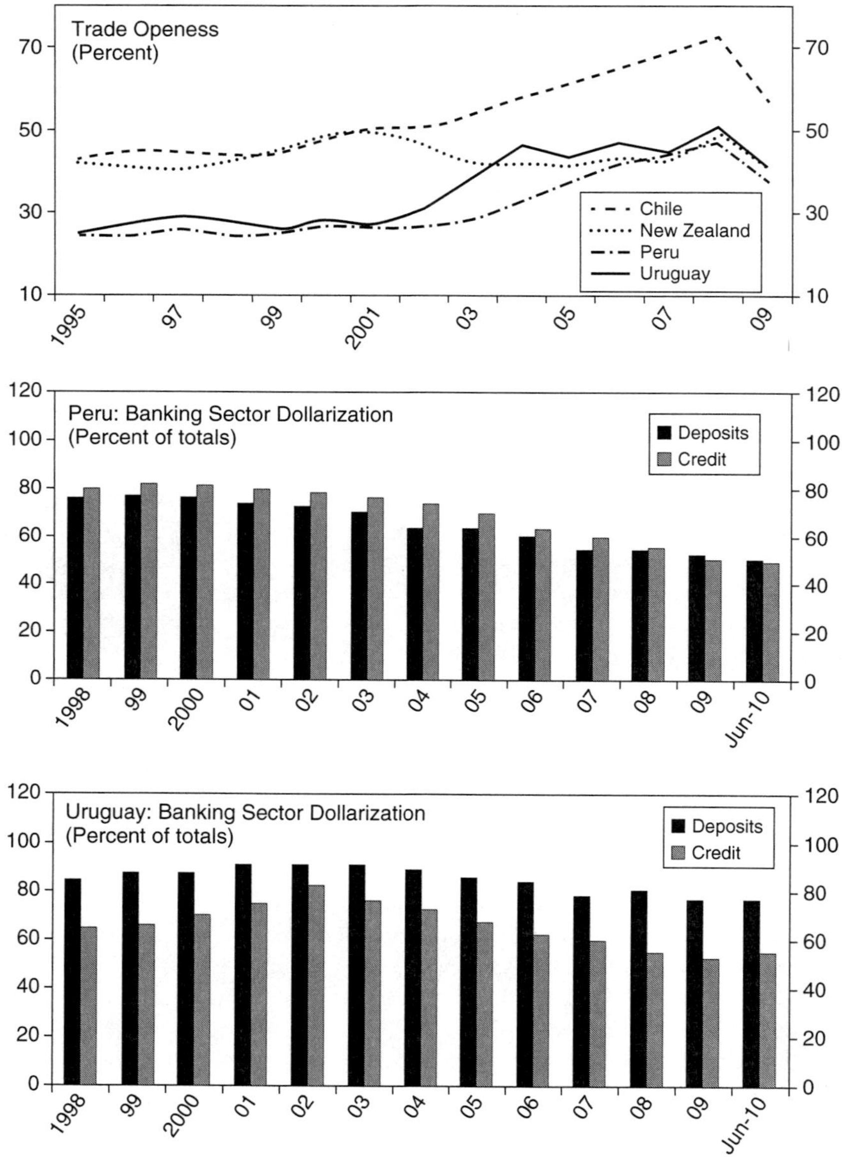

Sources: Country authorities; and authors' calculations.

TABLE 8.1

Volatility of Selected Variable (Standard deviations of annual changes, percent)

	REER		NER		Output		CPI Inflation		Expected Inflation (12 months ahead)		Foreign Reserves to GDP	
	(1)	(2)	(1)	(2)	(1)	(2)	(1)	(2)	(1)	(2)	(1)	(2)
Chile	6.4	7.6	5.0	17.2	1.0	3.8	1.4	4.1	0.3	1.1	7.1	34.2
New Zealand	8.0	12.2	10.1	22.8	1.1	1.8	0.6	1.0	0.2	0.7	20.2	12.8
Peru	2.3	2.9	3.4	7.3	1.8	4.7	0.9	2.3	0.3	0.6	15.5	31.4
Uruguay	6.1	6.9	6.8	14.8	8.2	8.4	1.5	0.8	0.5	0.5	15.8	25.0

Sources: Country authorities; and authors' calculations.
Note: (1) January 2005 to December 2007; (2) January 2008 to November 2010. CPI = consumer price index; NER = nominal exchange rate; REER = real effective exchange rate.

degree of output volatility relative to all other countries.[8] In the case of Peru, output volatility has been lower than in Uruguay, yet still above that observed in Chile and New Zealand. Somewhat surprisingly, however, the volatility of CPI inflation has recently decreased in Uruguay, contrary to the other three economies, where it has trended upward.[9] Expected inflation has followed a similar pattern: in all countries except Uruguay, its volatility increased over time. Interestingly, the evidence indicates a relatively more active use of foreign exchange interventions in these three Latin American countries in recent years. This contrasts with the case of New Zealand, where the volatility of reserves has decreased over time.

Although Uruguay's consumer price index (CPI) inflation has been relatively more stable, it has also remained at a higher level relative to the other three countries, particularly during 2010 (Figure 8.2). A similar pattern arises when considering different measures of core inflation (not shown). Furthermore, actual and expected inflation have remained systematically in the upper band of (or above) the target range in Uruguay, whereas in all the other cases, both variables have hovered around their respective midpoint target ranges. As expected, inflation expectations have moved in tandem with actual inflation, yet showing a lower variability. In addition, in all four cases, the policy rate has closely tracked the inflation rate, suggesting that monetary policy has been active in trying to curb inflation pressures.

[8]The IMF's 2010 Article IV Staff Report for Uruguay also states that Uruguay's output volatility tends to be high relative to a number of selected peer countries.

[9]This trend is partially explained by the evolution of certain prices in Uruguay that are somewhat controlled by economic authorities, notably transport prices and a number of selected utilities, limiting to some extent the variability of inflation in the country.

[10]Policy rates are taken from the website of each central bank, and reflect a target publicly announced by the central bank on the overnight interbank interest rate of each country.

Figure 8.2 Actual Inflation, Expected Inflation, Target Bands, and Policy Rates (Year-over year percent change)

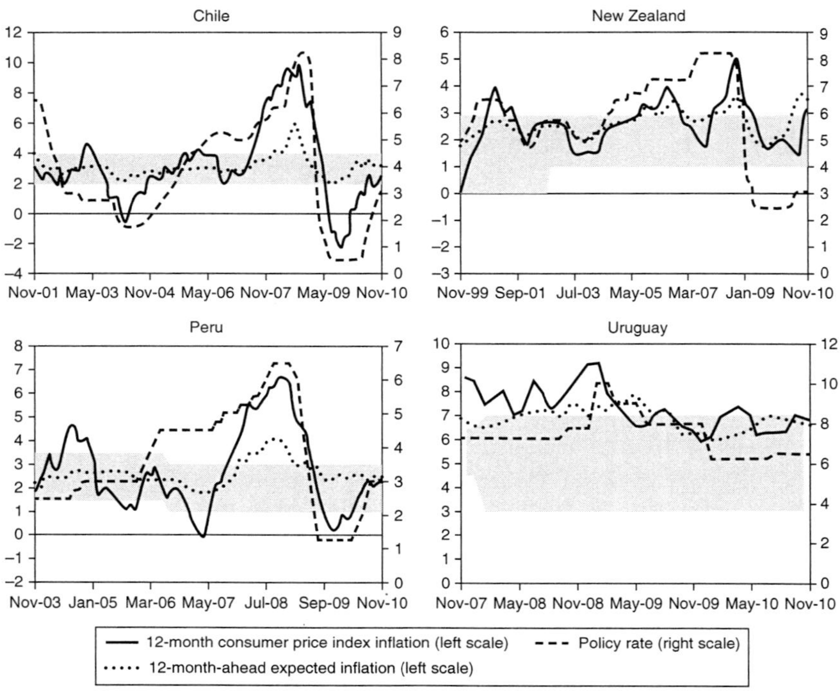

Sources: Country authorities, and authors' calculations.

There are, however, important differences in the evolution of the policy rate.[10] The sample considered here is divided into two periods: the first period extends from September 2003—the introduction of the policy rate as the main monetary policy instrument in Peru—to August 2007; the second period extends from its introduction in Uruguay—in September 2007—to the latest available observation—November 2010. Interestingly, Chile shows the most active use of monetary policy, measured by the number of policy rate changes observed during these periods. This contrasts with the case of Uruguay, which had the fewest number of modifications—although the median change was the largest whenever there was a change in the policy rate. In addition, as Uruguay has had the highest average inflation rate, the policy rate has accordingly taken the highest value after its implementation. These results differ substantially from those of Peru, where evidence suggests a more active use of monetary policy and a lower change in the policy rate whenever it was modified (Table 8.2). Overall, evidence points to the absence of a clear pattern in terms of the use of the policy rate across countries regardless of the level of dollarization and the date on which the inflation targeting regime was implemented.

TABLE 8.2

Inflation and Policy Rate (Percent, unless otherwise specified)

	CPI Inflation	Policy Rate		Policy Rate Changes[1]			
					Minimum	Maximum	Median
	Average	Average	Standard Deviation	No. of Times	(Basis Points)		
		September 2003–August 2007					
Chile	2.5	3.7	1.4	29	6	58	15
New Zealand	2.7	6.7	0.9	13	25	25	25
Peru	2.1	3.5	0.8	10	25	25	25
Uruguay	7.3	n.a.	n.a.	n.a.	n.a.	n.a.	n.a.
		September 2007–November 2010					
Chile	3.8	3.7	2.9	23	8	261	33
New Zealand	2.7	4.7	2.5	9	25	150	50
Peru	3.5	3.8	2.0	19	25	100	25
Uruguay	7.3	7.4	1.0	8	25	225	100

Sources: Country authorities; and authors' calculations.
Note: CPI = consumer price index; n.a. = not available.
[1]Minimum, maximum, and median are based on the absolute value of the policy rate change.

THE INTEREST RATE PASS-THROUGH

Under an inflation targeting regime, the transmission of monetary policy the decisions initially takes place through the modification of the policy rate, which in turn affects interbank rates on impact. Changes in the latter are then transmitted to deposit and lending rates, thus affecting the consumption and saving decisions of individuals and firms, and hence aggregate demand and inflation. Likewise, the change in the policy rate may affect the overall availability of credit as well as different asset prices that react to short-term interest rates, thereby enhancing the transmission through the so-called credit and asset price channels. Additionally, as domestic and foreign interest rates may differ for comparable assets, arbitrage between them gives rise to nominal exchange rate fluctuations, which in turn affect inflation and economic activity through the so-called exchange rate channel.

As expected, Figure 8.3 shows that in all countries, the policy rate and the money market (interbank) rate almost completely overlap. The only exception took place in Uruguay between October 2008 and November 2008, a period when the central bank explicitly avoided large interventions in a disrupted interbank market as part of a strategy to deal with the global financial turmoil triggered by the collapse of Lehman Brothers. Besides this exception, Figure 8.3 shows that the interest rate pass-through from the policy rate to the interbank rate tends to be immediate and complete across countries.

Figure 8.3 also shows that the co-movement between the policy rate and the deposit and lending rates is strong in Chile and New Zealand. This relationship is somewhat weaker in the cases of Peru and Uruguay, suggesting that the effectiveness of the policy rate in signaling the stance of monetary policy might not be that strong in these countries.

Figure 8.3 Local Currency Deposit, Lending, and Policy Rates (Year-over-year percent change)

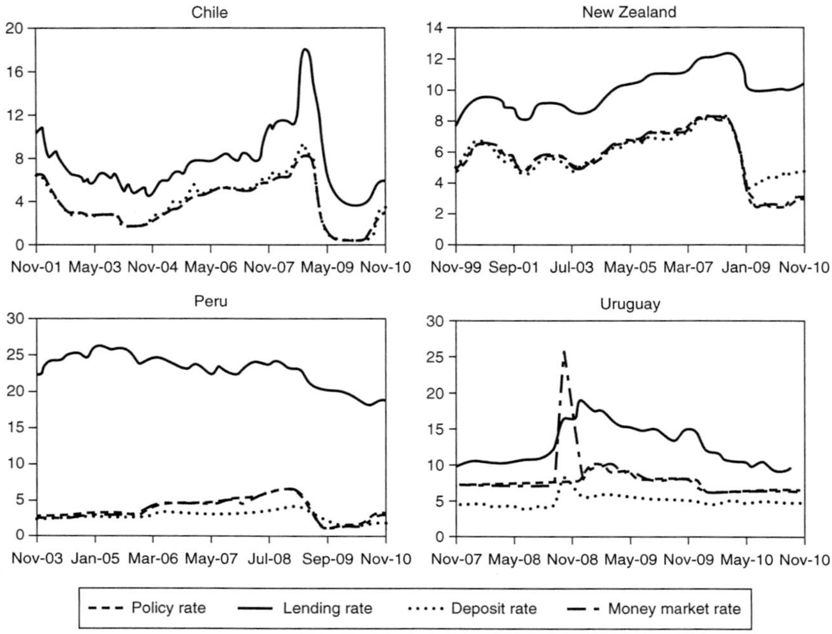

Source: Country authorities.

To evaluate formally the relationship between these key interest rates, the following simple regression is conducted:

$$y_{it} = c_i + \alpha_i x_{it} + \varepsilon_{it},$$

where for any country i and period t, y_{it} is the change in either the deposit or the lending rate, c_i is a constant, x_{it} is the change in the money market rate, and ε_{it} is an error term. The short-term effect of a money market rate change on the other interest rates is thus given by α_i. Tables 8.3 and 8.4 summarize the main results of the estimations.

As visually suggested by Figure 8.3, the overall interest rate pass-through in the cases of Chile and New Zealand is large. In these two countries, the change in the policy rate has a sizable and significant effect on both the deposit and lending rates through changes in the interbank rate. In contrast, for Peru and Uruguay, the policy rate pass-through tends to be much weaker, suggesting a somewhat larger impact on the deposit rather than the lending rate.[11] The weaker relationship between these interest rates in the cases of Peru and Uruguay is likely to reflect differences in the structure, depth, and degree of dollarization of their financial systems.

[11]These results should be treated with some caution owing to the relatively short sample period for the estimation in the case of Uruguay. In any case, the results obtained here are broadly consistent with other studies that show a low pass-through from the interbank rate to active and passive interest rates in this country.

TABLE 8.3

Pass-Through from Money Market Rate to Deposit Rate

	Constant (*c*)	Short-Term Pass-Through (α)	Cross-Correlation	R-Squared	Sample
Chile	0.00	0.78*	0.87	0.76	Sept. 1999–Nov. 2010
t-Statistic	−0.08	20.72			
New Zealand	0.01	0.67*	0.71	0.50	Apr. 1999–Oct. 2010
t-Statistic	0.70	11.68			
Peru	−0.01	0.32*	0.75	0.57	Sept. 2003–Oct. 2010
t-Statistic	−1.49	10.54			
Uruguay	0.03	0.20*	0.30	0.91	Sept. 2007–Nov. 2010
t-Statistic	0.71	19.91			

Source: Authors' estimations.
Note: * denotes statistical significance at the 5 percent level.

TABLE 8.4

Pass-Through from Money Market Rate to Lending Rate

	Constant (*c*)	Short-Term Pass-Through (α)	Cross-Correlation	R-Squared	Sample
Chile	−0.01	0.67*	0.72	0.51	Sept. 1999–Nov. 2010
t-Statistic	−0.21	11.88			
New Zealand	0.03*	0.62*	0.84	0.70	Apr. 1999–Oct. 2010
t-Statistic	3.18	17.94			
Peru	−0.03	0.19	0.13	0.02	Sept. 2003–Oct. 2010
t-Statistic	0.05	0.16			
Uruguay	0.03	0.10*	0.32	0.00	Sept. 2007–Oct. 2010
t-Statistic	0.14	2.05			

Source: Authors' estimations.
Note: * denotes statistical significance at the 5 percent level.

EMPIRICAL ANALYSIS OF THE TRANSMISSION OF MONETARY POLICY

After the initial transmission of the policy rate to the different interest rates of the economy, the monetary policy change is transmitted through the various channels discussed previously to the rest of the economy. This section specifically analyzes how this monetary policy innovation affects inflation and output in each country. In a nutshell, the effectiveness of monetary policy is assessed, with consideration given to the way inflation—the primary concern of the central bank—reacts to a policy-driven increase in the money market rate (a contractionary monetary policy shock). Since the stance of aggregate demand also determines the evolution of inflation, the response of output to the same innovation is studied as well. With this objective in mind, the following VAR model is estimated:

$$Y_t = A(L)Y_{t-1} + B\,(L)\,X_t + U_t, \tag{8.1}$$

where $A(L)$ and $B(L)$ are $n \times n$ and $n \times k$ polynomial matrices in the lag operator L, respectively, Y_t is an $n \times 1$ vector of endogenous variables, X_t is a $k \times 1$ vector of exogenous variables, and U_t is an $n \times 1$ vector of estimated residuals. X_t is included to control for those disturbances that are not directly managed by the monetary authority and may somewhat affect the dynamics of the model. The benchmark specification takes the following form:

$$Y_t = \left[R_t \;\; IP_t \;\; \pi_t - \pi_t^w \right]', \tag{8.2}$$

where R_t is the money market rate, IP_t is the year-over-year change of an index of economic activity, and $\pi_t - \pi_t^w$ is a measure of the year-over-year headline inflation that is effectively under the control of the monetary authority.[12] Intuitively, as these economies are small and open, world headline inflation will have a significant effect on their respective inflation rates. To effectively strip domestic inflation of external factors, the gap between domestic and external inflation is considered. This approach helps eliminate the so-called price puzzle problem often encountered in the empirical literature (see Sims, 1992). The vector of exogenous variables is in turn given by:

$$X_t = \left[FF_t \;\; WCPI_t \;\; IP_t^{us} \right], \tag{8.3}$$

where FF_t is the U.S. federal funds rate, $WCPI_t$ is the year-over-year change of the world commodity price index, and IP_t^{us} is the U.S. industrial production index gap in logs. In terms of identification, the model uses a standard Cholesky decomposition, with the variables ordered as in vector Y_t.[13] This implies, for instance, that R_t is contemporaneously affected only by its own shock, whereas $\pi_t - \pi_t^w$, being the most endogenous variable, is affected on impact by all structural innovations of the model.

The estimations consider monthly data, with the sample period tailored to each particular country. In the case of Chile, the sample starts with the introduction of the inflation targeting regime in September 1999 and ends in November 2010. For New Zealand, it starts in April 1999, when the so-called cash rate was set as the main policy instrument, and ends in September 2010.[14] For Peru, the sample starts in September 2003, the month in which the full-fledged inflation targeting regime was implemented, and ends in November 2010. Finally, for Uruguay, even though the inflation targeting regime began to be implemented with the use of the policy rate as the main instrument only in September 2010, the sample starts in January 2006 and ends in November 2010. This was done to have a larger sample to estimate the VAR model to obtain relatively more robust results. The model is estimated with two lags for all countries, as suggested by standard tests.

Figure 8.4 illustrates that the strength of the transmission of interest rate changes varies significantly across countries. The figure presents impulse-response (IR) functions for a 100 basis point increase in the money market rate—a contractionary

[12]See Appendix 8.1 for details on the different variables used in the VAR model.

[13]For robustness, estimations are compared with those obtained from a structural VAR model using an identification structure similar to that proposed in Kim and Roubini (2000), without showing major differences in results. In addition, the analysis considered all other possible orders in the Cholesky decomposition. The main conclusions of this section remain unaffected in all these cases.

[14]In the case of New Zealand, information is mostly available on a quarterly basis. Quarterly data have been converted to monthly data by taking a linear trend between each pair of consecutive quarters. At the time of running the estimations, quarterly data were available through the third quarter of 2010.

Figure 8.4 Impulse-Response Functions for a 100 Basis Point Increase in the Policy Rate (Percent, error bounds at 68 percent confidence)

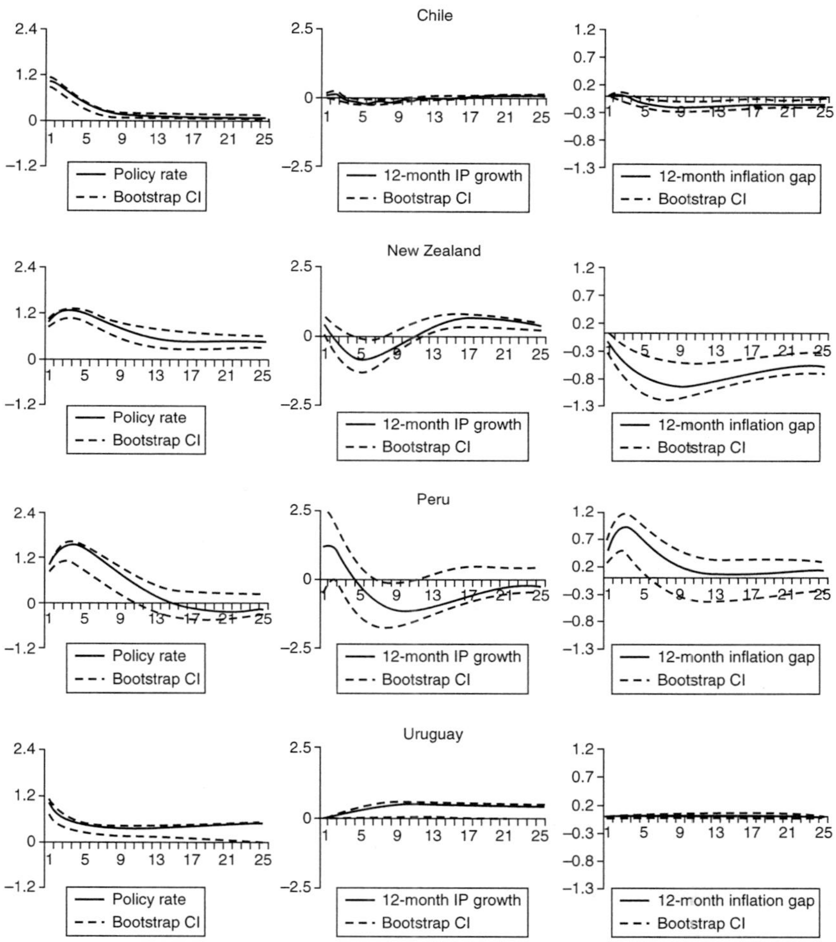

Source: Authors' estimations.

Note: IP = an index of economic activity (see text). All confidence intervals are computed using standard bootstrapping procedures with 1,000 replications.

monetary policy shock. In New Zealand, there is a significant and persistent contraction in the growth rate of output and inflation, in line with intuition. In Chile, the negative impact on output takes about three months to materialize, yet it tends to be persistent. In addition, the effect on inflation in Chile is more immediate than on output, and it also tends to be persistent.

The two dollarized economies analyzed here appear to have distinct results. In Peru and Uruguay, the interest rate hike leads to either a short-term increase in economic activity for about five months (Peru) or a slightly positive but not significant effect (Uruguay). In addition, the effect of the shock on inflation is either counterintuitive (Peru) or rather insignificant (Uruguay). In fact, the absence of a contraction in economic activity after the rise in the interest rate may be related to the existence of balance sheet effects in these economies. That is, the associated exchange rate appreciation that follows the interest rate hike may lead to an improvement in the balance sheets of those agents indebted in the foreign currency, thus generating an indirect positive effect on aggregate demand. This latter effect may outweigh the contractionary effect initially produced by the traditional interest rate channel (Figure 8.4).[16]

To analyze whether the exchange rate channel—rather than the interest rate channel—is relatively more relevant in Peru and Uruguay, a slightly different version of the VAR model is estimated. In this case, the vector of endogenous variables becomes:

$$Y_t = \left[neer_t \quad IP_t \quad \pi_t \quad R_t \right]', \tag{8.4}$$

where $neer_t$ indicates the year-over-year change in the nominal effective exchange rate (NEER), IP_t is the year-over-year change in an index of economic activity, π_t represents the annual CPI inflation rate, and R_t is the money market rate, as before. The rest of the model remains as in the baseline specification.

To explore formally the role of the exchange rate in the monetary transmission, the IR functions in Figure 8.5 evaluate how a NEER depreciation affects CPI inflation and output. As expected, Peru and Uruguay have the largest exchange rate pass-through, likely reflecting their high degree of dollarization. For instance, in Peru a 10 percent depreciation of the NEER raises CPI inflation up to 1.8 percent five months after the shock. This effect tends to also be persistent. In the case of Uruguay, CPI inflation tends to increase more quickly, to about 1.2 percent after three months, and the effect remains positive for a long period of time. These results contrast with those of Chile and New Zealand, where the NEER depreciation appears to have a small and short-lived effect on inflation.[17] There is also a relatively larger negative effect of the exchange rate depreciation on output in Peru and Uruguay, which again appears to be consistent with the presence of adverse balance sheet effects in these countries. In fact, in the cases of Chile and New Zealand the output

---

[16]Rossini and Vega (2007) point out that the presence of balance sheet effects may explain why economic activity seems to expand after the increase in the policy rate in the case of Peru.

[17]Although inflation patterns in Uruguay and Chile look relatively similar in Figure 8.5, there is a key important difference worth mentioning. The initial positive response of inflation in Chile vanishes seven months after the shock and turns negative immediately afterward. This behavior contrasts with that of Uruguay, where the inflation response to the currency depreciation remains positive about 20 months after the shock. Therefore, the overall exchange rate pass-through, conceived as the response of inflation to a currency depreciation over the medium term, becomes substantially larger in Uruguay relative to the case of Chile.

Figure 8.5 Impulse-Response Functions for a 10 Percent Depreciation in the Nominal Effective Exchange Rate (NEER; percent, error bounds at 68 percent confidence)

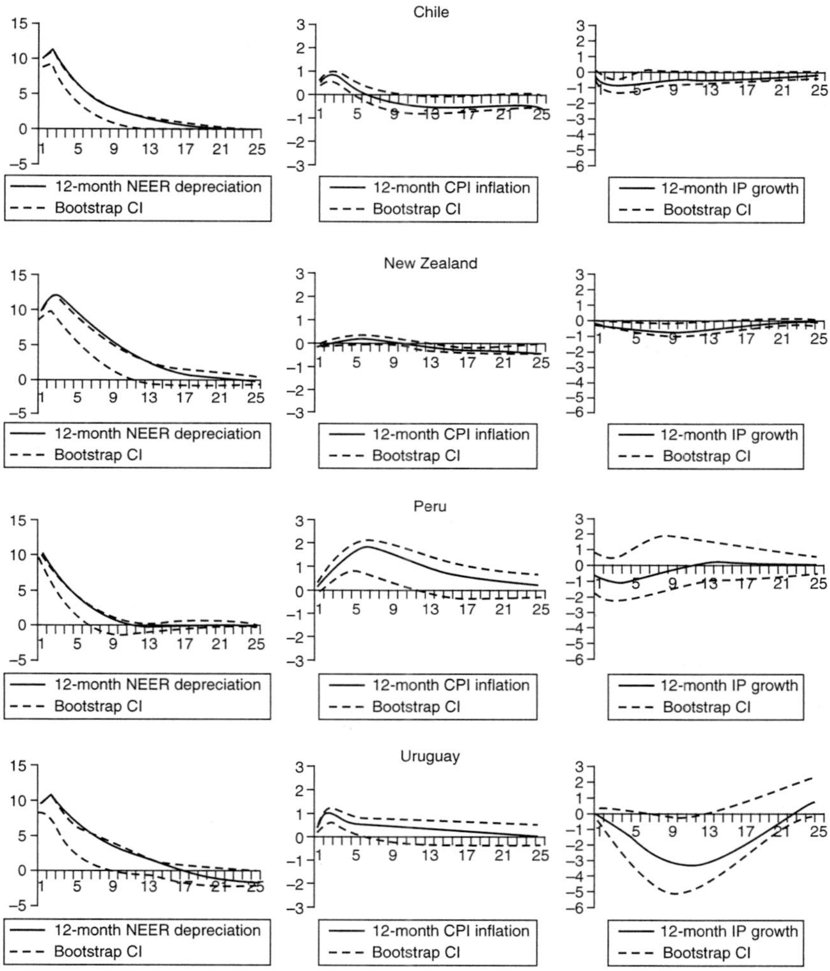

Source: Authors' estimations.
Note: CPI = consumer price index; IP = an index of economic activity (see text).

response is rather limited, suggesting from a different angle the larger effectiveness of monetary policy in these countries in controlling inflation at a lower output cost.

ROLE OF FINANCIAL FACTORS IN THE TRANSMISSION OF MONETARY POLICY

The overall strength of the monetary transmission depends on various factors, with some being specific to each country. This section explores to what extent the characteristics of the domestic financial system, notably its depth and degree of dollarization, may help explain the cross-country differences in the inflation response to the interest rate shock discussed previously.

Notice first that with a low degree of financial deepening, the traditional interest rate channel may not be operative, as a low degree of development of domestic credit markets may impinge on the ability of the monetary authority to control the flow of credit and thereby aggregate demand. In addition, if capital markets have only a modest relevance in the country, the strength of the transmission from asset prices to aggregate demand might be rather scant, thus limiting also the overall impact of the policy rate change on inflation. If the economy is also dollarized, in the sense that a large share of credit to the private sector is denominated in foreign currency, the monetary transmission may turn out to be even weaker due to the relatively lower influence of the monetary authority on modifying the key interest rates that affect foreign currency lending and thereby consumption and investment.

Table 8.5 presents a number of parameters for each country to evaluate the differences in the development of their respective financial system. The table illustrates that Uruguay ranks low in terms of credit to the private sector over GDP, a ratio that is closely followed by that of Peru. Particularly striking is the small size of the stock market capitalization in Uruguay. Not surprisingly, Uruguay also has the largest share of international debt issuance over GDP, followed by Peru, reflecting the still limited scope for funding in local markets. This trend has recently started to reverse, in line with the significant dedollarization process experienced by these two economies. Overall, the evidence suggests that credit markets are somewhat more developed in Chile and New Zealand, which may help explain the larger significance of the interest rate channel in these countries.

To formally evaluate whether the development of domestic credit markets may affect the transmission of monetary policy, we perform a different set of exercises, considering again our benchmark VAR model. Specifically, we explore whether the three-month response of inflation to a 100 basis point increase in the money market rate is affected when the credit-to-output ratio varies across countries.

TABLE 8.5

Financial System Indicators

	Total Deposits[1]	Credit to Private Sector[1]	Stock Market Capitalization[2]	International Debt Issuance[3]
		Percent of GDP[4]		
Chile	49.5	74.3	154.2	6.3
New Zealand	82.2	142.8	29.3	7.4
Peru	32.3	24.5	67.4	10.2
Uruguay	44.8	20.9	0.4	21.9

Sources: Bank for International Settlements (BIS); country authorities; Federacion Iberoamericana de Bolsas; New Zealand Exchange; and authors' calculations.

[1]As of November 2010.

[2]As of December 2010.

[3]International debt securities of all issuers (amortizations outstanding) from BIS Securities Statistics (Table 12A) as of December 2010.

[4]2010 GDP taken from IMF *World Economic Outlook* forecasts.

Regarding the econometric approach, the VAR model is estimated recursively. That is, for each country, the first window of the sample period is set to three years (36 observations). The impulse-response function to an interest rate shock is then calculated to pick the three-month response of inflation to the shock.[18] The process continues, adding one additional observation to the sample each time. The last (and largest) subsample for each country then coincides with that of the benchmark VAR model presented in the previous section. Once the three-month responses of inflation considering all the different subsamples are collected, a scatter plot is constructed including also the ratio of credit to the private sector over GDP for each country.[19]

Figure 8.6 illustrates that the credit-to-output ratio does not provide conclusive evidence regarding the role of credit in affecting the extent of the monetary policy transmission. The reason is that a higher credit-to-output ratio should be associated with a more negative response of inflation to the interest rate shock, because more developed financial markets should allow for better functioning of the credit channel and thus of the overall effectiveness of the interest rate shock

Figure 8.6 Credit to Private Sector and Inflation Response to a 100 Basis Point Policy Shock (Third-period response, percent)

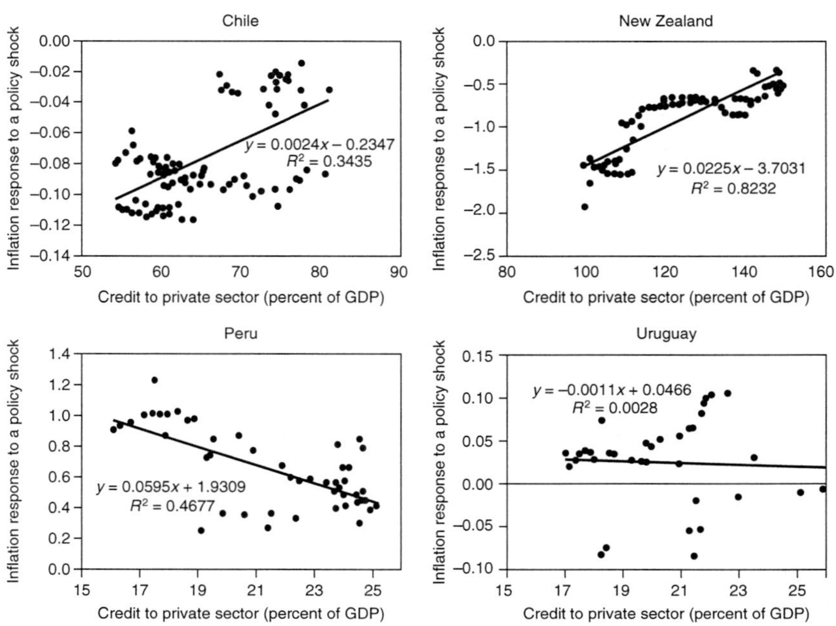

Source: Authors' estimations.

[18]The three-month response of inflation was chosen to account for the delay between the period in which the policy rate is changed and its final effect on inflation.

[19]The credit-to-output ratio of each particular point in the scatter plot coincides with the stock of credit available at the end of the sample period of the associated rolling VAR.

in affecting inflation. Whereas results for the case of Chile and New Zealand are counterintuitive, those of Peru and Uruguay suggest that the effectiveness of monetary policy in curbing inflation pressures may have increased when more credit was available. In any case, the absence of conclusive results is in line with those of Saizar and Chalk (2008). They do not find clear-cut evidence showing a positive relationship between the credit-to-GDP ratio and the strength of the transmission of interest rate shocks in a set of developing economies.

A similar recursive VAR exercise is also conducted to assess whether the recent dedollarization trend in Peru and Uruguay has somewhat strengthened their transmission of monetary policy. With this objective, the three-month response of inflation to the interest rate shock is again analyzed following the steps outlined before. Additionally, two different measures of dollarization are used to construct the scatter plots used for each country: local currency credit to the private sector (as percent of total credit) and local currency deposits (as percent of total deposits).[20]

Results suggest that the recent dedollarization process of Peru and Uruguay is likely to have improved the effectiveness of monetary policy (Figure 8.7). In fact,

Figure 8.7 Credit and Deposits in Domestic Currency and Inflation Response to a 100 Basis Point Policy Shock (Third-period response, percent)

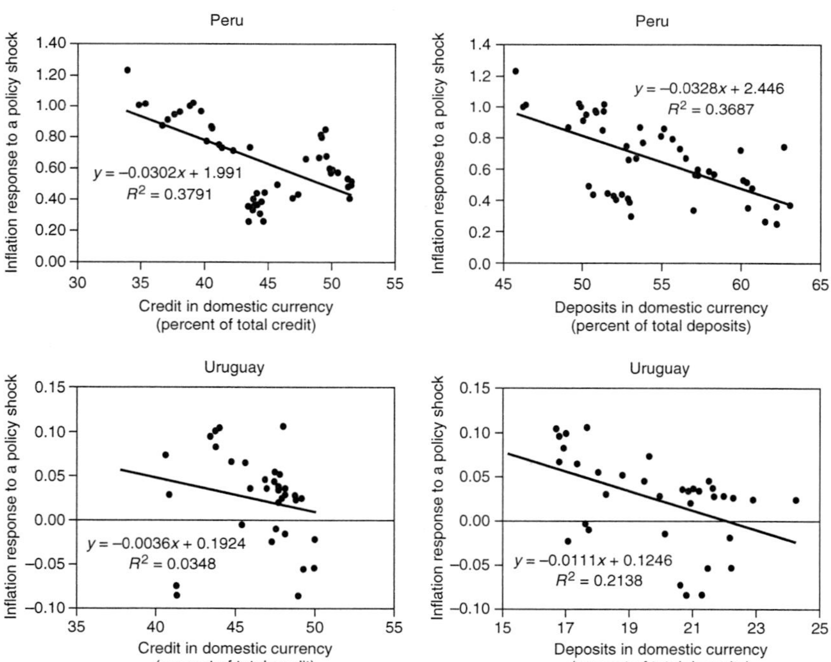

Source: Authors' estimations.

[20]Owing to data availability, we were not able to run the exercise considering only local currency dev

the figure indicates that the positive response of inflation to the interest rate hike (that is, the so-called price puzzle) has decreased substantially when the share of either credit or deposits in local currency increased, thus suggesting a better transmission of interest rate shocks in these economies as the process of dedollarization strengthened. Notwithstanding these results, for Uruguay, the findings are still relatively weak, a fact that is likely to be associated with the relatively shorter sample used in this latter case. A relevant exercise left for further research is therefore to evaluate whether the robustness of these findings rises as more data become available.

CONCLUSION

This chapter conducts a comparative study of the interest rate and exchange rate channels in two economies that run a well-established inflation targeting regime—Chile and New Zealand—vis-à-vis two economies that operate under relatively newer inflation targeting regimes and are exposed to a significant degree of dollarization—Peru and Uruguay. We found significant differences among these countries in terms of their respective transmission of monetary policy decisions. Whereas the traditional interest rate channel appears to operate to a large extent in Chile and New Zealand, evidence indicates instead that it is the exchange rate channel that still plays a more substantial role in controlling inflationary pressures in Peru and Uruguay. This result follows from the still limited impact of the policy rate in controlling inflation in these countries, in combination with their relatively large and persistent exchange rate pass-through. The latter is in turn likely to be associated with the substantial dollarization that still prevails in these economies. Importantly, however, since they have embarked on a significant dedollarization process, the relevance of the exchange rate channel is likely to decrease over time. In fact, the preliminary results presented in this chapter suggest that the interest rate channel is having a more significant role in their transmission of monetary policy as they tend to dedollarize their financial systems. Consequently, other channels of transmission may need to be further strengthened to curb inflation pressures more effectively over the medium term in these countries.

APPENDIX 8.1. SOURCES AND DATA DESCRIPTION

Table A8.1 provides sources, frequency, and samples for the data used in this chapter.

TABLE A8.1

Data Sources

Country	Variable	Description	Sample	Frequency	Source
Chile	CPI inflation	Consumer price index	Jan-2005 to Nov-2010	Monthly	National Bureau of Statistics
Chile	Credit to the private sector	Credit to the private sector in local currency	Sep-1999 to Nov-2010	Monthly	Central Bank of Chile
Chile	Deposit rate	Deposit rate	Sep-1999 to Nov-2010	Monthly	International Financial Statistics database, IMF
Chile	Expected inflation	Inflation expectations, 12 months ahead	Jan-2005 to Nov-2010	Monthly	Central Bank of Chile
Chile	Foreign reserves	Reserve assets	Jan-2005 to Nov-2010	Monthly	Central Bank of Chile
Chile	Lending rate	Lending rate	Sep-1999 to Nov-2010	Monthly	International Financial Statistics database, IMF
Chile	Money market rate	Average overnight interbank rate	Sep-1999 to Nov-2010	Monthly	Central Bank of Chile
Chile	NER	Nominal exchange rate, local currency per U.S. dollar	Jan-2005 to Nov-2010	Monthly	Central Bank of Chile
Chile	Nominal GDP	Gross domestic product at current prices	1995–2010	Annually	Central Bank of Chile
Chile	Openness	Export plus imports over GDP	1995–2009	Annually	Central Bank of Chile
Chile	Output	Monthly indicator of economic activity, IMACEC	Jan-2005 to Nov-2010	Monthly	Central Bank of Chile
Chile	Policy rate	Monetary policy rate	Sep-1999 to Nov-2010	Monthly	Central Bank of Chile
Chile	REER	Real effective exchange rate, index 2005 = 100	Jan-2005 to Sep-2010	Monthly	International Financial Statistics database, IMF
Chile	NEER	Nominal effective exchange rate, index 2005 = 100	Jan-2005 to Sep-2011	Monthly	International Financial Statistics database, IMF
Chile	Target bands	Inflation target bands	Sep-1999 to Nov-2010	Monthly	Central Bank of Chile
New Zealand	CPI inflation	Consumer price index	Jan-2005 to Nov-2010	Monthly	Reserve Bank of New Zealand
New Zealand	Credit to the private sector	Claims on private sector	April-1999 to Nov-2010	Monthly	International Financial Statistics database, IMF
New Zealand	Deposit rate	Deposit rate	April-1999 to Nov-2010	Monthly	International Financial Statistics database, IMF
New Zealand	Expected inflation	Inflation expectations, 12 months ahead	Jan-2005 to Nov-2010	Monthly	Reserve Bank of New Zealand
New Zealand	Foreign reserves	Total reserves minus gold	Jan-2005 to Nov-2010	Monthly	International Financial Statistics database, IMF
New Zealand	Lending rate	Base lending rate	April-1999 to Nov-2010	Monthly	International Financial Statistics database, IMF
New Zealand	Money market rate	Money market rate	April-1999 to Nov-2010	Monthly	International Financial Statistics database, IMF
New Zealand	NER	Nominal exchange rate, local currency per U.S. dollar	Jan-2005 to Nov-2010	Monthly	International Financial Statistics, IMF
New Zealand	Nominal GDP	Gross domestic product at current prices	1995–2010	Annually	Statistics New Zealand

New Zealand	Openness	Export plus imports over GDP	1995–2009	Annually	Statistics New Zealand
New Zealand	Output	Gross domestic product at constant prices	Jan-2005 to Sep-2010	Quarterly converted to monthly	Statistics New Zealand
New Zealand	Policy rate	Monetary policy rate	April-1999 to Nov-2010	Monthly	Reserve Bank of New Zealand
New Zealand	REER	Real effective exchange rate, index 2005 = 100	Jan-2005 to Sep-2010	Monthly	International Financial Statistics database, IMF
New Zealand	NEER	Nominal effective exchange rate, index 2005 = 100	Jan-2005 to Sep-2010	Monthly	International Financial Statistics database, IMF
New Zealand	Target bands	Inflation target bands	April-1999 to Nov-2010	Monthly	Reserve Bank of New Zealand
Peru	CPI inflation	Consumer price index	Jan-2005 to Nov-2010	Monthly	National Bureau of Statistics
Peru	Credit in domestic currency	Credit to the private sector in local currency	Sep-2003 to Nov-2010	Monthly	Central Bank of Peru
Peru	Credit in foreign currency	Total credit in foreign currency	1995–2009	Annually	Central Bank of Peru
Peru	Credit to the private sector	Total credit to the private sector	Sep-2003 to Nov-2010	Monthly	Central Bank of Peru
Peru	Deposit rate	Average deposit rate in local currency (TIPMN)	Sep-2003 to Nov-2010	Monthly	Central Bank of Peru
Peru	Deposits in domestic currency	Liquidity of the banking system in local currency minus vault cash	Sep-2003 to Nov-2010	Monthly	Central Bank of Peru
Peru	Deposits in foreign currency	Total deposits in foreign currency	1995–2009	Annually	Central Bank of Peru
Peru	Expected inflation	Inflation expectations, 12 months ahead	Jan-2005 to Nov-2010	Monthly	Central Bank of Peru
Peru	Foreign reserves	Net international reserves	Jan-2005 to Nov-2010	Monthly	Central Bank of Peru
Peru	Lending rate	Average lending rate in local currency (TAMN)	Sep-2003 to Nov-2010	Monthly	Central Bank of Peru and IMF
Peru	Money market rate	Interbank rate	Sep-2003 to Nov-2010	Monthly	Central Bank of Peru
Peru	NER	Nominal exchange rate, local currency per U.S. dollar	Jan-2005 to Nov-2010	Monthly	Central Bank of Peru
Peru	Nominal GDP	Gross domestic product at current prices	1995–2010	Annually	Central Bank of Peru
Peru	Openness	Export plus imports over GDP	1995–2009	Annually	Central Bank of Peru
Peru	Output	Gross domestic product at constant prices	Jan-2005 to Nov-2010	Monthly	Central Bank of Peru
Peru	Policy rate	Monetary policy rate	Sep-2003 to Nov-2010	Monthly	Central Bank of Peru
Peru	REER	Real effective exchange rate, index 2005 = 100	Jan-2005 to Sep-2010	Monthly	International Financial Statistics database, IMF
Peru	NEER	Nominal effective exchange rate, index 2005 = 100	Jan-2005 to Sep-2010	Monthly	International Financial Statistics database, IMF
Peru	Target bands	Inflation target bands	Sep-2003 to Nov-2010	Monthly	Central Bank of Peru

(Continued)

TABLE A8.1 (*Continued*)

Data Sources

Country	Variable	Description	Sample	Frequency	Source
Peru	Total credit	Total credit	1995–2009	Annually	Central Bank of Peru
Peru	Total deposits	Total deposits	1995–2009	Annually	Central Bank of Peru
Uruguay	CPI inflation	Consumer price index	Jan-2005 to Nov-2010	Monthly	National Bureau of Statistics
Uruguay	Credit in domestic currency	Credit to the private sector in local currency	Jan-2006 to Nov-2010	Monthly	Central Bank of Uruguay
Uruguay	Credit in foreign currency	Total credit in foreign currency	1995–2009	Annually	Central Bank of Uruguay
Uruguay	Credit to the private sector	Total credit to the private sector	Jan-2006 to Nov-2010	Monthly	Central Bank of Uruguay
Uruguay	Deposit rate	Deposit rate in local currency	Sep-2007 to Nov-2010	Monthly	Central Bank of Uruguay
Uruguay	Deposits in domestic currency	Total deposits in local currency	Jan-2006 to Nov-2010	Monthly	Central Bank of Uruguay
Uruguay	Deposits in foreign currency	Total deposits in foreign currency	1995–2009	Annually	Central Bank of Uruguay
Uruguay	Expected inflation	Inflation expectations, 12 months ahead	Jan-2005 to Nov-2010	Monthly	Central Bank of Uruguay
Uruguay	Foreign reserves	Reserve assets	Jan-2005 to Nov-2010	Monthly	Central Bank of Uruguay
Uruguay	Lending rate	Lending rate (ordinary)	Sep-2007 to Nov-2010	Monthly	International Financial Statistics database, IMF
Uruguay	Money market rate	Interbank overnight rate (call)	Sep-2007 to Nov-2010	Monthly	Central Bank of Uruguay
Uruguay	NER	Nominal exchange rate, local currency per U.S. dollar	Jan-2005 to Nov-2010	Monthly	National Bureau of Statistics
Uruguay	Nominal GDP	Gross domestic product at current prices	1995–2010	Annually	Central Bank of Uruguay
Uruguay	Openness	Export plus imports over GDP	1995–2009	Annually	Central Bank of Uruguay
Uruguay	Output	Industrial production index volume (excludes refinery)	Jan-2006 to Nov-2010	Monthly	National Bureau of Statistics
Uruguay	Policy rate	Monetary policy rate	Sep-2007 to Nov-2010	Monthly	Central Bank of Uruguay
Uruguay	REER	Real effective exchange rate, index 2005 = 100	Jan-2005 to Sep-2010	Monthly	International Financial Statistics database, IMF
Uruguay	NEER	Nominal effective exchange rate, index 2005 = 100	Jan-2005 to Sep-2010	Monthly	International Financial Statistics database, IMF
Uruguay	Target bands	Inflation target bands	Sep-2007 to Nov-2010	Monthly	Central Bank of Uruguay
Uruguay	Total credit	Total credit	1995–2009	Annually	Central Bank of Uruguay
Uruguay	Total deposits	Total deposits	1995–2009	Annually	Central Bank of Uruguay

Source: Authors' compilation.

REFERENCES

Aghion, Philippe, P. Bacchetta, and A. Banerjee, 2000, "A Simple Model of Monetary Policy and Currency Crises," *European Economic Review*, 44, pp. 728–38.

Céspedes, Luis, R. Chang, and A. Velasco, 2004, "Balance Sheets and Exchange Rate Policy," *American Economic Review*, Vol. 94, No. 4, pp. 1183–93.

García-Escribano, Mercedes, and S. Sosa, 2011, "What Is Driving Financial De-dollarization in Latin America?" IMF Working Paper No. 11/10 (Washington: International Monetary Fund).

Kim, Soyoung, and N. Roubini, 2000, "Exchange Rate Anomalies in the Industrial Countries: A Solution with a Structural VAR Approach," *Journal of Monetary Economics*, Vol. 45, pp. 561–86.

Leiderman, Leonardo, R. Maino, and E. Parrado, 2006, "Inflation Targeting in Dollarized Economies," IMF Working Paper No. 06/157 (Washington: International Monetary Fund).

Mishkin, Frederic, 1996, "The Channels of Monetary Transmission: Lessons for Monetary Policy," NBER Working Paper No. 5464 (Cambridge, Massachusetts: National Bureau of Economic Research).

Peersman, Gert, and F. Smets, 2001, "The Monetary Transmission Mechanism in the Euro Area: More Evidence from VAR Analysis," Working Paper No. 91 (Frankfurt: European Central Bank).

Rossini, Renzo, and M. Vega, 2007, "El mecanismo de transmisión de la política monetaria en un entorno de dolarización financiera: El caso del Perú entre 1996 y 2006," Working Paper No. 17 (Lima: Banco Central de Reserva del Perú).

Saizar, Ana Carolina, and N. Chalk, 2008, "Is Monetary Policy Effective when Credit Is Low?" IMF Working Paper No. 08/288 (Washington: International Monetary Fund).

Sims, Christopher, 1992, "Interpreting the Macroeconomic Time Series Facts," *European Economic Review*, 36, pp. 975–1011.

Index

Page numbers followed by *f, n,* or *t* refer to figures, footnotes, or tables, respectively.

E

F

G

I